Learning to Pass

Complete New CLAIT

Using Office 2000

Angela Bessant

Heinemann Educational Publishers
Halley Court, Jordan Hill, Oxford OX2 8EJ
Part of Harcourt Education

Heinemann is the registered trademark of Harcourt Education Limited

© Angela Bessant, 2003

First published 2003
07 06 05 04 03
10 9 8 7 6 5 4 3 2 1

British Library Cataloguing in Publication Data is available from the British Library
on request.

ISBN 0 435 46289 X

Designed by Artistix, Thame, Oxon

Typeset by Techtype, Abingdon, Oxon

Printed in the UK by Thomson Litho Ltd

Websites
Please note that the examples of websites suggested in this book were up to date at
the time of writing. It is essential for tutors to preview each site before using it to
ensure that the URL is still accurate and the content is appropriate. We suggest
that tutors bookmark useful sites and consider enabling students to access them
through the school or college intranet.

Acknowledgements
This book is the result of a team effort and I would like to thank all involved.
These include all those at or associated with Heinemann, especially Gillian Burrell
for her efficient professionalism; all past and present students and colleagues; my
family who always give untiring support and encouragement.

Every effort has been made to contact copyright holders of material reproduced in
this book. Any omissions will be rectified in subsequent printings if notice is given
to the publishers.

The author and publishers would like to thank the following people and
organisations for permission to reproduce photographs: Corbis/David H Wells –
page 19; Epson – page 3; Anthony King, MedImage – page 1; Photodisc – page 4.

Screenshots reprinted with permission from Microsoft Corporation

Tel: 01865 888058 www.heinemann.co.uk

Contents

Introduction

In order to become proficient in using a computer, it is necessary to practise. This book enables you to do that, leading you through Microsoft Office 2000 applications step by step so that you can build up confidence. Currently, Microsoft Office 2000 is the most commonly used suite of applications. It contains word processor (Word), spreadsheet (Excel) and database (Access) applications (amongst other things) that can be used together to produce documents. The documents are created and saved within the particular applications and then sections can be inserted into a final integrated document. This is very useful for generating reports, presentations and longer documents where graphics and sections from spreadsheets and databases need to be combined. Applications in the Microsoft Office suite have many things in common making them user friendly.

This book, which has been endorsed by OCR, covers units for OCR Level 1 Certificate for IT Users (New CLAIT*), but it would be equally suitable for anyone wanting to learn Microsoft Office 2000. The book covers Units 1 (core), 2, 3, 4, 5, 6, 7, 9 and 10 (as detailed in the contents page) of the OCR syllabus for New CLAIT.

* CLAIT: Clued up About IT.

Using this book

With the aid of the quick reference guides at the end of each chapter, and referring back through the sections for points you are unsure of, there is ample practice material for you to attempt, including sample full practice assignments. In this way, you will consolidate your understanding of the methods used. Answers to exercises are provided on the accompanying CD-ROM as PDF files. You will need Acrobat® Reader™ to access these files. The CD-ROM also contains files that you will need as you progress through the practical work. You need to make copies of these files to your own storage medium, eg hard disk, to work on (see Appendix for instructions on how to do this). Instructions on copying the database files can be found under the section Accessing the CD-ROM. The Appendix on the CD-ROM contains information that is useful to know but not essential.

There are many ways of performing a task in Windows 98 and Office 2000 applications, for example via the keyboard, using the mouse or using the menus. For simplicity, the practical exercises demonstrated usually show one method. However, there are instructions given for other methods at the end of the chapters or in the Appendix. You will then be able to decide which is the best method for you.

Default settings

Default settings are those that are automatically chosen the first time you use Office 2000. In the main, this book uses default settings. It is easy to change settings to suit your way of working. Instructions of how to change the most common settings are included in the Appendix.

Getting Help

In addition to the quick reference guides at the end of chapters and useful information in the Appendix, there is a Help menu in all Office 2000 applications. Pressing the **F1** key will activate help. There is also the Office Assistant. Throughout the book, I have hidden the Office Assistant so as not to be distracted from the main objectives. More details of the Office Assistant are found in the Appendix.

Accessing the CD-ROM

The answers to the exercises can be found as PDF files on the accompanying CD-ROM. The answers have been saved by chapter with each chapter being a separate folder.

To access the CD-ROM contents:

1 Insert the CD-ROM into your CD-ROM drive.
2 From the Windows desktop **Start** menu, Select: **Run**.
3 Key in the name of your CD-ROM drive – eg **D:**
4 Click on: **OK**.
5 The CD-ROM contents will be displayed.
6 Double-click on the folder or file that you want to access.

Copying Access database files

1 Copy the files onto your hard drive as instructed in the section on using this book.
2 Before you open each file, in My Computer or Windows Explorer, right-click on it and select: **Properties** at the bottom of the drop-down list.
3 At the bottom of the properties dialogue box click in the **read-only** box to remove the tick, then click on: **Apply** and then **OK**.

About OCR New CLAIT

New CLAIT – Level 1 Certificate for IT Users
The scheme

New CLAIT has been developed from the RSA CLAIT qualification, the most widely recognised basic qualification in practical computing and information technology at Level 1. It is aimed at IT users everywhere of all ages, all abilities and needs.

The syllabus

In order to gain full accreditation for New CLAIT, candidates must achieve the mandatory core unit plus four additional units. This book covers the knowledge and skills that are necessary to achieve competence in the applications covered.

New CLAIT assessment

- Each unit is assessed separately.
- There is one assignment, lasting two hours, for each unit.
- The core unit is assessed externally by an OCR-appointed examiner-moderator.
- All other units are assessed locally (usually by your tutor) and externally moderated by an OCR-appointed examiner-moderator. As an alternative, computer-based assessment is available for some units.
- When your work has been externally moderated and you have been deemed successful in the core unit plus four other units, you will receive a New CLAIT certificate. Certificates can also be issued for individual units.
- Candidates who are not successful may resit individual units using different assignments.

If you require more details of assessment you will need to ask your tutor.

The syllabus for OCR New CLAIT can be found on the OCR website www.ocr.org.uk or you can contact OCR by phone, telephone 01223 552552 for more details.

1

Using a computer (Unit 1)

1 Getting started

This section introduces the knowledge and understanding associated with Unit 1 that is not fully covered in the practical sections. There is also other background information to help you grasp some of the computer jargon.

1.1 Information and communication technology

Information and communication technology (ICT) is the term commonly used to cover the range of computer and telecommunications technologies involved in the transfer and processing of information.

There has always been a need for accurate up-to-date information, even before the advent of computer technologies, but it used to be a time-consuming process to gather and process relevant information. The advent of very large mainframe computers, relying on specialised staff to operate them, brought a change in the ways that big businesses handled information. Increasingly over the past decades, as the cost and size of computers have decreased, the mainframes have been replaced by powerful, inexpensive desktop personal computers on a colossal scale. Linking these computers together via the Internet has resulted in an explosion in the amount of data being manipulated every day. Today, almost all businesses rely on information communication technology and this has generated an ever-increasing demand for ICT skills in the workplace.

1.2 The computer system

There are two commonly used personal computers. The most widespread of the two is the computer based on the IBM PC, and all clones of this machine are referred to as *PCs*. The PC is predominant in business and commerce. The other common computer is the Apple Macintosh, also known as the *Mac*. This has a niche in creative fields such as music and design.

The computer system consists of *hardware* and *software*. Computer equipment that you can touch and handle is called *hardware*. It is the name given to all the devices that make up the computer system. These devices include the *input devices* (how we get the information into the computer), such as disk drives and keyboards. It also includes the processor (housed in the *system box*) – the 'brains' of the system that carries out all the instructions received from the operator or the program.

Figure 1.1 A typical computer system

Finally, it includes the *output devices* (how we get the information out of the computer), such as monitors and printers.

Computer systems can be standalone (not connected to any other computer), or they can be linked together to form a network so that information can be exchanged and items such as printers can be shared. Networked computers do not have to be in the same building. Using telecommunications, a computer can be linked to another computer anywhere in the world. Computers that are connected together on a network within an organisation are often referred to as *workstations*.

In order for the hardware to do a useful job, it needs to be instructed what to do. *Software* is the name given to the programs, each made up of a series of instructions that tell the computer what to do. There are different types of software: *operating system* software and *applications* software. The operating system software runs the computer and is used to load and run applications software: MS-DOS (*Microsoft Disk Operating System*), Windows, Mac OS and Linux are examples of operating system software. MS-DOS was a typical early operating system for PCs and it is not very user-friendly because it is necessary to key in commands (that you need to remember or look up) so that the computer can carry out the command.

However, Windows operating systems, developed later, are much more user-friendly. Windows is an example of a popular *graphical user interface* (*GUI* – pronounced 'gooey') operating system. It uses *icons* (small pictures), a *mouse* and *menus* (you will learn how to use these and other GUI components as you progress through the practical tasks). These make it more intuitive to use and reduce the need to remember complicated commands. Another advantage of the GUI is that what you see on the screen is what you will see when a document is printed. This is known as *WYSIWYG* (What You See Is What You Get).

Word processing, spreadsheet, database and *drawing programs* are all examples of applications software. *Microsoft Office* and *WordPerfect Office* are examples of integrated applications software. They have popular applications bundled together in one *suite.*

Hardware	Computer equipment that you can touch and handle, eg the monitor, keyboard
Software	Programs that allow the computer to do a useful task

Printers

There are two main types of printer commonly in use: *inkjet* and *laser*. Both inkjets and lasers are quiet in operation and print to a high quality. Lasers are generally quicker and produce the highest-quality output. All types have models available to print in black and white and/or colour. Printers come with a recommendation for types of paper, since the quality of paper used has an effect on the quality of output produced. There is sometimes an option of using continuous or single sheet paper. You can choose a specific paper size from the selection available in the software application.

Care of printers

- Do not overload with paper since this could cause a paper jam.
- Ensure that paper is loaded straight so avoiding skewed printouts.
- Avoid spilling drinks and crumbs on the printer by not eating or drinking near it.
- Do not pile things on top of it.

Figure 1.2 Inkjet and laser printers

1.3 Storage of data

Data stored on a computer can be saved to various mediums, eg hard disk, floppy disk and compact disk (CD). These are accessed using alphabetically named *drives*.

Hard disks (usually Drive C)	Most computers have hard disks installed. A hard disk is a fixed disk positioned inside the computer system box that can hold a large number of programs and a large amount of data.
Floppy disks (for use in Drive A or B)	The $3^1/_2$" floppy disk (Figure 1.3) has become the norm. It is a removable storage medium (it can be taken away and used on another computer). The amount that can be stored on a floppy disk depends on whether it is single or double sided and whether it is single, double or high density. The $3^1/_2$" disk has a hard plastic case (protecting its floppy interior) with a metal cover which slides back when the disk is placed in the disk drive so that it can be read or written to. Some disks come ready formatted, but if not, the first time you use a new floppy disk, you must *format* it so that it is configured for your particular system (see Appendix for how to do this). On floppy $3^1/_2$" disks there is a small tab in one corner that slides across to write-protect it so that anything stored on it cannot be deleted or amended.
CD (for use in Drive D)	CD is an acronym for compact disc. A compact disc is a removable storage medium that holds huge quantities of data, eg an entire encyclopaedia. There are different types of CD. A *CD-R* is a recordable CD that can be recorded on once only. A *CD-RW* allows unlimited recordings. A *CD-ROM* is for reading from only. Software such as Microsoft Office is usually distributed on CD-ROM.

Care of removable disks

- Handle disks with care at all times.
- Always store disks carefully.
- Keep the disks away from anything magnetic.
- Keep the disks away from direct heat, eg radiators or sunlight.
- Do not touch the exposed recording surface.

Figure 1.3 Floppy disk

1.4 Backing up

It is always a good idea to produce a *backup* (exact copies) of your files on a regular basis. (See the Appendix on the CD-ROM for how to produce a backup.) Things can go wrong and, if they do and your files become *corrupted* (damaged) or deleted, you will be able to revert to the safely stored versions. It is best to store the backups in a safe and separate place, away from your computer or office. Backups can be created as often as you want depending on how often you update your files. Generally the more often files are updated, the more often you will need to make backups so that you have a very recent copy to fall back on.

If there is a power cut when you are using your computer, the documents and information that you have not saved to disk will be lost. It is important that you save your work regularly so that you will minimise the amount of effort required to redo the work in such situations. Occasionally the computer may just *crash* (sometimes called *freezing* or *hanging*), ie cease to function, either because there is a program error or a more serious system problem. You may be able to recover your work. If it is a program problem, restart the program. If it is a system problem, restart the computer by pressing the keys **Ctrl**, **Alt** and **Delete** (all at the same time). If this does not have any effect, try the **Reset** button (this does a *warm boot*, ie the power supply is not turned off). As a last resort, turn the computer off and then restart it (a *cold boot*). Specialised disk recovery programs are available for retrieving all or part of the data from damaged files.

1.5 Limiting access

For security reasons, you should be aware of how you can limit access to your computer and files that are confidential or that you do not want changed. Computers can be password protected so that only an authorised user can access the data on them. In some organisations several passwords are needed to access strictly confidential data, giving added extra security. Document files can also be password protected. Screen savers can be useful so that people walking past do not see what is on your screen. These can be password protected too. It is always good practice to use a password that is not easy for anyone to guess and it must not be divulged to anyone. Taking such precautions makes it difficult for *hackers* (unauthorised illegal users) to break into the system to steal or alter confidential information or plant *viruses* (see page 5).

Computers should be sited in places that:

- are not easily accessible, so that they cannot be stolen (they should be security marked so that they can be easily traced if necessary);
- have fire and smoke alarms;
- are kept clean and dust free; and
- do not flood.

1.6 Viruses

A *computer virus* is a destructive program that is buried within other programs received from disk or e-mail. Viruses are written by people with programming skills who want to cause widespread havoc for computer users. Once an infected program is run, the virus coding is activated and usually attaches copies of itself to other programs. Infected programs then copy the virus to other programs. In this way the virus can spread quickly causing irritating effects (such as displaying messages on screen) to severe damage (destroying complete disk contents) to computers and networks. To protect against viruses, always know the source of your software. When downloading software from the Internet, always save it and virus check it before running it. Also be wary when opening e-mails and attachments. If in doubt, do not open a suspect e-mail but delete it. In May 2000 the *Iloveyou* virus affected 10% of business computer systems in the UK alone and many more throughout the world, costing millions of pounds. It was spread via e-mail. The reason the virus spread so quickly was because people rushed to click on the e-mail attachment; it opened their Address Book and was then e-mailed to everyone listed.

Antivirus utility programs are available and can alert you to a virus and remove (*disinfect*) it. They are a good 'insurance' investment. They must be updated on a regular basis to cope with any new viruses. If you are unfortunate enough to have a virus on your computer, close down the computer and restart it using a write-protected floppy *boot disk* (a disk that contains the essential elements of the operating system) and then run an antivirus utility. Always remember to backup your files. Then even if the worst has happened and your files have been destroyed, you will be able to replace them with the backup copies.

1.7 Data Protection Act 1998

The UK Data Protection Act was first passed in 1984 and has since been updated (1998) to give full effect to the European Directives on Data Protection. It now not only sets rules for processing personal information on computers but also extends to paper-based records. It gives individuals the right to know about the information held on them. Personal data is kept for many reasons, eg by tax offices, personnel departments, banks and hospitals. Everyone who processes and stores information should register as a data controller with the Data Protection Commissioner. If an individual feels that information is not being properly used, he or she can contact the Data Protection Commissioner who will investigate the claim. There are strict penalties (unlimited fines) for anyone who does not comply with the rules. There are eight principles to ensure that information is handled properly. These are:

Personal data shall be:

- Fairly and lawfully processed.
- Obtained only for one or more specified purposes.
- Adequate, relevant and not excessive.
- Accurate and where necessary kept up to date.
- Not kept for longer than necessary.

- Processed in line with the rights of data subjects.
- Kept secure.
- Not transferred to countries outside the European Economic Area without adequate protection.

1.8 Health and safety

Computing environments must conform to the *Health and Safety at Work* (*HASAW*) legislation. An employer is responsible for providing a safe and comfortable working environment. When you are using a computer it is important that you make yourself comfortable otherwise you may become easily fatigued, ill or injured. *Repetitive strain injury* (*RSI*), an injury arising from making awkward movements or the prolonged use of particular muscles, is a recognised condition. Eyestrain and headaches have also been linked to working with computers. Minimise any risks by being aware of the following:

Positioning of the screen	All screens should be adjustable so that you can set them up for your requirements in order to avoid muscle strain in the neck and shoulders. The screen should be directly in front of you, roughly at arm's length. The top of the screen display should be just above eye level.
Positioning of documents	To prevent visual fatigue and muscle tension and to minimise re-focusing and twisting the neck, these should be near to the screen, at the same height and distance.
Positioning of keyboard	If your keyboard is not comfortable – ie it is placed too near to the edge of the desk so that there is nowhere to rest your wrists – you could put unnecessary strain on your wrists causing RSI. Wrist rests are available.
Using the mouse	Ensure that you are using the mouse correctly. Keep it in a comfortable position and rest your fingers lightly on the buttons. Do not grip it too tightly.
Type of chair	An adjustable chair is essential. Your back should be straight and your feet should rest on the floor. Your forearms should be roughly horizontal when using the keyboard.
Lighting	Screen glare should be avoided by adjusting background lighting and using window blinds or positioning the screen so that it is unaffected. Anti-glare filters are available. Flickering of the screen should be optimised by selecting a high scan rate.
Ventilation	Adequately ventilated working areas should be provided.
Frequent breaks	When working at the computer for prolonged periods, it is important to take frequent breaks every hour to stretch and walk around. Give your eyes a rest so that they do not become tired and sore from staring intently at the small screen area. Focus them in the distance. Consider the possibility that spectacles may be helpful even if you do not normally wear them.
Ensure equipment is safe	It is important to have equipment checked periodically to ensure that it is safe to use. Power cables should be secured so that they cannot be tripped over and power sockets should not be overloaded. Any cable damage should be repaired.
Look after your computer	Do not eat and drink while using your computer. Crumbs can become lodged in the keyboard and spilled drinks can cause quite serious damage. Do not pile things on top of the monitor, system box or printer as this could block air vents. Computers should not be moved when they are in use since this may cause damage to the hard disk.

Working with Windows

This section contains practical exercises to familiarise you with your computer and Windows 98. You will learn how to:

- switch the computer on
- recognise parts of the Windows desktop
- recognise parts of a Window
- shut down the computer
- work with passwords and login to a system
- use the mouse
- access Help

2.1 Switching the computer on

Exercise 1

Switch on the computer.

Method

1   Ensure that the computer is plugged into the electricity socket.
2   Press the button on the computer system box (and on the monitor, if it has a separate button) to switch the power on.
3   The computer will perform its start-up checks and load Windows 98 and accessories (this is sometimes called *powering up* or *booting up*). This can take some time during which there will be whirring noises from the system box and text will scroll across the screen. Eventually you will see the Windows 98 desktop displayed. The items that appear on this screen depend on how your computer is set up. It will look something like Figure 1.4.

Note: The small pictures that Windows 98 uses to represent things, eg programs, documents that you have saved (files) and so on are called *icons*.

 If you are using a password-protected computer, you will need to find out what the procedure is to login and what user name and password you should use. Typically something like the boxes shown below appear on screen.

| New password: | [   ] | New password: | [********] |
| Confirm new password: | [   ] | Confirm new password: | [|] |

If you choose/change your own password, you should use something that you will remember but, at the same time, something that is not easy for anyone else to guess. Your password may be restricted to a certain number of characters.

When you enter your password, it will appear in a form similar to that shown so that no one can take a sneaky look at it. You will be asked to confirm your password by keying it in again. This ensures that you keyed it in correctly.

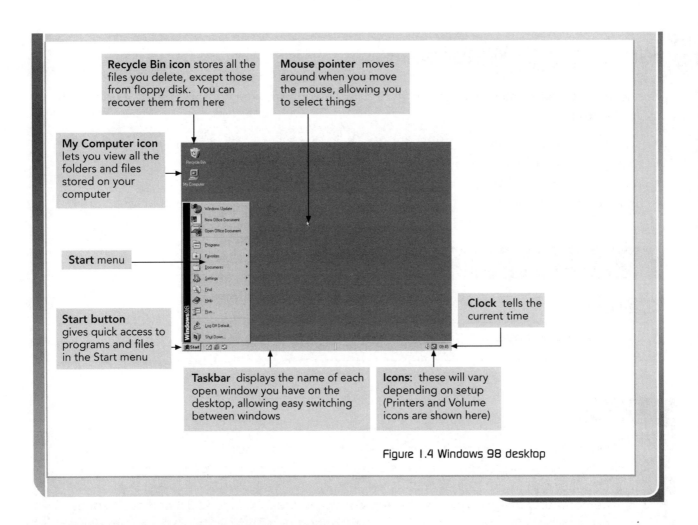

Recycle Bin icon stores all the files you delete, except those from floppy disk. You can recover them from here

Mouse pointer moves around when you move the mouse, allowing you to select things

My Computer icon lets you view all the folders and files stored on your computer

Start menu

Start button gives quick access to programs and files in the Start menu

Clock tells the current time

Taskbar displays the name of each open window you have on the desktop, allowing easy switching between windows

Icons: these will vary depending on setup (Printers and Volume icons are shown here)

Figure 1.4 Windows 98 desktop

2.2 Using the mouse

The mouse lets you select and move items on the screen. When you move the mouse on your desk, the mouse pointer ⟨ moves on the screen in the same direction. You will notice that the mouse pointer changes depending on where it is and what it is doing. A typical mouse has a left and a right button. These can both be used to select and choose options. In Windows 98, the right mouse button is usually used to access alternative context-sensitive pop-up menus. Some mice have a wheel that is very useful for scanning through documents.

Mouse terms

Click: Press and release a mouse button.

Double-click: Quickly press and release a mouse button twice.

Drag and drop: When the mouse pointer is over an object on your screen, press and hold down the left mouse button. Still holding down the button, move to where you want to replace the object. Release the mouse button.

Hover: Place the mouse pointer over an object for a few seconds so that something happens, eg another menu appears, or a *ToolTip*.

Exercise 2

An excellent way of practising mouse skills is to play the game *Solitaire* that comes with Windows 98. Practise now.

1 To start Solitaire follow the directions given in Figure 1.5.

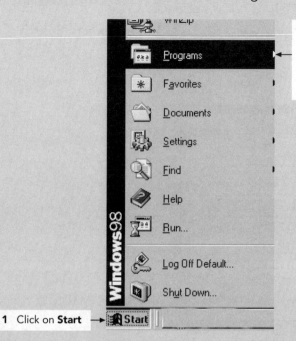

2 Hover the mouse over **Programs** – another menu appears.
Hover the mouse over **Accessories**, then **Games**, then click on **Solitaire**

1 Click on **Start**

Figure 1.5 Starting Solitaire

 If you do not have *Solitaire* on your computer, load any other **Accessories** program and practise some of the skills shown below.

2 The **Solitaire** window appears (Figure 1.6). Notice that the taskbar, at the bottom of your screen, now displays a button for Solitaire.

Minimise button: reduces window from the screen. Redisplay by clicking the left mouse over its button on the title bar

Menu bar

Title bar

Maximise button: window fills screen

Close button: closes the window

Drop-down menu

Mouse pointer

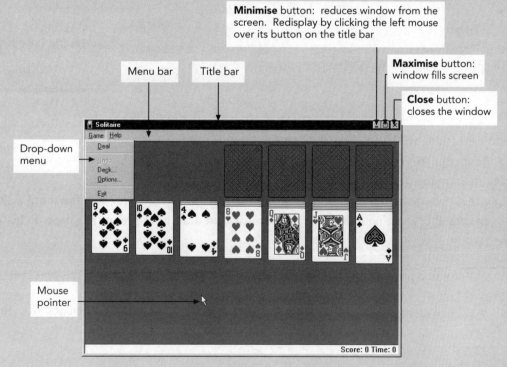

Figure 1.6 Parts of a Window

To play Solitaire:

3 On the **Menu** bar, click on: **Help**; a menu appears.

4 Click on: **Help Topics**; the **Solitaire Help** window appears.

5 Click on: the **Contents** tab, if not already selected (on top of **Index** and **Search** tabs).

6 Click on: **Playing Solitaire** (Figure 1.7).

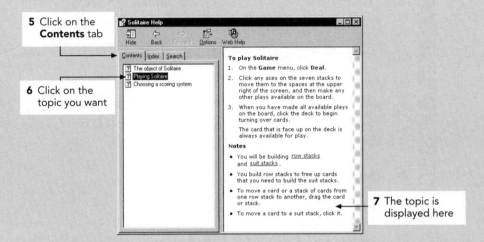

Figure 1.7 Solitaire Help Window

7 The rules of the game are displayed in the right-hand pane.

8 When you have read the rules, click on: the **Close** button of the **Solitaire Help** window (Figure 1.8).

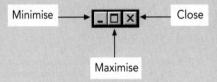

Figure 1.8 The Close button

You are now ready to play Solitaire!

Practise:

- The mouse actions whilst playing the game.
- Using the menus to get Help and choose other options for the game.
- Moving the window by pointing to the Title bar and dragging and dropping.
- Resizing the window by moving the mouse pointer over the edge of the window until a double arrow appears. Press and hold down the left mouse and drag to the required shape. Release the mouse.

Note: To keep the same proportions of the window, drag from a corner.

When you have had enough practising, from the **Game** menu, click on: **Exit** or click on: the **Close** button.

Exercise 3

Practise getting help with any topic from Windows 98 Help, as follows.

Method

1 Click on: the **Start** button, then on: **Help**. The **Windows Help** window appears (Figure 1.9).

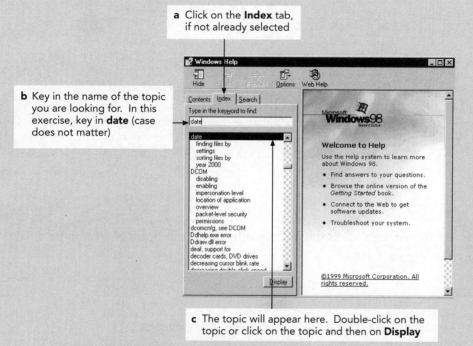

a Click on the **Index** tab, if not already selected

b Key in the name of the topic you are looking for. In this exercise, key in **date** (case does not matter)

c The topic will appear here. Double-click on the topic or click on the topic and then on **Display**

Figure 1.9 Windows Help

2 The **Topics Found** box appears (Figure 1.10). A list of date-related topics is given.

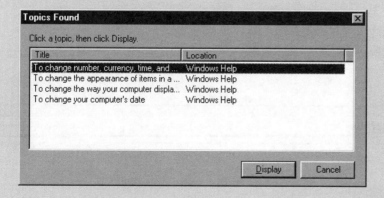

Figure 1.10 Topics Found

3 Choose a topic by double-clicking on it. I have chosen *'To change your computer's date'* and the **Windows Help** appears displaying help in the right-hand pane (Figure 1.11).

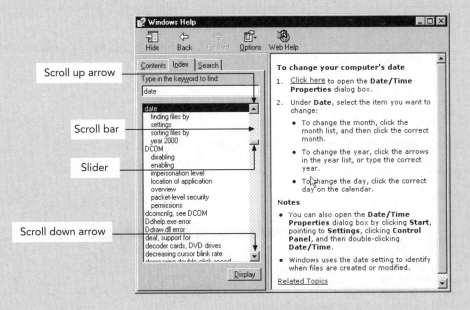

Figure 1.11 Specific windows help is displayed

Scroll bars

When a window is not big enough to display all the information in it, scroll bars appear, vertically and/or horizontally (see Figure 1.11).

Practise:

- Clicking on the scroll bar arrows to move through the index entries.
- Dragging the slider along the scroll bar to move more quickly through the entries.
- Searching for other Help topics.

When you have finished searching for Help topics, close the Help window by clicking on: the **Close** button.

2.4 Shutting down the computer

Exercise 4

Shut down the computer correctly.

1   From the **Start** menu, click on: **Shut Down**. The **Shut Down Windows** dialogue box appears (Figure 1.12).

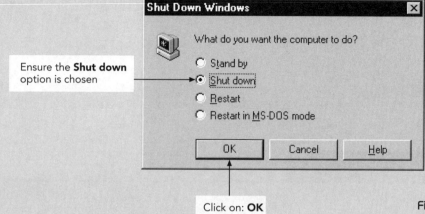

Ensure the **Shut down** option is chosen

Click on: **OK**

Figure 1.12 Shutting down Windows

2   A message *'It's now safe to turn off your computer'* is displayed. Your computer may then switch off automatically. If not you can now switch off using the button on the system box.

It is important that you shut down Windows correctly when you have finished your work. If not, files may become corrupted. If you have any work that you have not saved, you will be asked if you want to save it before shutting down. Any work that has not been saved will be lost when the computer is switched off.

It seems odd to use the **Start** menu when you want to stop using the computer. What you are actually doing is 'starting' the shut down process.

Section 2: checklist

Are you familiar with the following?	
Starting the computer	
Using the mouse	
Recognising parts of the desktop and parts of an application window	
Using Help functions	
Reducing/enlarging a window	
Resizing, rescaling and closing a window	
Moving windows on a desktop	
Shutting down the computer	

3 Windows Explorer

This section contains practical exercises to familiarise you with *Windows Explorer*. Windows Explorer allows you to view all the folders and files on your computer. It is useful for disk and file management. You will learn how to:

- start Windows Explorer
- recognise folders and files
- use the Recycle Bin
- close Windows Explorer

3.1 Starting Windows Explorer

Method 1

From the **Start** menu, select: **Programs**, then: **Windows Explorer**.

Method 2

Right-click on: **Start**. Select: **Explore** from the pop-up menu.

The **Exploring** window appears. In the example (Figure 1.13), $3^1/_2$ Floppy (A:) drive is selected in the left (**Folders**) pane and the contents of the disk in Drive A are displayed in the pane on the right. Your window may not look the same since Drive C may be selected. Do not be concerned about this.

Note: If your window has a different layout, you may be in Web Page View. From the **View** menu, select: **as Web Page** so that there is no tick next to it.

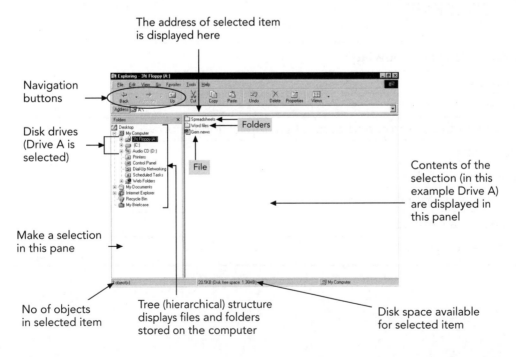

The address of selected item is displayed here

Navigation buttons

Disk drives (Drive A is selected)

Folders

File

Make a selection in this pane

Contents of the selection (in this example Drive A) are displayed in this panel

No of objects in selected item

Tree (hierarchical) structure displays files and folders stored on the computer

Disk space available for selected item

Figure 1.13 Windows Explorer

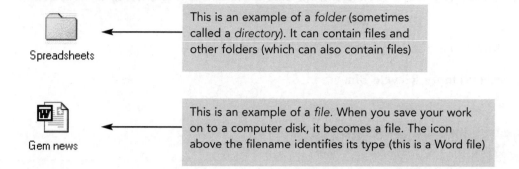

Spreadsheets — This is an example of a *folder* (sometimes called a *directory*). It can contain files and other folders (which can also contain files)

Gem news — This is an example of a *file*. When you save your work on to a computer disk, it becomes a file. The icon above the filename identifies its type (this is a Word file)

Displaying the contents of a folder

Double-click on: the folder.

 It is better to double-click the icon rather than the text as sometimes you will not get the action you expect (if you have not double-clicked properly). Instead a box may appear round the text, waiting for your input. If this happens, press: **Esc** and try again.

Creating a new folder

You can create new folders in which to store related documents. This is always good practice as it makes for easier location at a later date.

Example

To create a new folder on the disk in Drive A:

1   In the left-hand (**Folders**) pane, click on: $3^1/_2$ **Floppy (A:).**

2   The contents of the floppy disk in Drive A are displayed in the right-hand pane.

3   Right-click in: the white space of this pane. A menu appears.

4   Select: **New** and then: **Folder.**

5   Key in the name for the new folder and press: **Enter.**

Deleting a file/folder

Select the file/folder you want to delete by clicking on it. Press: the **Delete** key. You will be asked to confirm file delete. Click on: **Yes.**

Note: When you delete a folder, its contents are also deleted.

You can restore a deleted file (*not one deleted from a floppy disk*) from the **Recycle Bin** by clicking on: the **Recycle Bin,** selecting the file you want to restore and selecting: **Restore** from the **File** menu.

Emptying the Recycle Bin

It is a good idea to remove files from the Recycle Bin from time to time to save cluttering up the hard disk. To do this:

1   Click on: the **Recycle Bin** to select it.

2   From the **File** menu, select: **Empty Recycle Bin**.

3.4 Closing Windows Explorer

From the **File** menu, select: **Close**.

Section 3: checklist

Are you familiar with the following?	
Starting Windows Explorer	
Recognising folders/files	
Understanding file/folder structure	
Closing Windows Explorer	

4 ## Inputting data using Word

This section contains practical exercises to familiarise you with the keyboard, more general Windows skills and the application *Word*. Word is a word processing application. You will learn how to:

- load Word
- use the keyboard
- key in text, numbers and symbols
- insert text, numbers and symbols
- delete text, numbers and symbols
- save your work
- close Word

Note: Unit 1 assesses basic text-editing skills. Therefore an application such as *Notepad* or *WordPad* could be alternatives for this unit. Word is covered in more detail in Chapter 2.

4.1 Loading Word

Exercise 1

Load Word.

Method

1   Switch on your computer and wait until the **Windows 98 desktop** screen appears. (*Note:* You may need a password to login.)

2   Hover the mouse pointer over the **Start** button and click the left mouse button – a menu appears (Figure 1.14).

Figure 1.14 Selecting from the Start menu

3   Select: **Programs** by hovering the mouse over it – another menu appears.

4 Select: **Word** by clicking the left mouse on it (Figure 1.15).

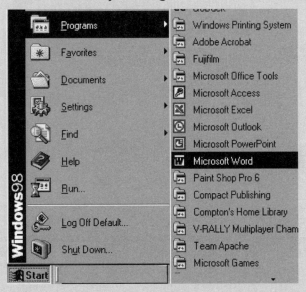

Figure 1.15 Selecting Word

5 The Word window will be displayed on screen looking similar to Figure 1.16.

Cursor positioned where your text will appear

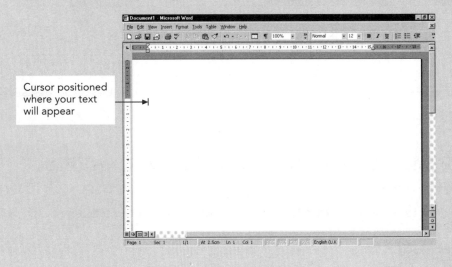

Figure 1.16 Word window

4.2 Examining the keyboard

Exercise 2

Examine the keyboard.

Before keying anything in to Word, take some time to have a close look at the keyboard. Most keyboards are quite similar so it will look something like Figure 1.17. Those who have used typewriters in the past or who can touch type will recognise the standard QWERTY keyboard layout (QWERTY refers to the first six letters on the top row). A computer keyboard has extra keys.

The ones that you need to know about at this stage are labelled in Figure 1.17. They include the following.

Shift key

There are two Shift keys, one at either side of the character keys. They perform the same task so you can use either, whichever is most convenient. Press the Shift key down at the same time as the character key you require to produce an uppercase (capital letter), ie holding down **Shift** and pressing **R** produces uppercase R.

Space bar   Shift   Enter (or Return)

Figure 1.17 Keyboard layout

Some keys have two characters, eg the number keys above the QWERTY row. For instance the number 1 key also has an exclamation mark !; the number 5 key, a % symbol. To produce the upper part of these keys, hold down the **Shift** key and at the same time press the required key.

Enter (or Return) key

When the text is too long to fit within the space available, it will automatically be carried over to the next line. This is known as *word wrap*. However, if you have not reached the end of a line and you want to move to the next line, you need to press the **Enter** key. If you want to leave a blank line, say after headings or between paragraphs, press the **Enter** key twice.

Space bar

Use the space bar to create a space in between words. Try to be consistent. One space after a comma and one space after a full stop is acceptable, looks neat and is easy to read.

4.3 Keying in text

Exercise 3

Key in the following letters (at this stage do not worry if you make mistakes, you will learn how to correct them later):

qwerty
Leave a space (press the space bar once) and key in:

QWERTY
Move to the next line by pressing: **Enter**.

The keyed in text will look similar to Figure 1.18. Notice how the *cursor* moves with you as you key in.

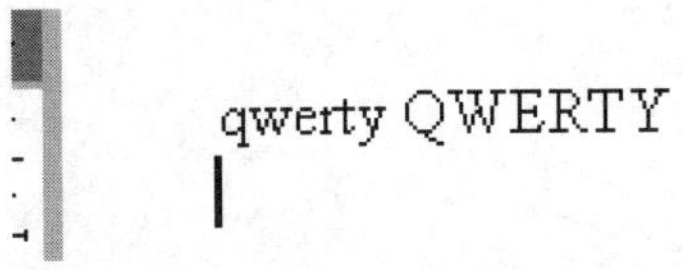
qwerty QWERTY

Figure 1.18 Text keyed in

Exercise 4

Key in the following text that uses all the letters of the alphabet plus a full stop:

The quick brown fox jumps over the lazy dog.

Exercise 5

Leave a line space by pressing: **Enter** twice and key in your name.

Exercise 6

Leave a line space and key in the following numbers and symbols. Leave a space between each one.

2 ! 4 = 1 / & 3 – 8 # 6 @ 7 : 5 ? £ % * + , 9

Results of your keying in will now look like Figure 1.19.

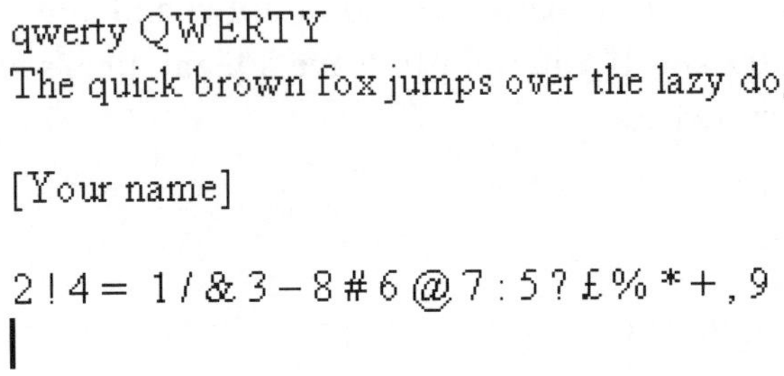
qwerty QWERTY
The quick brown fox jumps over the lazy dog.

[Your name]

2 ! 4 = 1 / & 3 – 8 # 6 @ 7 : 5 ? £ % * + , 9

Figure 1.19 More keying in

4.4 Moving around

Exercise 7

Now that you have some text keyed in, practise moving around your document.

Here we will learn three methods to move around the document:

1 Using the arrow keys.

2 Using the mouse.

3 Using two keys together, **Ctrl + Home**, and **Ctrl + End**.

1 Moving around your text using the arrow keys

The arrow keys ← ↑ → ↓ (located at the bottom right of the main keyboard) allow you to move the cursor (a flashing black vertical line) in the direction of the arrows. You can move one space forwards or backwards at a time, or you can move up or down one line at a time. If you keep an arrow key pressed down, the cursor will automatically move quickly through the document. Remember to release the arrow key when you reach the required place.

2 Moving around your text using the mouse

As you move the mouse pointer around the screen, you will notice that it turns into an I-beam and moves with you. Move it until you have reached the required position, click the left mouse button once and the cursor will appear where you clicked.

3 Using **Ctrl + Home** and **Ctrl + End**

Hold down: the **Ctrl** key at the same time as the **Home** key to move to the start of your document.

Hold down: the **Ctrl** key at the same time as the **End** key to move to the end of your document.

4.5 Inserting text

Exercise 8

Insert the word **cub** between **fox** and **jumps**.

Method

1 Position the cursor at the point where you want to insert text (in this case after the space after the word **fox**), and then key in **cub** and a space (Figure 1.20).

2 Notice how the text to the right of the cursor moves to make room for the new text.

 If your text does not move across but overwrites text already there, check that **OVR** is not displayed on the status bar. If it is, press: **Insert** to remove overwrite.

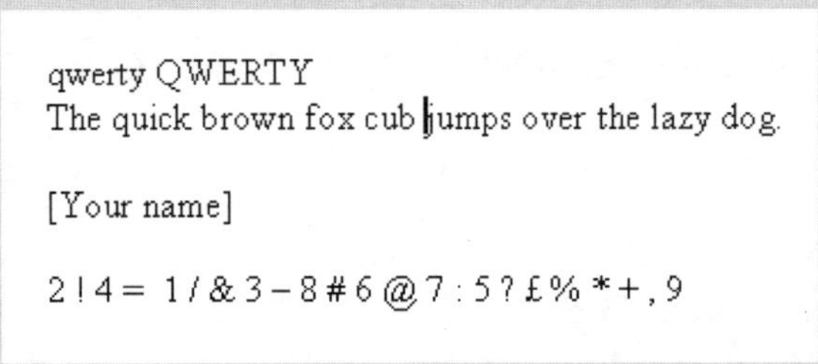

```
qwerty QWERTY
The quick brown fox cub jumps over the lazy dog.

[Your name]

2!4= 1/&3−8#6@7:5?£%*+,9
```

Figure 1.20 Inserting text

4.6 Deleting text

Exercise 9

Delete the word **quick**. Three methods are shown below. Try each one, reinserting the word **quick** after each deletion in order to delete by another method.

Method 1

Position the cursor to the left of the first character that you want to delete, ie the **q** of **quick** and press: **Delete** until all the letters of **quick** (and the space) have been deleted.

Method 2

Position the cursor to the right of the last character you want to delete and press: ← **Del** (Backspace) key (top right of main keyboard) until all the letters of **quick** (and the space) have been deleted.

Method 3

Double-click on the word **quick** and press: **Delete**.

4.7 Saving

Exercise 10

Save the document using the filename **keyboard**.

The great thing about using a computer is that you can save your work so that you can recall it at a later date to make alterations, update it and so on. Note that the document, when saved, is referred to as a *file*.

1   From the **File** menu, select: **Save As** (Figure 1.21).

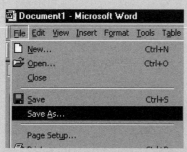

Figure 1.21 Saving a file for the first time using Save As

2   The **Save As** dialogue box is displayed (Figure 1.22).

Click on the down arrow
and then on a location
to store your document

Key in the new
filename here

Figure 1.22 The Save As dialogue box

3   Click on: the down arrow as shown in Figure 1.22 and click on the location where you want to save your document. (If you are saving to a floppy disk, select: **A:** and remember to have your disk inserted in the drive. See INFO box below.)

4   In the **File name** box, double-click on the filename that is already there, ie **qwerty QWERTY**, and delete it by pressing: **Delete**.

5   Key in the filename **keyboard** (case does not matter).

6   Click on: **Save**.

Inserting a floppy disk into the disk drive

Insert the disk metal slider first and with the label side uppermost until it clicks and the eject button pops out.

To eject a disk from a drive

Press: the Eject button on the drive.

Note: Sometimes there are problems when using Drive A because the application program you are using may try to access it when there is no disk in it. If this happens try reinserting the disk into the drive.

Notice that the default filename (**qwerty QWERTY**) has been replaced with the new filename (**keyboard**) on the Title bar.

4.8 Closing the file and exiting Word

Exercise 11

Close the file and exit Word.

Method

Either

From the **File** menu, select: **Close**
From the **File** menu, select: **Exit**

or

Click on: the **Close** button in the top right-hand corner.

i In Word, if you forget to save the document, you will be prompted to do so.

Inputting data practice

Practice 1

1 Load Word.

2 Enter the following leaving line spacing as shown:

   Arithmetic/Addition & Subtraction?

   6 + 2 – 4 = 4*

   ***Correct answer!**

   Your name and today's date

3 Save the document using the filename **prac1sums**.

4 Close Word.

Practice 2

1 Load Word.

2 Enter the following leaving a line space between each line as shown:

   Sales July 01: 25% increase

   Profit: £37,000@supplies-2-U

   Your name and today's date

3 Save the document using the filename **prac2sales**.

4 Close Word.

In this section you will learn how to:

- open an existing file
- amend an existing document
- resave a previously saved file
- switch on a printer
- load paper
- print a document
- create a new document
- save a document with a different filename

5.1 Opening an existing file

Exercise 1

Load Word and open the file **keyboard** saved in Section 4.

Method

1 Load Word.

2 From the **File** menu, select: **Open** (Figure 1.23).

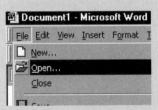

Figure 1.23 Opening a file

3 The **Open** dialogue box appears (Figure 1.24).

Figure 1.24 The Open dialogue box

4 In the **Look in** box, click on the down arrow and then on the location of the file, eg $3^{1}/_{2}$ Floppy (A:).

5 Click on: the filename, ie **keyboard**.

6 Click on: **Open**.

Exercise 2

Using skills learnt in the last section, add the following at the end of the document as shown below, leaving a line space after the existing text:

Learning the keyboard.

Method

1 Move the cursor to the end of the document using one of the methods shown in the previous section.

2 To leave a line space, press: **Enter** twice.

3 Key in the text.

Exercise 3

Delete the symbol @ from the line with the numbers.

Method

Use one of the deletion methods from the previous section. Your document will now look like Figure 1.25. *Note:* Ensure that you still have one space between each character after deletion.

qwerty QWERTY
The brown fox cub jumps over the lazy dog.

[Your name]

2 ! 4 = 1 / & 3 − 8 # 6 7 : 5 ? £ % * + , 9

Learning the keyboard.

Figure 1.25 Document after amendments

 It is very important that you pay attention to keying in accurately. Mistakes are easily transferred, eg gas bills for £1,000,000 because someone keyed in too many 0s. There is a computer saying *garbage in garbage out* (GIGO), ie if you key in incorrect information, incorrect information will be stored and printed. Correct any mistakes as you go along.

5.3 Resaving a previously saved file

Exercise 4

Resave the document with the amendments.

 Since you have already saved the first draft of this document, you will now be able to do a quick save instead of using **Save As**. This will overwrite your original with the changes you have made, but still keep the same filename, **keyboard**. If you wanted to keep the original document intact you would need to save the document with a different name using **Save As**. You would then have two files, the original and the amended one.

Method

From the **File** menu, select: **Save**.

5.4 Printing

Note: You will need to ask your tutor or refer to your printer manual for the next exercise.

Exercise 5

Prepare the printer for printing.

Method

1   Locate the printer that is connected to your computer and that is the default printer to be used with Word. (*Note*: There can be more than one printer connected to a computer. The default printer is the one the computer assumes it is printing to unless you tell it otherwise.)
2   Switch the printer on.
3   Load the printer with paper.

Exercise 6

Print the file **keyboard**.

1   From the **File** menu, select: **Print** (Figure 1.26).

Figure 1.26 Printing

2   The **Print** dialogue box is displayed.
3   Click on: **OK**.

5.5 Creating a new document

Exercise 7

Create the following new document and save with the filename **symbols** and print:

Your name and today's date

I am learning about symbols on the computer keyboard. They are:

* + % = – & £ # / @ ! ? :

I need to be very accurate!

Method

1   With Word loaded, from the **File** menu, select **New** (Figure 1.27).

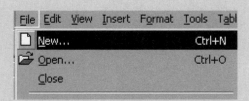

Figure 1.27 Creating a new document

2   The **New** box is displayed.

3   Click on: the **General** tab, then on **Blank Document**, then on **OK**.

Note: Instead of steps 1–3, you could click on: the ▯ **New** button.

4   Create, save and print the document in the normal way.

5.6 Close Word

Editing, saving and printing practice

Practice 3

1 Load Word and open the file **prac1sums** saved in Section 4, Practice 1.

2 Print one copy.

3 On the first line, delete the question mark.

4 Resave the document with the same filename.

5 Print one copy.

6 At the end of the document, leave a line space and on a new line add the following:

10@£3.99

7 Resave the document with the filename **prac3sums**.

8 Print one copy.

9 Close Word.

Practice 4

1 Load Word and open the file **prac2sales** saved in Section 4, Practice 2.

2 Print one copy.

3 On the first line change **July** to **June**.

4 Resave the document with the filename **prac4sales**.

5 Print one copy.

6 Close Word.

6 | # Locating and amending files

In this section you will learn how to locate files using file search facilities.

Note: For the exercises in this section you will need to have access to the files **Minutes3**, **Tasks** and **Profits**. These are on the CD-ROM that accompanies this book. In the examples that follow, I have copied the files to a floppy disk.

6.1 Locating files

Exercise 1

Using the operating system's **Find** facility, find the text file **Minutes3**.

Method

1 From the Windows 98 desktop **Start** menu, select: **Find**.

2 From the menu that appears, click on: **Files or Folders** (Figure 1.28).

Figure 1.28 Finding files

3 The **Find: All Files** dialogue box is displayed (Figure 1.29).

Figure 1.29 Find: All Files dialogue box

4 With the **Name & Location** tab selected (it is positioned in front of the other tabs when selected. If it is not selected, click on it to select it), in the **Named** box, key in: **Minutes3**. (*Note:* Case does not matter but it is important to key in the name correctly.)

5 If you know where it is, eg on a floppy disk, you can select the location by clicking on the down arrow in the **Look in** box and clicking on the location. Otherwise clicking on **My Computer** will ensure that a complete search is made in order to locate it.

6 Click on: **Find Now**.

7 The computer will start to search and when it finds a file with the filename you entered, it will list it in the window below together with the file's location (Figure 1.30). Make a note of the location. (You may need to use the scroll bar to see it in full.)

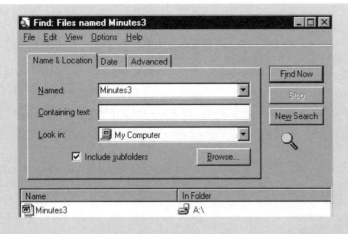

Figure 1.30 File found is listed

8 Double-click on the filename to open the file.

9 It will open in Word.

 In the examples used in this section, files open in Word. If a file does not open in Word but in another application:

1 Close the application.

2 Load Word.

3 From the **File** menu, select: **Open**.

4 The **Open** dialogue box is displayed.

5 Click on the down arrow in the **Look in** box to access the drive where your file is located.

6 Click on the appropriate drive so that the files are listed.

7 Double-click on the file.

If there are still problems opening the file in this way, you will need to discuss it with your tutor.

10 Close the **Find** box by clicking on it (it has minimised) on the taskbar (Figure 1.31), then click on: the ☒ **Close** button.

 Figure 1.31 Find Box – minimised on taskbar

6.2 Amending the file

Exercise 2

Add your name, your centre number and today's date at the end of the document.

Method

Use the methods in the preceding sections to do this.

6.3 Resaving the file with a different filename and print

Exercise 3

Resave the file with the filename **Minutes4**.

Method

Resave and print as in the previous sections.

Locating and amending files practice

Note: For the following exercises you will need access to the files **Tasks** and **Profits** on the CD-ROM.

Practice 5

1 Using the Find facility, find the text file **Tasks**.

2 Using an application that will allow you to read text files (ie Word), open the file **Tasks** in the application.

3 Add your name, your centre number and today's date at the end of the document.

4 Save the document with its original filename **Tasks**.

5 Print the document.

Practice 6

1 Using the Find facility, find the text file **Profits**.

2 Using an application that will allow you to read text files, open the file **Profits** in the application.

3 Add your name, your centre number and today's date at the end of the document.

4 Save the document with its original filename **Profits**.

5 Print the document.

Using a computer quick reference for New CLAIT (Windows Explorer)

Action	Keyboard	Mouse	Right-mouse menu	Menu
Create a new folder	Select where you want the new folder to be			
			New, **F**older	**F**ile, **N**ew, **F**older
Create a subfolder	Select the folder in which you want the subfolder to be and follow the steps for creating a new folder			
Delete a file/folder	Select the file/folder			
	Delete		**D**elete	**F**ile, **D**elete
Display contents of folder		Double-click: the folder		
Exit Windows Explorer		Click: the ⊠ **Close** button		**F**ile, **C**lose
Format a floppy disk	Select drive			
			Format	
Load Windows Explorer	In the Windows 98 desktop			
		Double-click: the **Windows Explorer** shortcut icon		**Start, Programs, Windows Explorer**

Using a computer quick reference for New CLAIT (Word)

Action	Keyboard	Mouse	Right-mouse menu	Menu
Close a file	**Ctrl + W**	Click: the ⊠ **Close** button		**F**ile, **C**lose
Exit Word		Click: the ⊠ **Close** button		**F**ile, E**x**it
Load Word		Double-click: the **Word** shortcut icon		**Start, Programs, Microsoft Word**
Open a new file	**Ctrl + N**	Click: the ▭ **New** button		**F**ile, **N**ew
Open an existing file	**Ctrl + O**	Click: the ☞ **Open** button		**F**ile, **O**pen
	Select the appropriate drive, directory and filename Click: **Open**			
Printing	**Ctrl + P**	Click: the 🖨 **Print** button		**F**ile, **P**rint
Saving a document for the first time or an existing document with a different filename	Select the appropriate drive and directory and change the filename if relevant			
		Click: the 🖫 **Save** button		**F**ile, **Save As**

Action	Keyboard	Mouse	Right-mouse menu	Menu
Saving an existing document with the same filename	Ctrl + S			File, Save

Using a computer quick reference Windows Desktop

Action	Keyboard	Mouse	Right-mouse menu	Menu
Find files/ folders	**Start**, **Find**, **Files or Folders** *or* in Windows Explorer **File** menu, **Find**			
Login	Enter your user name and password in the appropriate boxes (depending on your system)			
Recycle Bin, restore files	Double-click on the **Recycle Bin** icon Select the file you want to restore			
			Restore	File, **Restore**
Recycle Bin, empty			**Empty Recycle Bin**	
Switch on the computer	Ensure that the computer is plugged into the electricity socket. Press the button on the system box to turn the computer on, and on the monitor (if it has one)			
Shut down the computer	**Start**, **Shut Down**			

Hints and tips

- Ensure that you save the documents with the correct filenames.
- Proofread for errors in keyed-in text. In this unit data entry errors are counted per character (max allowed three).
- Can't find a file? Have you keyed it into the **Search** box correctly?
- Password not accepted? Have you keyed it in correctly? Are you using the correct case for each character?

Using a computer: sample full practice assignment

Note: If you want to practise this assignment using a password-protected file you can use **Health1** on the CD-ROM. The password is **Doctor23**. (You must match case when keying in the password.)

For this assignment you will need to use the file **Health** on the CD-ROM. No passwords will be required in this assessment but in an actual assessment they will be. Check that you know how to use them.

Scenario

You are looking to change your role within the large organisation where you work. You have been asked to work through the following tasks to demonstrate that you can use a computer.

Your computer has been set up ready for you to use. You have been given a password to gain access to any files that you need for the tasks. Your tutor will tell you when the password is needed.

1   Switch on the computer and monitor correctly and safely.

2   Wait for the operating system to load fully.

3   Using the operating system's 'find file' or 'search' facility, find the text file **Health**.

4   Using an application that will allow you to read text files, open the file **Health** in the application.

5   Using the mouse and keyboard (or alternatives if available) add your name, your centre number and today's date at the end of the document.

6   Save the document using the original filename, **Health**.

7   Switch on your printer and load a few sheets of paper.

8   Print the document using the default printer settings.

9   Close the Health document.

10   Create a new text document using the same software that you used to edit Health.

11   Enter the following data as shown, leaving a space between each line:

Computer chairs: Stock Code CC/59#2

@ £95.00-£150 with 10% discount

your name, your centre number and today's date

12   Save this document using the filename orders.

13   Print the document using the default printer settings.

14   Close the document orders.

15   Exit the application software and shut down the operating system safely.

Word processing using Word (Unit 2)

Getting started

In this section you will become familiar with Word and discover the advantages of using a word processor. You will learn how to:

- load Word
- set margins
- enter text
- delete text
- close a file

- understand the parts of the document window
- set text alignment
- insert text
- save a document
- exit Word

Note: Some skills covered in Chapter 1 are repeated here for those who have used an alternative software application for Unit 1. They will act as a refresher for those who have not.

1.1 What is a word processor?

Word processing software applications are the most commonly used computer applications. They allow you to create documents by keying in and manipulating text on screen. The documents can be saved as files and printed. These documents can be stored on disk so that they can be recalled and edited at a later date. Once the basics have been learnt, it is easy to produce professional-looking documents. Microsoft Word is a word processing program. Compared with a text editor (eg *Notepad*), Word has many powerful features, for example formatting text (eg its size, appearance and position), checking spelling, creating indexes and handling graphics. The screen display of the document is usually the same as the printout display. This is known as **WYSIWYG** (What You See Is What You Get). You will learn more about some of these features as you progress through the chapter.

1.2 Loading Word

Exercise 1

Load Word.

Method

1 Switch on your computer and login until the Windows 98 desktop screen appears.

2 Move the mouse cursor over the **Start** button and click the left button – a menu appears.

3 Select: **Programs** by moving the mouse over it – another menu appears.

4   Select: **Microsoft Word** and click the left button (Figure 2.1).

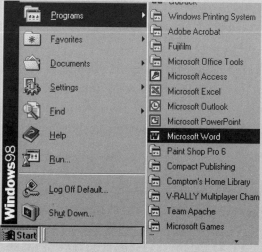

Figure 2.1 Loading Word

 If you have a shortcut icon to Word on your desktop, you can load Word
by clicking or double-clicking on: the [W] **Word** icon.

The Word Document window will be displayed on screen (Figure 2.2) showing a new blank document
with default values, ie pre-programmed settings such as line spacing, width of margins and font type.
These will remain unchanged unless you alter them.

If there is no Document window, click on: the [ ] **New** button at the top left of the
Standard toolbar

or

Select: **New** from the **File** menu; the **New** window will appear. Click on: **General** tab,
Blank Document and **OK**.

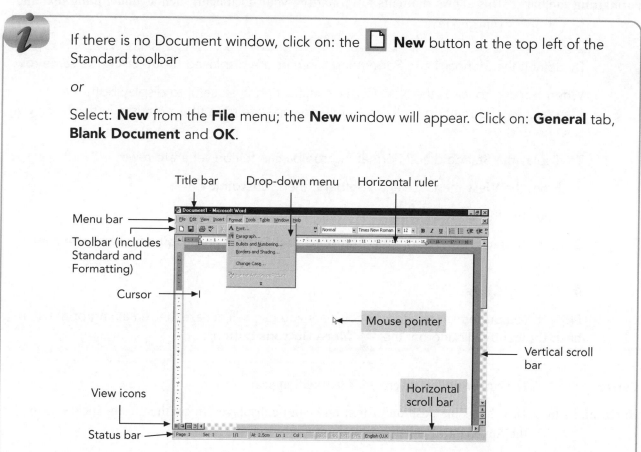

Figure 2.2 The Word Document window

Title bar | This shows the name of the application being used, Microsoft Word, and the current document name, **Document1** (this is the default name).

Menu bar | This has menu names that can be selected using the mouse/keyboard. A *drop-down menu* then gives you further options. This initially displays options used most recently. After a few seconds, the drop-down menu expands to include all available options. These menus will personalise to display your most recently selected options as you progress through your work.

Standard toolbar | This contains shortcut buttons for frequently made actions. For example, to open an existing file, click on: the button shown in Figure 2.3.

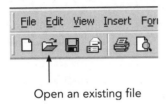

Open an existing file

Figure 2.3 Standard toolbar buttons

To find out quickly what each button on the toolbar does, hover the mouse over the button and wait for a few seconds. A *ToolTip* will appear giving a brief explanation of the button. Try this now.

Formatting toolbar | This allows shortcuts to formatting your document, such as underlining text and centring text.

By default the Standard and Formatting toolbars are displayed together on the same row.

When working towards the New CLAIT qualification it is useful to display both the Standard and Formatting toolbars, in full, on separate rows (the exercises in this book will assume this).

To display the Standard and Formatting toolbars in full on separate rows:

1   From the **View** menu, select: **Toolbars**, then: **Customize**.

2   Click on: the **Options** tab.

3   Click to remove the tick in the **Standard and Formatting toolbars share one row box**.

4   Click on: **Close**.

Note: If you prefer not to alter the toolbars you can still access the remaining options on each toolbar by clicking on: the ⏬ **More Buttons** buttons.

Cursor | The cursor flashes where your text will appear.

Horizontal ruler | This shows the position of text and can be displayed in centimetres or inches. (See the Appendix to change the default.)

Mouse pointer | This will move when you move the mouse – use to select items in the window. The mouse pointer changes shape depending on where it is on the screen.

Scroll bars | You can scroll quickly through your document using the scroll bars.

Status bar	This provides information about the position of the cursor and the text displayed on your screen.
View icons	These allow for different ways of viewing your text. We will be using **Normal View** (the furthest left of the View icons). Click on this now. This view allows fast editing.

1.4 Setting margins

Margins are the blank space at the top, bottom and sides of text that will be printed on your document. In this exercise you will learn how to set the left and right page margins. You can set margins before or after you have keyed in text. Setting margins before keying in text and making adjustments after keying in text are requirements for New CLAIT.

Exercise 2

Set the left and right page margins to 2 cm.

Method

Note: Before following these instructions, have a look at the horizontal ruler (Figure 2.2). This shows the default width that text entered on the page will be (line length). Make a note of this measurement so that you can see the difference after resetting the margins.

1   From the **File** menu, select: **Page Setup** (Figure 2.4).

Figure 2.4 Selecting Page Setup

2   The **Page Setup** dialogue box is displayed (Figure 2.5). With the **Margins** tab selected, this shows the default margins set by Word, ie **Left** and **Right** margins are 3.17 cm.

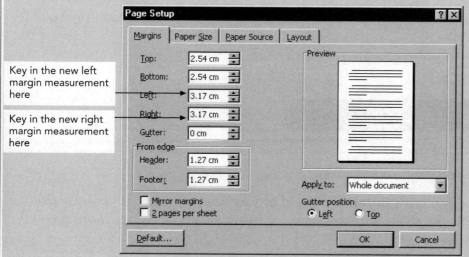

Figure 2.5 Setting margins

3   Click in: the **Left** box, delete 3.17 cm and key in: **2 cm**.

4   Do the same in the **Right** box.

5   Click on: **OK**.

6   You are returned to the document window.

7   Check the horizontal ruler to see the change. The left and right margins are now narrower so the line length is longer.

1.5 Setting alignment

Exercise 3

Set an unjustified right margin and a justified left margin.

 There are four types of alignment. They can be accessed via the **Formatting** toolbar (Figure 2.6). Alignment can be set before and after text has been keyed in. When text is fully justified the spacing between words may change slightly to ensure a straight right edge. You do not need to be concerned about this, but should be aware of it.

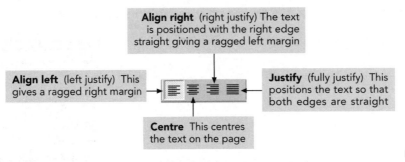

Align right (right justify) The text is positioned with the right edge straight giving a ragged left margin

Align left (left justify) This gives a ragged right margin

Justify (fully justify) This positions the text so that both edges are straight

Centre This centres the text on the page

Figure 2.6 Types of alignment

Method

Click on the appropriate toolbar button. In this case **Align Left** (this is the default so should be already selected).

1.6 Entering text

 Before you begin entering text you should be aware of the following:

- You do not need to press **Enter** at the end of each line, because if the text is too long to fit within the space available, it will automatically be carried over to the next line. This is known as *word wrap*.

- To create a space, press: the **space bar** (the wide key at the bottom centre of the keyboard) once.

- You should be consistent with spaces after commas and full stops. One space after a comma and one/two space(s) after a full stop is acceptable, looks neat and is easy to read. You can check that you have been consistent by clicking on: the ¶ **Show/Hide** button. This displays spaces as dots. So one space appears as one dot. To turn Show/Hide off, click on: the **Show/Hide** button again.

- To make documents easier to read, you should leave a blank line after headings and between paragraphs. To do this press: **Enter** twice.

- Organisations have specific *house styles*. These determine how documents should look and when working for an organisation you will need to be aware of their document layout rules.

- To key in capital letters, hold down: **Shift** at the same time as the key for the letter you want to key in.

- If you are keying in a block of capital letters, press: the **Caps Lock** key to start keying in capitals and press: **Caps Lock** again to stop. (See **Change Case** in the quick reference at the end of this chapter.)

- Do not worry if you make mistakes, you can correct them later.

- You may notice that sometimes wiggly lines appear under text that you have keyed in. This is due to the default spellchecking option. To turn this off: from the **Tools** menu, select: **Options**. Click on: the **Spelling and Grammar** tab. In the **Spelling** section, click in: the **Check spelling as you type** box to remove the tick. Click on: **OK**.

For more information on layout, see the Appendix.

Exercise 4

Key in the following text:

Wisdom teeth are so called because they do not appear until the age of 18 to 20 when we are supposed to have become wiser.

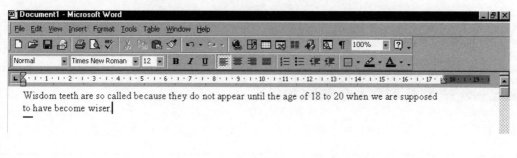

Figure 2.7 The keyed in text will look similar to this

1.7 Moving around your text

Here, we will learn three methods to move around the text:

1   Using the arrow keys.

2   Using the mouse.

3   Using two keys together, **Ctrl + Home**, and **Ctrl + End**.

1 Moving around your text using the arrow keys

The arrow keys ← ↑ → ↓ (located at the bottom right of the main keyboard) allow you to move the cursor (a flashing black vertical line) in the direction of the arrows.

You can move one space forwards or backwards at a time, or you can move up or down one line at a time. If you keep an arrow key pressed down, the cursor will move quickly through the document. Remember to release the arrow key when you reach the required place.

2 Moving around your text using the mouse

As you move the mouse around the screen, you will notice that the I-beam moves with you. Move it until you have reached the required position, click the left mouse button once and the cursor will appear where you have clicked.

3 Using **Ctrl + Home** and **Ctrl + End**

Hold down: the **Ctrl** key at the same time as the **Home** key to move to the top of your text.

Hold down: the **Ctrl** key at the same time as the **End** key to move to the bottom of your text.

 There are other ways to move around the document and these are included in the quick reference at the end of this chapter.

1.8 Inserting text

Exercise 5

Insert the word **usually** between the words **not** and **appear**.

Method

Position the cursor at the point where you want to insert text (in this case immediately before the letter **a** of the word **appear**), and then key in **usually** and a space (Figure 2.8).

> Wisdom teeth are so called because they do not usually |appear until the age of 18 to 20 when we are supposed to have become wiser.

Figure 2.8 Inserting text

Notice how the text to the right of the cursor moves to make room for the new text and some text at the end of the line has automatically moved to the next line.

 If your text does not move across but overwrites text already there, check that **OVR** is not displayed on the Status bar. If it is, press: **Insert** to remove overwrite.

1.9 Deleting text

Exercise 6

Delete the word **of**.

There are three methods:

Method 1

Position the cursor to the left of the first character that you want to delete, ie the **o** of **of** and press: **Delete** until the letters **of** (and the space) have been deleted.

Method 2

Position the cursor to the right of the last character you want to delete and press: **Del** ← (Backspace) key (top right of the main keyboard) until the letters **of** (and the space) have been deleted.

Method 3

Double-click on the word **of** to select it and press: **Delete**.

Try each method. Reinsert the word **of** after each method by clicking on: the ↰ **Undo** button.

Exercise 7

Now try keying in a longer piece of text. Set the left and right margins to 3 cm. Use a justified left margin and an unjustified right margin.

Method

1   Click on: the ▯ **New** button.
2   Set the margins as specified.
3   Set the alignment as specified.

4   Key in the following text:

(*Note*: The line endings will not necessarily be in the same place.)

Better Travel & Co Information

The cathedral of Pisa in Tuscany, Italy, has a bell tower known as the leaning tower of Pisa. It is a big attraction to visitors to the area.

Why does it lean? Work started on the tower in 1173. When the building was half finished the sandy soil under one half of the circular structure began to subside and the tower tipped. Work was discontinued for a century.

Architects devised a plan to counteract the 5.5% tilt. They decided that two storeys should be built slightly askew so as to alter the tower's centre of gravity. When the bell tower section was added at the top, the extra weight increased the tilting even more!

Ten years ago the tower was on the brink of collapse and closed to visitors. The tower underwent major restoration work at a cost of £3 million. Thirty tonnes of subsoil were removed from underneath it. This allowed the tower to settle under its own weight in a more stable but still leaning position. The tower reopened in June 2000.

1.10 Saving documents

Exercise 8

Save the document.

Method

 Note that the text will now be referred to as a file.

1   From the **File** menu, select: **Save As** (Figure 2.9).

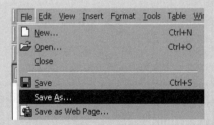

Figure 2.9 Saving a file for the first time using Save As

2   The **Save As** dialogue box is displayed (Figure 2.10).

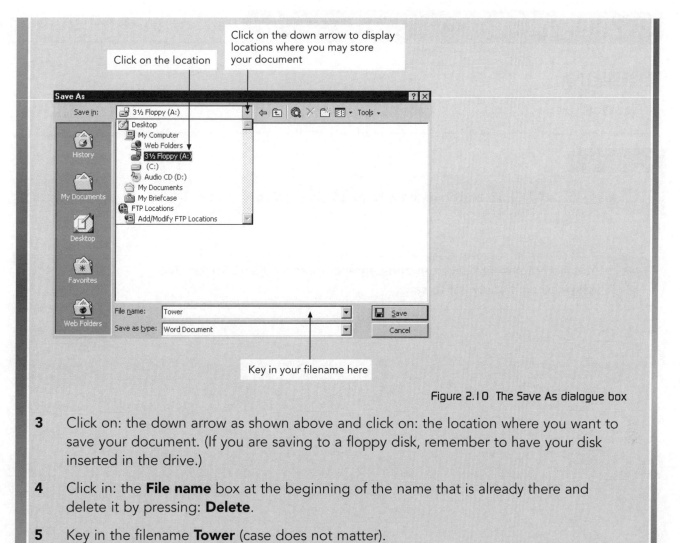

Click on the location

Click on the down arrow to display locations where you may store your document

Key in your filename here

Figure 2.10 The Save As dialogue box

3 Click on: the down arrow as shown above and click on: the location where you want to save your document. (If you are saving to a floppy disk, remember to have your disk inserted in the drive.)

4 Click in: the **File name** box at the beginning of the name that is already there and delete it by pressing: **Delete**.

5 Key in the filename **Tower** (case does not matter).

6 Click on: **Save**.

> Notice that the default filename (**Documentx**) has been replaced with the new filename (**Tower**) on the **Title** bar.

1.11 Closing a file

Exercise 9

Close the file **Tower**.

Method

From the **File** menu, select: **Close**.

1.12 Exiting Word

Exercise 10

Exit Word.

Method

Click on: the **Close** button in the top right-hand corner.

You do not need to save the one-sentence practice file. Click on: **No** when asked if you want to save.

Word processing practice

Practice 1

1 Create a new word processing document.

2 Set the left and right margins to 2 cm.

3 Enter the following text with an unjustified right margin and a justified left margin:

Electronic Mail Etiquette

It is believed that 87% of Internet users use e-mail. Some businesses cite that they make savings of at least £5,000 per year by communicating in this way.

You should not expect an immediate response to your e-mails. If you require an immediate response, use the telephone. E-mail is there for the user's convenience and not to cause inconvenience!

There has been much debate about e-mail etiquette. There are unwritten rules of business behaviour. These include being polite, being brief and not shouting. Shouting in e-mail terms means using capital letters to make a point stand out. Using too much punctuation, such as repeated exclamation marks to add emphasis is also bad form. Try to express what you want to say in your text.

When using abbreviations, try to stick to the more common ones, such as BTW, meaning by the way, and FYI, meaning for your information. If you received a message would you understand what ROTFL meant? What would be your response?

4 Save your document with the filename **P1 sec1 email**.

Practice 2

1 Create a new word processing document.

2 Set the left and right margins to 2.5 cm.

3 Enter the following text fully justified:

Computer Passwords

It is most important at ABC Financial Services that passwords are used routinely when creating documents that are of a sensitive nature. These include all internal reports, personal letters to customers and to other financial institutions.

All computer systems within this department have recently been upgraded at a cost of £150,000. We estimate that this will be of benefit to 90% of ABC's computer users. This upgrade includes new security access.

Typing in of passwords is now required to access individual workstations. It is very important that you choose your password so that others cannot easily guess it. For example, your boyfriend's name is not a good idea or, indeed, your birth date.

Passwords can be a mixture of letters and numbers to a maximum of fifteen. They are case sensitive. When typing in passwords the characters appear as asterisks on the screen. However, ensure that nobody can see what you are typing in. Always remain vigilant.

4 Save your document with the filename **P2 sec1 passwords**.

Editing, formatting and printing 1

In this section you will practise and learn how to:

- reload a saved file
- spellcheck
- print preview and print
- change font size
- insert a block of text
- save document with a new filename

- proofread and correct errors
- resave a previously saved file
- change font
- emphasise text – embolden, italicise, underline
- move text
- insert a paragraph break

2.1 Reloading a saved file

Exercise 1

Load Word and open the file **Tower** saved in Section 1.

Method

1 Click on: the ⬆️ **Open** button.

2 The **Open** dialogue box appears (Figure 2.11).

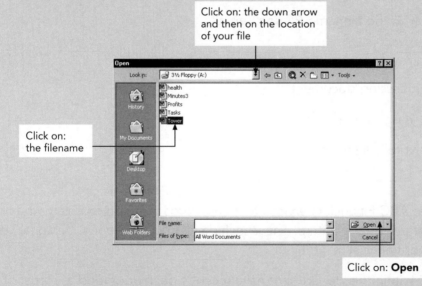

Click on: the down arrow and then on the location of your file

Click on: the filename

Click on: **Open**

Figure 2.11 Opening a file

3 In the **Look in** box, click on: the down arrow and then on the location of your file.

4 Click on: the filename.

5 Click on: **Open**.

It is important to proofread your work carefully against the hard copy. Correct any errors in the text using the methods described in Section 1.

2.3 Spellchecking

It is always useful to run the spellchecker through a document before you print as it will pick up most misspelt words and provide you with the chance to correct them. It will also pick up repeated words, eg the the, so that you can delete one of them. Word provides an option to check spelling and grammar together, or check spelling and grammar as you type, but at this stage it is more straightforward to check spelling only and I have set this option in the examples (see the Appendix for changing the default).

Note: There are limitations to the spellchecker's abilities and it may not pick up wrong usage of words (eg where and were, stair and stare). Although these words are spelt correctly it may be that they are being used in the wrong context.

Always check that you are using the English (UK) spellchecker. From the **Tools** menu, select: **Language**, **Set Language**, **English (UK)**.

Note: Using the spellchecker is advisable, but is not a requirement for New CLAIT.

Exercise 2

Run the spellchecker through the document.

Method

1 Position the cursor at the start of the document by pressing: **Ctrl + Home**.

2 Click on: the ABC ✓ **Spelling and Grammar** button.

3 The **Spelling and Grammar** dialogue box is displayed (Figure 2.12).

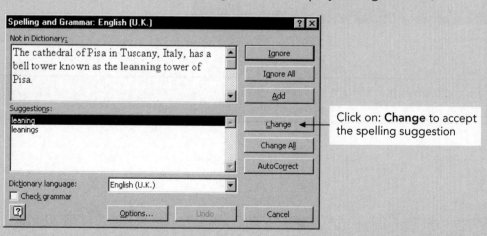

Figure 2.12 Spelling and Grammar dialogue box

The spellchecker will go through your text and match it with the words in its dictionary. It will highlight unrecognisable words and offer suggestions. (You may not have made any spelling errors!) In the example above, the spellchecker has highlighted the word **leanning** and it is offering its preferred replacement, **leaning**, also highlighted in the lower box. In this case accept the suggestion by clicking on: **Change**.

If you do not want to accept a suggestion that the spellchecker has made, click on: **Ignore**.

If you want to accept one of the other suggestions, click it to select it and then click on: **Change**.

The spellchecker will repeat this process until it has finished checking all the text. It will then display a message telling you that the spellcheck is complete.

2.4 Resaving a previously saved file

Exercise 3

Resave the file **Tower**.

As you have already saved the first draft of this document, you will now be able to do a quick save instead of using **Save As**. This will overwrite your original with the changes you have made, but still keep the same filename, **Tower**.

Method

To resave

Click on: the 💾 **Save** toolbar button.

2.5 Print Preview

Exercise 4

Print Preview your document.

Method

If you want to see how your document is going to look on the page before printing it, you can use Word's **Print Preview** facility.

1   Click on: the 🔍 **Print Preview** button. The **Print Preview** screen appears (Figure 2.13).

Click on: **Close** to return
to the document window

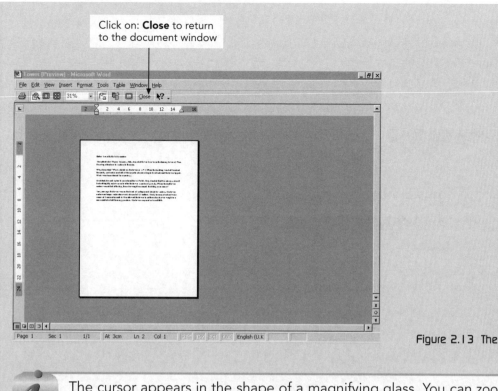

Figure 2.13 The Print Preview screen

The cursor appears in the shape of a magnifying glass. You can zoom in to any part of the document by clicking over it with the left mouse button. To zoom out, click again.

2   Press: **Esc** or click on: **Close** to return to the document window.

2.6 Printing a document

Exercise 5

Key in your name and the date a few lines below the end of the text. Resave the document using the **Save** toolbar button. Print one copy of the document.

Method

1   Move to the end of the document using one of the methods you have learnt.

2   Leave a few line spaces by pressing: **Enter** for each line space.

3   Key in your name and press: **Enter**.

4   Key in the date and press: **Enter**.

5   Resave the file.

Printing

1   From the **File** menu, select: **Print** (Figure 2.14).

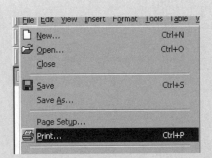

Figure 2.14 File menu, Print

2   The **Print** dialogue box is displayed (Figure 2.15).

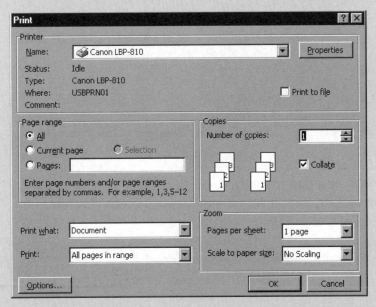

Figure 2.15 Print dialogue box

3   Check that the printer is turned on, ready and loaded with paper.

4   There are several default control options concerning printing, such as number of copies and page range (shown in the **Print** dialogue box). At this stage, you should not need to change any settings, so just click on: **OK**.

Quick method to print

On the toolbar, click on: the ⬛ **Print** button.

Use this if you know that you do not need to alter anything in the Print dialogue box.

2.7 Changing font and font size

Exercise 6

Change the font of the main heading to **Arial** and the size to **16 pt**, ie so that it is larger than the rest of the text.

Changing font type

 The term *font* refers to the design of the characters in the character set. In Word there are numerous fonts to choose from. The default font is *Times New Roman*. This is a **serif** font. Serifs are small lines that stem from the upper and lower ends of characters. Serif fonts have such lines. *Sans serif* fonts do not have these lines. Examples:

Times New Roman is a serif font
Arial is a sans serif font

The vertical height of fonts is measured in *points* (*pt*). The default point size is 12 so when asked for a font size larger than the rest of the text, 14 pt or 16 pt would be good choices. Below are some example point sizes:

6 pt
10 pt
12 pt
18 pt
28 pt
36 pt
44 pt

1   Select the heading **Better Travel & Co Information** so that it is highlighted. To do this:

   a   Position the cursor at the beginning of the text to select – in this case the **B** of **Better**.

   b   Hold down the left mouse button and drag the I-beam pointer across the heading so that it is highlighted.

   c   Release the mouse.

 There are many ways to select text. These are given in the quick reference at the end of this chapter. There is no right or wrong way. Experiment to find your own preferred method.

2   Click on the down arrow in the **Font** box (where *Times New Roman* is displayed, shown in Figure 2.16) to display fonts that are available on your computer.

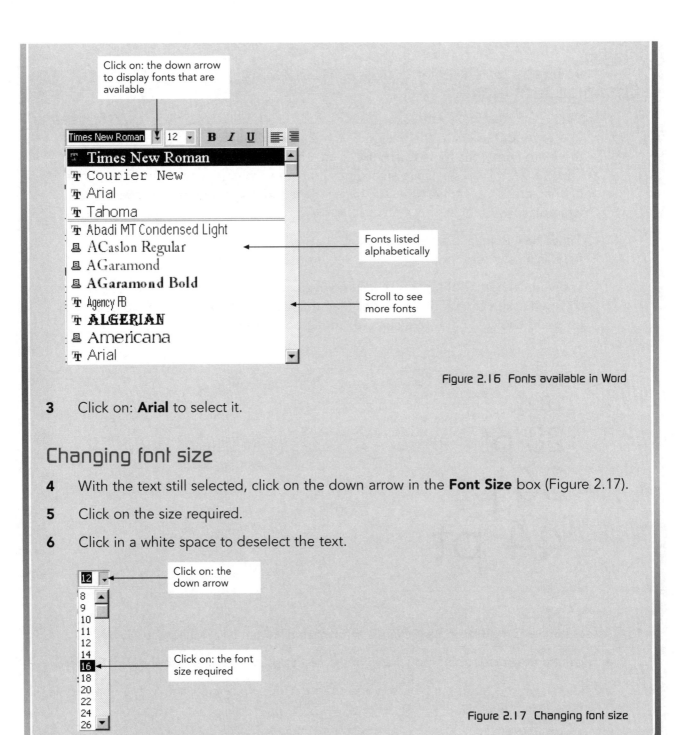

Click on: the down arrow to display fonts that are available

Times New Roman | 12 | **B** *I* <u>U</u>

T **Times New Roman**
T Courier New
T Arial
T Tahoma
T Abadi MT Condensed Light
A ACaslon Regular
A AGaramond
A **AGaramond Bold**
T Agency FB
T **ALGERIAN**
A Americana
T Arial

Fonts listed alphabetically

Scroll to see more fonts

Figure 2.16 Fonts available in Word

3 Click on: **Arial** to select it.

Changing font size

4 With the text still selected, click on the down arrow in the **Font Size** box (Figure 2.17).

5 Click on the size required.

6 Click in a white space to deselect the text.

12

Click on: the down arrow

8
9
10
11
12
14
16
18
20
22
24
26

Click on: the font size required

Figure 2.17 Changing font size

2.8 Emphasising text

Emboldening, italicising or underlining text is a way of giving emphasis to the text.

Emboldening text

Exercise 7

Embolden the heading **Better Travel and Co Information**.

1 Select the text to be emboldened.

2 Click on: the **B** **Embolden** button.

Italicising text

Exercise 8

Italicise the word **Tuscany** in the first paragraph.

Follow the method shown above except at step 2 click on: the **I** **Italic** button.

Underlining text

Exercise 9

In the second sentence of the final paragraph underline **£3 million**.

Follow the method shown above except at step 2 click on: the **U** **Underline** button.

When underlining, do not extend the underline before or beyond the words to be underlined as shown in the examples below:

<u>Your name</u> is correct

<u>Your name </u>is incorrect.

2.9 Inserting a block of text

Exercise 10

Using the instructions for inserting text in Section 1.8 and below, insert the new text (shown below) at the end of the first paragraph ending **... attraction to visitors to the area.**

Many people visit Pisa just so that they can have their photograph taken beside the leaning tower. How many visitors would want to see the upright tower of Pisa?

Method

1 Position the cursor after the full stop after the word **area**.

2 Create a space between the sentences by pressing the space bar once/twice (depending on your preferences).

3 Key in the text.

 Remember: When you insert or delete text, check that the spacing between words, sentences and paragraphs is still consistent. Use the ¶ **Show/Hide** button to check this.

2.10 Moving text

Exercise 11

Move the first sentence of the second paragraph: **Why does it lean?** so that it then becomes the final sentence of the first paragraph.

Method

1 Select the sentence by dragging the mouse over it as in Section 2.7.

2 Click on: the ✂ **Cut** button. The text will be saved on to a clipboard (you will not see or be told this).

3 Position the cursor where you want the text to reappear, click on: the 📋 **Paste** button.

 Remember to check that spacing is still consistent. Delete any extra spaces by positioning the cursor in front of them and pressing: **Delete**. Insert spaces as necessary by positioning the cursor where you want the space to appear and pressing the **space bar**.

Note: You can also use the above method for copying. In this case, at step 2, click on: the **Copy** button.

If you have good control of the mouse you can use the *drag and drop* method to move text. To do this:

1 Select the text as above.

2 Hold down the left mouse button over the selected text and drag the block of text to the required position.

3 Release the mouse button.

4 Check for spacing consistency.

This is quite difficult to master! Use the **Undo** button if you have problems.

2.11 Inserting a paragraph break

Exercise 12

Insert a paragraph break and clear line space in the first paragraph after the
text **... to the area.**

Method

1   Position the cursor immediately in front of the word **Many**.

2   Press: **Enter** twice.

3   Check for consistency of spacing.

2.12 Saving the document

Exercise 13

Save the document with the filename **Tower1** (as shown in Section 1.10) and
print one copy.

 By saving your file as **Tower1**, you will ensure that the original file is not overwritten.
This is important when working through New CLAIT assignments because you will then
be able to go back and correct any errors should this be necessary.

2.13 Exiting Word

Exercise 14

Close the file and exit Word.

Editing, formatting and printing practice 1

Practice 3

1   Reload the file **P1 sec1 email**, saved in Practice 1, Section 1.

2   Enter your name, centre number and today's date a few lines below the end of the text.

3   Format the heading so that it is larger than the rest of the text.

4   Save the document with the filename **P3 sec2 email** and print one copy.

5   Insert a paragraph break and clear line space in the third paragraph after the words **...point stand out.**

6   Insert the following text as the last sentence of the last paragraph after the text **...be your response?**

   For your information, ROTFL means rolling on the floor laughing.

7   Change only the heading to a different font.

8   Embolden the words **at least** in the second sentence of the first paragraph.

9   In the paragraph beginning **You should not...**, move the last sentence beginning **E-mail is there...** so that it is the first sentence of this paragraph.

10 Save the document with the filename **email step 10** and print one copy.

Practice 4

1   Reload the file **P2 sec1 passwords**, saved in Section 1.

2   Enter your name, centre number and today's date a few lines below the end of the text.

3   Format the heading so that it is larger than the rest of the text.

4   Save the document with the filename **P4 sec2 passwords** and print one copy.

5   Insert a paragraph break and clear line space in the final paragraph after the words **...case sensitive.**

6   Insert the following paragraph after the first paragraph:

   Accessing unauthorised information is a serious matter. Passwords should not be divulged to anyone. They should be changed on a regular basis.

7   Change only the heading to a different font.

8   Underline the word **most** in the first sentence of the first paragraph.

9   In the final paragraph move the sentence **Always remain vigilant** so that it is the second sentence of the first paragraph.

10 Save the document with the filename **passwords step 10** and print one copy.

3 Editing, formatting and printing 2

In this section you will practise and learn how to:

- delete blocks of text
- amend margins
- realign text

- replace specified text
- change line spacing

3.1 Reload the file Tower1 saved in Section 2

3.2 Deleting blocks of text

We have already learnt how to delete text using the **Delete** or ← Del (Backspace) key. However, this is not the quickest method to delete whole sentences or longer portions of text. To do this we need to select the text to be deleted.

Exercise 1

In the last paragraph, delete the sentence beginning: **Thirty tonnes of...**.

Method

1 Move the cursor to the beginning of the text you want to delete – in this case the **T** of **Thirty** (Figure 2.18).

> t a cost of £3 million. |Thirty tonnes of subsoil were
> lowed the tower to settle under its own weight in a

Figure 2.18 Positioning the cursor

2 Hold down the left mouse button and drag the I-beam pointer across the sentence (Figure 2.19).

> underwent major restoration work at a cost of £3 million. Thirty tonnes of subsoil were
> removed from underneath it. This allowed the tower to settle under its own weight in a

Figure 2.19 Selecting text

3 Release the mouse button. The highlighting shows the text that is selected. If you need to cancel the selection, click anywhere on the screen or press any arrow key.

4 Press: **Delete**.

5 Check for consistency of spacing.

 If you want to undo the last action(s), click on: the ↰ **Undo** button on the toolbar. This button is very useful and can be used at any time.

3.3 Replacing text

 There is no need for you to scan through text manually to replace it because Word can automatically find and replace text. It is thorough in its searching and saves time.

Exercise 2

The word **visitors** appears three times in the text. Replace the word **visitors** with the word **tourists** each time it appears.

Method

1   Move your cursor to the top of the document (**Ctrl** + **Home**).

2   From the **Edit** menu, select: **Replace** (Figure 2.20).

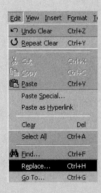

Figure 2.20 Edit menu, Replace

3   The **Find and Replace** dialogue box is displayed.

4   Click on: the **Replace** tab (if not already selected).

5   Click in: the **Find what** box; key in the word **visitors**. *NB:* Do not press enter yet.

6   Click in: the **Replace with** box; key in the word **tourists** (lower case).

7   Click on: **Replace All** (Figure 2.21).

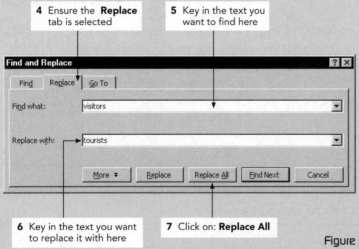

4 Ensure the **Replace** tab is selected

5 Key in the text you want to find here

6 Key in the text you want to replace it with here

7 Click on: **Replace All**

Figure 2.21 The Find and Replace dialogue box

8 A box appears telling you how many replacements have been made (Figure 2.22).

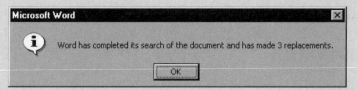

Figure 2.22 You are advised how many replacements have been made

9 Click on: **OK**.

10 Click on: **Close**.

 There are options available within Find and Replace. The commonly used option is **Match Case**. Use this if you are replacing a word consisting of capital letters. If you do not use it, the replacement word will also have capital letters (it will not have matched the case you have keyed in). To set Match Case, in the **Find and Replace** dialogue box, click on: **More**, click on: **Match Case** and proceed as before.

3.4 Changing line spacing

Exercise 3

Change the whole document to double line spacing.

 Word lets you apply a variety of line space settings (the distance between individual lines of text). Examples are:

Single line spacing   this is the default.
Double line spacing   one blank line is left between the lines of text.

This is an example of single line spacing. The default setting is single line spacing. If the specification for a document is single line spacing, then usually you need do nothing.

This is an example of double line spacing. There is one blank line left between lines of

text. It is often used when a section needs extra emphasis.

Method

1 Select all the text using the quick method (press: **Ctrl + A**).

2 From the **Format** menu, select: **Paragraph**. The Paragraph dialogue box is displayed (Figure 2.23).

3 Ensure the **Indents and Spacing** tab is selected.

4 In the **Spacing** section, **Line spacing** box, click on the down arrow and click on: **Double**.

5 Click on: **OK**.

6 Click in a white space to remove highlighting.

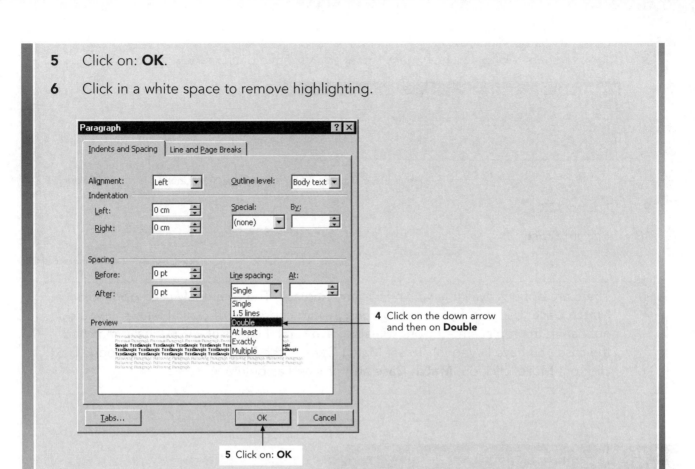

Figure 2.23 The Paragraph dialogue box – selecting double line spacing

 In double line spacing there are usually three lines between paragraphs. If you look on the Status bar you may notice that your document now takes up 2 pages (depending on how many line spaces you have left between the main text and your name) since 1/2 is displayed. When you scroll through your document you will see a dotted line across the page indicating that Word has inserted a page break.

3.5 Amending margins

Exercise 4

Change the left and right margins from 3 cm to 2 cm.

Method

Follow the method in Section 1.4.

3.6 Realigning text

Exercise 5

Centre the heading.

Method

1   Select the text to be centred or click on the line to centre.
2   Click on: the ☰ **Center** button.

Exercise 6

Fully justify only the fourth paragraph beginning **Architects devised...**

Method

1   Select the paragraph to justify.
2   Click on: the ☰ **Justify** button.

3.7 Save the file with the name Tower2 and print one copy

3.8 Close the file and exit Word

Editing, formatting and printing practice 2

Practice 5

1 Reload the file **email step 10**, saved in Practice 3, Section 2.

2 In the third paragraph, which begins **There has been...**, delete the sentence:

   These include being polite, being brief and not shouting.

3 Replace all occurrences of the word **response** with the word **reply** (three times in all).

4 Centre the heading **Electronic Mail Etiquette**.

5 Fully justify all except the heading.

6 Set the final paragraph in double line spacing.

7 Change the left and right margins from 2 cm to 3 cm.

8 Save the document with the filename **P5 sec3 email**.

9 Print a final copy.

10 Close the document and exit the application securely.

Practice 6

1 Reload the file **passwords step 10**, saved in Practice 4, Section 2.

2 In the third paragraph, which begins **All computer systems...**, delete the sentence:

   We estimate that this will be of benefit to 90% of ABC's computer users.

3 Replace all occurrences of the word **typing** with the word **keying** (three times in all).

4 Centre and embolden the heading **Computer Passwords**.

5 Left justify the first paragraph only.

6 Set the heading and first two paragraphs in double line spacing.

7 Change the left and right margins from 2.5 cm to 1.5 cm.

8 Save the document with the filename **P6 sec3 passwords**.

9 Print a final copy.

10 Close the document and exit the application securely.

Word processing quick reference for New CLAIT (Word)

Action	Keyboard	Mouse	Right-mouse menu	Menu
Bold text	Select text to embolden			
	Ctrl + B	Click: the **B** **Bold** button	Font	**Format, Font**
			Select: **Bold** from the **Font style:** menu	
Capitals (blocked)	**Caps Lock** Key in the text **Caps Lock** again to remove			Select text to be changed to capitals: **Format, Change Case, UPPERCASE**
Centre text	Select the text to centre			
	Ctrl + E	Click: the ≡ **Center** button	**Paragraph**	**Format, Paragraph**
			Select: **Centered** from the **Alignment:** drop-down menu	
Change case	Select the text to be changed From the **Format** menu, select: **Change Case** Select the appropriate case			
Close a file	**Ctrl + W**	Click: the ✕ **Close**		**File, Close**
Cut text	Select the text to be cut			
	Ctrl + X	Click: the ✂ **Cut** button	**Cut**	**Edit, Cut**
Delete a character	Press **Delete** to delete the character to the right of the cursor Press ← (Backspace) to delete the character to the left of the cursor			
Delete a word	Double-click: the word to select it. Press: **Delete**			
Delete/cut a block of text	Select the text you want to delete			
	Delete or **Ctrl + X**	Click: the ✂ **Cut** button	**Cut**	**Edit, Cut**
Exit Word		Click: the ✕ **Close** button		**File, Exit**
Font size	Select the text you want to change			
		Click: the ▼ down arrow next to the **Font Size** box Select: the font size you require	Font	**Format, Font**
			Select: the required size from the **Size:** menu	
Font	Select the text you want to change			
		Click: the ▼ down arrow next to the **Font** box Select: the font you require	Font	**Format, Font**
			Select: the required font from the **Font:** menu	
Help	**F1**			**Help, Microsoft Word Help**
	Shift + F1			**Help, What's This?**
Insert text	Position the cursor where you want the text to appear Key in the text			

Action	Keyboard	Mouse	Right-mouse menu	Menu
Italics	Select text to italicise			
	Ctrl + I	Click: the *I* **Italic** button	Font	**Format**, **Font**
			Select: **Italic** from the **Font style:** menu	
Justified margins	Select the text you want to change			
	Ctrl + J	Click: the ≣ **Justify** icon	**Paragraph**	**Format**, **Paragraph**
			Select **Justified** from the **Alignment:** drop-down menu	
Line spacing			**Paragraph**	**Format**, **Paragraph**, **Indents and Spacing**
			In the **Spacing** section, select the options you require	
Load Word	In the Windows 98 desktop			
		Double-click: the **Word** shortcut icon		**Start**, **Programs**, **Microsoft Word**
Margins				**File**, **Page Setup**, **Margins**
Move a block of text	Select: the text to be moved Cut and paste the text where you want it *or* Select: the text to be moved Click and drag: the text to the correct position Release the mouse button			
Moving around the document	Use the cursor keys (see separate table for more)	Click: in the required position		
New file, creating	**Ctrl + N**	Click: the ▯ **New** button		**File**, **New**
Open an existing file	**Ctrl + O**	Click: the 📂 **Open** button		**File**, **Open**
	Select the appropriate directory and filename Click: **Open**			
Page display	Click: the appropriate ≣⬚▤⬚ **View** button (at the bottom of the Word window)			**View**
Page Setup				**File**, **Page Setup** (choose from **Margins**, **Paper Size**, **Paper Source**, **Layout**)
Paper size	(See Page Setup)			
Paragraphs – splitting/ joining	*Splitting:* Move the cursor to the first letter of the new paragraph Press: **Enter** twice *Joining:* Move the cursor to the first character of the second paragraph Press ← (Backspace) twice (Press the space bar to insert a space after a full stop)			

Action	Keyboard	Mouse	Right-mouse menu	Menu
Print file	**Ctrl + P** Select the options you need Press: **Enter**	Click: the 🖨 **Print** button		**File**, **Print** Select the options you need and click: **OK**
Print Preview		Click: the 🔍 **Print Preview** button		**File**, **Print Preview**
Ragged right margin	**Ctrl + L**	Click: the ≣ **Align Left** button	**Paragraph** Select **Left** from the **Alignment:** drop-down menu	**Format**, **Paragraph**
Remove text emphasis	Select text to be changed			
	Ctrl + B (remove bold) **Ctrl + I** (remove italics) **Ctrl + U** (remove underline)	Click: the appropriate button: **B** **I** **U**	**Font** Select **Regular** from the **Font Style:** menu	**Format**, **Font**
Replace text	**Ctrl + H**			**Edit**, **Replace**
Save	**Ctrl + S**	Click: the 💾 **Save** button		**File**, **Save**
	If you have not already saved the file you will be prompted to specify the directory and to name the file If you have already done this, then Word will automatically save it			
Save using a different name or to a different directory	Select the appropriate drive and change the filename if relevant Click: **Save**			**File**, **Save As**
Save file in a different file format	Save as above, select from **Save as type**			
Spellcheck	**F7**	Click: the ✓ **Spelling** button		**Tools**, **Spelling and Grammar**
Toolbar, modify				**View**, **Toolbars**, **Customize**
Underline	Select text to underline			
	Ctrl + U	Click: the **U** **Underline** button	**Font**	**Format**, **Font**
			Select: **Underline** from the **Font style:** menu	
Undo	**Ctrl + Z**	Click: the ↺ **Undo** button		**Edit**, **Undo Typing**
Zoom	Click: the 100% ▼ **Zoom** button			**View**, **Zoom**

MOVING AROUND THE DOCUMENT	
Move	**Keyboard action**
To top of document	**Ctrl + Home**
To end of document	**Ctrl + End**
Left word by word	**Ctrl + ←**
Right word by word	**Ctrl + →**
To end of line	**End**
To start of line	**Home**

SELECTING TEXT	
Selecting what	**Action**
Whole document	**Ctrl + A**
One word	Double-click on word
One paragraph	Double-click in selection border (ie to the side of the text)
Any block of text	Click cursor at start of text, press: Shift. Click cursor at end of text and click
Deselect text	Click in any white space

See the Appendix for keyboard shortcuts.

Hints and tips

Common errors made when completing New CLAIT assignments:

- Not proofreading well enough – missing out words or longer portions of text. Omitting exclamation/question marks.
- Not using capital letters for the heading and centring it (where appropriate).
- Inconsistency of spacing – between words, between paragraphs.
- Not printing when instructed, resulting in too few printouts.

Check your work carefully. Have you done everything asked?

Word processing: sample full practice assignment

Scenario

You work as a Project Assistant for a travel company. Your job is to create and format reports as requested by the Department Manager.

Your Department Manager has asked you to create a report based on a recent survey.

1   Create a new word processing document.

2   Set the left and right margins to 3 cm.

3   Enter the following text with an unjustified right margin and a justified left margin:

CITY TRAVELLERS

City Travellers is a small company that specialises in short breaks to cities in the UK. It has an annual turnover in excess of £250,000. Last year City Travellers arranged city breaks for several thousand people.

During the month of September, representatives of City Travellers conducted a survey. A sample of five hundred people was taken. This was deemed sufficient to gain an overall picture of the number of people who would be likely to consider a short city break in the coming year.

An analysis of the results has revealed some interesting facts. Preferred destinations included Bristol, Leeds, London and Edinburgh. Most people preferred to take their own transport, 72%, and of the rest, 12%, favoured train travel. Only 10% opted for travel by coach.

Most of those questioned thought that hotel accommodation would be preferable to Bed and Breakfast, especially in the winter months. Half of those questioned said that they would consider a short break if the price was right.

4   Enter your name, centre number and today's date a few lines below the end of the text.

5   Format the heading so that it is larger than the rest of the text.

6   Save the report with the filename **City** and print one copy.

Your Department Manager has asked for amendments to be made to the report.

7   Insert a paragraph break and clear line space in the third paragraph, after the words, **London and Edinburgh**.

8   Insert the following text as the second sentence of the first paragraph, after the text **...cities in the UK**:

It currently employs one hundred staff.

9   Move the last sentence of the first paragraph:

Last year City Travellers arranged city breaks for several thousand people.
to become the first sentence of the first (ie same) paragraph.

10 In the second paragraph beginning **During the month…**, delete the sentence:

A sample of five hundred people was taken.

11 Replace all occurrences of the word **short** with the word **weekend** (three times in all).

12 Change only the heading **CITY TRAVELLERS** to a different font.

13 Italicise and centre the heading **CITY TRAVELLERS**. Make sure that the rest of the text is not italicised.

14 Fully justify all text except the heading.

15 Set the second paragraph only in double line spacing.

16 Change the left and right margins from 3 cm to 2 cm.

17 Save the report with the new filename **City2**.

18 Print a final copy of the report.

19 Close the document and exit the application securely.

Electronic communication using Outlook Express and Internet Explorer (Unit 3)

❘ Getting started

In this section you will learn about the terms Internet, World Wide Web and e-mail.

Note: Since answers to exercises in this chapter will vary, sample answers are only supplied for the full practice assignment.

❘.❘ Introduction

It really is no surprise that everyone is talking about the Internet. It has revolutionised the way we communicate with others and the way that we access information of all kinds.

❘.2 What is the Internet?

The *Internet* is made up of interconnected computer networks all over the world that send, receive and store information. An individual with a computer and the relevant communications equipment can gain access to this network by subscribing to an *Internet Service Provider* (*ISP*) so that he or she can connect to the Internet as often or as seldom as he or she likes (or can afford). Large companies, educational establishments and government offices have their own arrangements and they are usually connected to the Internet all the time.

❘.3 What is the World Wide Web?

The *World Wide Web* (*WWW* or *web* for short) is one of the services run on the Internet. It contains millions of *websites* – linked pages of words that sometimes include pictures, sounds and graphics. You can explore all these sites using a *web browser* (application software designed to view documents stored on websites on the Internet. This book uses Internet Explorer 5 in the examples). Web pages contain *hyperlinks* to other web pages and other websites so that users can navigate their route through depending on their area of interest. Moving through sites on the web in this way is known as *surfing*.

The number of websites is growing at a phenomenal rate. Each website is created and managed either by an organisation or an individual and each has its own unique address so that you can locate it. Websites are stored on computers connected to the Internet. In fact, with a little know-how, anyone can create a website and ISPs usually provide the facility and storage space to host one. Websites come and go and are constantly being updated. As a result, what you see on a site one day could be quite different from what you see the following week. The web addresses and screenshots of sites used in this book were correct at the time of writing but may have changed by the time you access them.

Websites are usually presented in an interesting and attractive way to encourage you to spend time exploring them. A wide selection of sites provide information on almost every subject imaginable. You can find information such as train times, weather forecasts, the latest news, or you can look up information as you might in an encyclopaedia. You can shop on the web, order groceries to be delivered to your home without stepping outside, or just browse through the latest items for sale in your favourite store. You should be aware that companies and organisations have specific policies on what their employees are allowed to access on the Internet. Remember that copyright legislation applies to website content too, so you must adhere to copyright rules if using any web material.

1.4 What is e-mail?

Electronic mail (e-mail) is a method of sending messages between computers located anywhere in the world. Using the appropriate application software (in this book the examples show Outlook Express 5) you can exchange the electronic equivalent of letters, faxes, pictures and sound with anyone who has an e-mail address. Some organisations have their own internal e-mail systems and are also connected to the Internet to send and receive e-mail locally and internationally. A typical home user has an ISP that allocates them an e-mail address, so people know where to send their messages. E-mail is a quick and efficient means of communication. It has the advantage that you can send and receive your messages when you choose (unlike telephone communication) and is cheaper because calls are charged at local rates (or sometimes free). To save money, you can compose and read messages when you are disconnected from the telephone line. In addition, you will usually be informed if your message has failed to reach its destination. All e-mail messages include dates and sender's details. Messages can be stored for recall at a later date.

 As you work through this chapter, you will need to access websites and use e-mail addresses. OCR provides dummy e-mail addresses (e-mails sent to these addresses are not read or assessed in any way) and the website www.progress-media.co.uk. This site may become very busy at times, making it difficult to access, so there are mirrors (duplicate sites) available as follows:

www.progress-mirror1.co.uk
www.progress-mirror2.co.uk

Section 1: checklist

Explain briefly the following terms in your own words (a couple of sentences):

● the Internet

● the WWW

● e-mail.

Sending and receiving e-mail

In this section you will learn how to:

- load Outlook Express
- use a spell checking tool (if available)
- copy a message
- reply to a message
- print messages
- close Outlook Express

- create a new message
- send a message
- access an incoming message
- forward a message
- delete messages

Note: Since Outlook Express can be configured to suit your specific needs the Outlook Express settings used in the examples may differ slightly from your settings.

2.1 Opening Outlook Express

Exercise 1

Open Outlook Express.

Method

1 From the **Start** menu, select: **Programs**, **Outlook Express** *or* click on the 🖳 **Launch Outlook Express** icon on the **Taskbar**.

2 Either method will result in the Outlook Express window being displayed on screen (Figure 3.1).

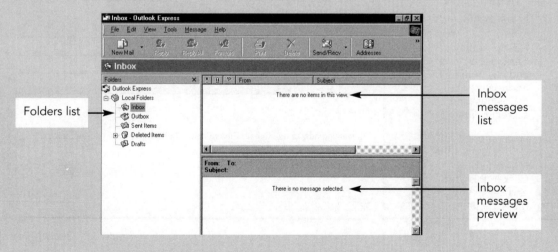

Figure 3.1 Outlook Express 5 window

3   The Folders list shows the e-mail storage system (mailbox) and contains:

- **Inbox** folder – where incoming messages are stored
- **Outbox** folder – where outgoing messages are stored
- **Sent Items** folder – where sent messages are stored
- **Deleted Items** folder – where deleted items are stored
- **Drafts** folder – where draft messages are stored.

2.2 Creating messages

Exercise 2

Create the message, shown below, and send it to someone you know who has an e-mail address.

Note: If you do not have anyone to send it to, to practise send it to your own e-mail address.

Hello there [insert person's name]

I am learning how to use e-mail. Please let me know if you have received this message.

Thanks.

[Insert your name]

Method

1   Click on the [New Mail] **New Message** button.

2   The New Message window appears (Figure 3.2).

3   Click in the **To:** box and key in the e-mail address of the person you are sending the message to. Check that you have keyed in the address correctly.

Header section: Click in the boxes and key in the e-mail address(es) of recipient(s) and subject here

Message box: Click in this area and key in your message here

Figure 3.2 Creating a message

  It is very important that the address is keyed in correctly, otherwise it will not reach its destination. Each dot (full stop, space, upper or lower case letter and so on) is important. If you have made an error, you can delete it and key it in again.

E-mail addresses are made up of the user's name, followed by the @ symbol, followed by the address of the user's service provider. This includes the domain

category, in this example, co, meaning a company or commercial organisation in the UK, followed by the country, in this example, uk (United Kingdom). For example:

A.Smith@somewhere.co.uk

Common domain categories include the following:
ac = academic community (in the UK)
co = company or commercial organisation (in the UK)
com = company or commercial organisation
edu = educational institution
org = non-profit organisation
gov = government organisation

Each country has its own unique code, eg fr = France, ca = Canada, se = Sweden.

4   Click in: the **Subject** box and key in: **Just testing**.

Note: Do not include **Re** or **Fw** in the Subject text since these are added automatically when you reply to or forward a message.

5   Click in: the **Message** box underneath and key in the message.

Note: The subject of your message 'Just testing' has replaced 'New Document' on the **Title** bar.

At this stage you can check spelling.

Use the button.

Spellchecking is not turned on by default. To turn it on so that spelling is checked automatically:

- From the **Tools** menu, select: **Options**.
- Click on: the **Spelling** tab.
- Click in: the **Always check spelling before sending** box.

6   Click on: the **Send** button.

Note: This may not send the message at this stage but will transfer it to your **Outbox** folder.

7   You are returned to the original Outlook Express window with the **Outbox** contents displayed (Figure 3.3)

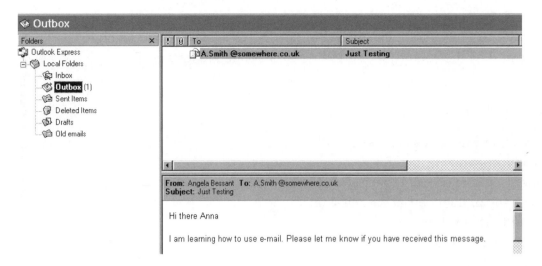

Figure 3.3 Outbox contents are displayed

 You have composed your message 'offline', ie not connected to the phone line and therefore not incurring phone costs. When you have learnt how to use e-mail, to reduce connection time it is a good idea to compose several messages and then send them all together. They will be stored in your **Outbox** folder until you are ready to send them. However, in this example for practice purposes there is just one message to send. Outlook Express will automatically check if you have received any incoming messages at the same time as sending your messages.

2.3 Transmitting and receiving messages

Exercise 3

Transmit and receive messages.

Method

1   Click on the ⬛ **Send/Recv** **Send and Receive All** button.

2   Outlook Express will send the message automatically and will display that it is sending the message.

3   When it has been transmitted, it is placed in the **Sent Items** folder. Click on the folder to check.

 At step 3, if the sent message does not appear in the **Sent Items** folder, from the **Tools** menu, select: **Options**, **Send** tab and click on the box to place a tick next to: **Save copy of sent messages in the 'Sent Items' folder**. This is very important for CLAIT assessments because you must save copies of all sent messages.

As well as saving messages in Outlook Express using the method above, you should be aware that it is a good idea to make backups of important messages (this is not tested in CLAIT). To do this:

1 Display the message in its own window.

2 From the **File** menu, select **Save As**.

3 Save in another location in the normal way.

Outlook Express can be set up automatically to connect/disconnect from the phone line. If this is not set you will need to do this manually and you should be prompted to do so. When you are connected to the phone line, an icon is placed on the **Taskbar** 🖥 .

Click the right mouse button on this icon for a menu with the option to disconnect.

2.4 Copying messages

Sending 'carbon copies'

1 In the **To:** box, key in the first person's e-mail address.

2 In the **Cc:** box, key in the second person's e-mail address.

The main recipient is the person in the **To:** box, with a 'carbon copy' sent to the second addressee. The message is transmitted at the same time to the different e-mail addresses.

2.5 Opening received mail messages

Exercise 4

Open received messages.

Note: If you have not yet received replies to your e-mails then you will need to practise by sending an e-mail to your own e-mail address so that there is a message received.

Method

1 Load Outlook Express (if not already loaded).

2 You will notice that there is a number (in this example, 2) next to your **Inbox** folder, indicating that two messages have been received (Figure 3.4).

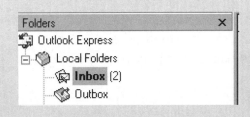

Figure 3.4 Messages have been received

3 The message(s) is displayed in the right-hand pane.

4 Click once on the message to see it in the **Preview** pane (bottom right), or double-click it to see it in a separate window (Figure 3.5).

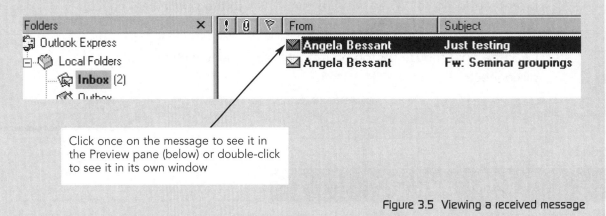

Click once on the message to see it in the Preview pane (below) or double-click to see it in its own window

Figure 3.5 Viewing a received message

2.6 Replying to a message

Exercise 5

Reply to a message.

Method

1 Double-click on: the message to reply to so that it appears in its own window.

2 Click on: the Reply **Reply to Sender** button. The address and subject are already entered. *Note:* The subject now automatically has **Re:** inserted before the main text.

3 Key in your reply. *Note:* It is usual to key this in above the original message so that a 'thread' is formed, ie the sequence of messages is maintained (Figure 3.6).

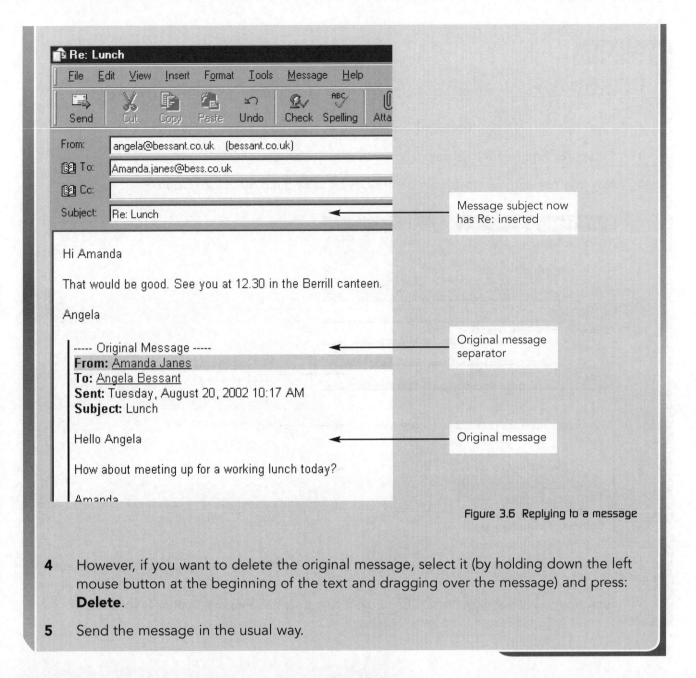

Figure 3.6 Replying to a message

Labels in figure:
- Message subject now has Re: inserted
- Original message separator
- Original message

Email window contents:
Re: Lunch

File Edit View Insert Format Tools Message Help

Send Cut Copy Paste Undo Check Spelling Atta

From: angela@bessant.co.uk (bessant.co.uk)
To: Amanda.janes@bess.co.uk
Cc:
Subject: Re: Lunch

Hi Amanda

That would be good. See you at 12.30 in the Berrill canteen.

Angela

----- Original Message -----
From: Amanda Janes
To: Angela Bessant
Sent: Tuesday, August 20, 2002 10:17 AM
Subject: Lunch

Hello Angela

How about meeting up for a working lunch today?

Amanda

4   However, if you want to delete the original message, select it (by holding down the left mouse button at the beginning of the text and dragging over the message) and press: **Delete**.

5   Send the message in the usual way.

2.7 Forwarding an e-mail message

Exercise 6

Forward a message. Add a short note about the message for the recipient that you are forwarding it to, for example:

For info

[Your name and centre number]

1   Double-click on: the message to forward on so that it appears in its own window.

2   Click on: the 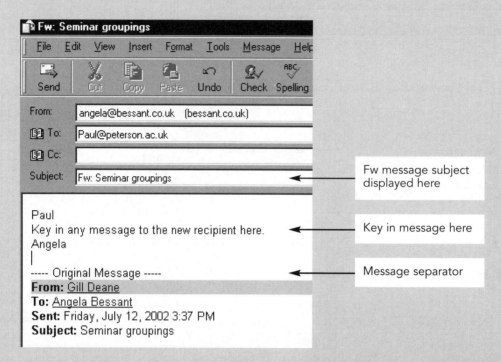 **Forward** button.

3   In the **To:** box, key in the new recipient's e-mail address.

4   Key in any message for the recipient above the original message (Figure 3.7).

Figure 3.7   Adding a message to a forwarding message

5   Send in the normal way. *Note:* The subject text now has **Fw:** automatically inserted.

2.8 Printing messages

Exercise 7

Print a message.

Method

1   Select the e-mail in the Inbox or open the e-mail in its own window.

2   Click on: the **Print** button or from the **File** menu, select: **Print**.

3   The Print dialogue box is displayed.

4   Make any relevant selections.

5   Click on: **OK**.

2.9 Deleting messages

Exercise 8

Delete a message.

Method

1 In the main window, select the message to delete by clicking on it. Press: **Delete**.

2 To select adjacent messages, hold down **Shift** when selecting.

3 To select non-adjacent messages, hold down **Ctrl** when selecting.

 Deleted messages are sent to the **Deleted Items** folder. It is a good idea to empty this folder from time to time to save space. To do this right-click on the folder and select: **Empty 'Deleted Items' Folder**.

2.10 Close Outlook Express

Exercise 9

Close Outlook Express.

Method

From the **File** menu, select: **Exit** or click on: the **Close** button.

Sending and receiving e-mail practice

Practice 1

Compose the following message and send it to someone:

Subject: New Staff Meeting

[Recipient's name]

I understand that the New Staff Meeting has been postponed and will now take place next Monday. Please can you let me know if you will still require the use of the Hemsley Conference Room?

Thank you

Regards

[Your name]

Practice 2

Ask your tutor or a friend to send you the following e-mail message:

Subject: Vending Machine

[Your name]

The hot drinks vending machine in the canteen area is not working. Please can you inform the relevant person so that arrangements can be made to repair it.

Many thanks

[Sender's name]

Practice 3

When you receive a reply to question 1, reply to the message as appropriate. (Use the **Reply to Sender** button.)

Practice 4

When you have received the message in Practice 2, forward to another person, copying it to the sender at Practice 2. Add the following above the received message:

This should be very useful for your meeting next week.

Regards

[Your name and centre number]

Practice 5

Print all the messages sent and received.

Practice 6

Delete all the messages.

3 Sending and receiving e-mail attachments

In this section you will learn how to:

- attach files to messages
- receive, save, view and print attachments
- delete attachments

Note: You will need to access the file **Tutor email** on the CD-ROM for exercises in this section.

3.1 Attaching files to messages

Sometimes you may want to enclose something with your message, eg a picture or a graph. In such cases you can add a file to your message. This is called an attachment. You can add more than one file. These then are called attachments.

Exercise 1

Send a message with an attachment.

Method

1. Load Outlook Express and key in the following new message:

   Hi [name of recipient]

   I am practising sending and receiving attachments to email messages. Please find the attached file Tutor email.

   Please could you let me know that you have received this and also please could you send me an example attachment?

   Thanks.

   [Your name]

   NB: *Do not click send yet.*

2. Click on: the **Attach File** button.

3. The Insert Attachment dialogue box appears (Figure 3.8).

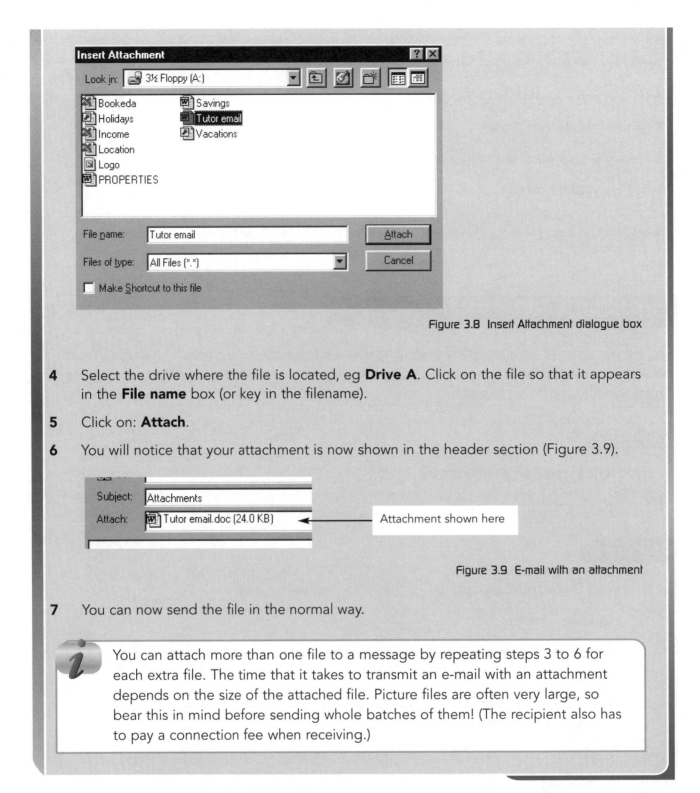

Figure 3.8 Insert Attachment dialogue box

4   Select the drive where the file is located, eg **Drive A**. Click on the file so that it appears in the **File name** box (or key in the filename).

5   Click on: **Attach**.

6   You will notice that your attachment is now shown in the header section (Figure 3.9).

Subject: Attachments

Attach: [W] Tutor email.doc (24.0 KB)   ◄————   Attachment shown here

Figure 3.9 E-mail with an attachment

7   You can now send the file in the normal way.

> *i* You can attach more than one file to a message by repeating steps 3 to 6 for each extra file. The time that it takes to transmit an e-mail with an attachment depends on the size of the attached file. Picture files are often very large, so bear this in mind before sending whole batches of them! (The recipient also has to pay a connection fee when receiving.)

3.2 Viewing attachments

Note: If you do not have virus-checking facilities in place and you are in any doubt about the sender, delete the message and attachment. Click once on the message to select it, then press: Delete.

Exercise 2

View an attachment.

Note: This is not recommended if you have any doubts about the sender's reliability.

1   When you receive a message with an attachment, the message has a paperclip icon next to it (Figure 3.10).

Paperclip icon indicates an attachment

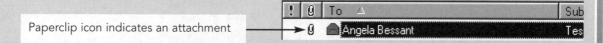

Figure 3.10 Receiving attachments

2   Double-click on the message to view it in a separate window.

3   In the **Attach** box, double-click on the attached file (Figure 3.11). The file will appear in its own program window.

Double-click on the attached file to view it

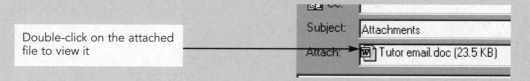

Figure 3.11 Viewing an attachment

4   When you have finished viewing the file, close its window in the normal way. You are returned to Outlook Express.

3.3 Saving a file attachment outside the mailbox

Exercise 3

Save an attachment to a different location.

Method

1   Double-click on the message with the attachment so that it appears in its own window.

2   From the **File** menu, select: **Save Attachments**.

3   The Save Attachments dialogue box is displayed (Figure 3.12).

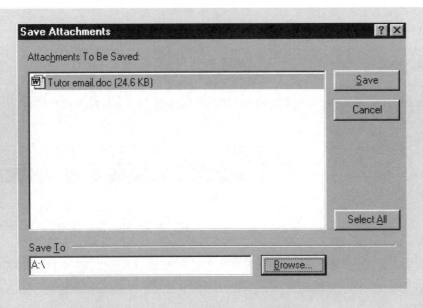

Figure 3.12 Saving attachments

4   Click on: **Browse** to choose where to save it.

5   Click on: **Save**.

or

Right-click on the attachment and select: **Save As** (Figure 3.13).

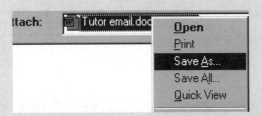

Figure 3.13 Saving the attachments by right-clicking

3.4 Printing an attachment

Exercise 4

Print an attachment.

Method 1

Once you have saved the attachment you can print it from its application window using the **File** menu, **Print** *or* the **Print** button.

Method 2

In Outlook Express, right-click on: the attachment and select: **Print** (Figure 3.13).

3.5 Deleting a file attachment from a message

Exercise 5

Delete a file attachment from a message.

Method

When sending attachments, if you have chosen the wrong one or need to delete one for any other reason, select the attachment by clicking on it. Press: **Delete**.

3.6 Close Outlook Express

Attachments practice

Note: For these exercises you will need the files **savings** and **rose** on the CD-ROM.

Practice 1

Compose and send the following message to someone. Attach the file **savings** to the e-mail.

Subject: Brochure info

[Recipient name]

Please find attached file that you will need to complete the brochure.

Regards

[Your name]

Practice 2

Ask someone to send you the following e-mail and the attachment filename **rose**.

Subject: Flower show leaflet

[Your name]

Please find attached file that you will need to complete the leaflet.

Regards

[Your name]

Practice 3

When you receive the e-mail in Practice 2, save the attachment onto a floppy disk or other location on your computer. Print the attachment only.

Practice 4

Print all the e-mails sent and received in the questions above.

4 The Address Book

When you have completed this task you will have learnt:

- about the Address Book

- about automatically adding addresses to the Address Book

- how to send messages using the Address Book

4.1 About the Address Book

The Outlook Address Book enables you to store addresses that you often use. Using the Address Book means that you do not have to remember all those cumbersome e-mail addresses and saves you having to key in addresses each time you send messages.

4.2 Adding an address to the Address Book when mail is received

Exercise 1

Add an e-mail address to the Address Book using a received message.

Method

1 Double-click on an e-mail that you have received but have not replied to.

2 From the **Tools** menu, select: **Add to Address Book**, **Sender** (Figure 3.14).

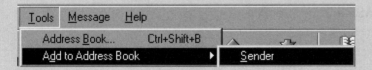

Figure 3.14 Adding received message's e-mail address to the Address Book

3 A summary of the sender's details will be displayed (Figure 3.15).

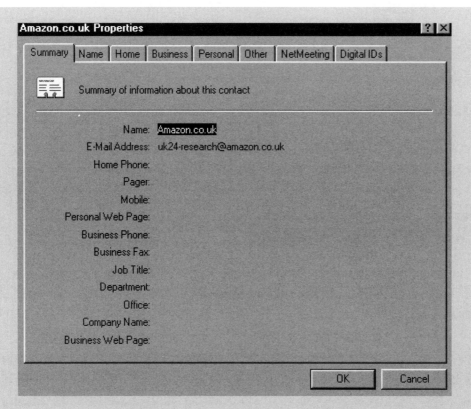

Figure 3.15 Sender's details summary

4 Click on: **OK**.

 Outlook Express can automatically add an address to the Address Book when you reply to messages as follows:

1 Open Outlook Express.

2 From the **Tools** menu, select: **Options**.

3 Click on: the **Send** tab.

4 Click next to **Automatically put people I reply to in my address book**.

4.3 Sending messages using the Address Book

Exercise 2

Send a message using an address stored in the Address Book.

Method

1 Click on the **New Message** button.

2 In the **Header** section, double-click in: the 📖 To: **To:** box.

3   The Select Recipients dialogue box is displayed.

4   Click on: the recipient's name and click on: the ⟦ To: -> ⟧ button.

5   Click on: **OK**.

 You can select as many recipients as you want and add them to the To: or Cc: boxes.

4.4 Close Outlook Express

Address Book practice

Select a couple of messages that you have received but have not replied to. Add the senders' e-mail addresses to the Address Book.

5 Using the web

In this section you will learn how to:

- connect to the Internet
- access web addresses
- save and print information
- exit Internet Explorer

- load Internet Explorer
- search for specific information
- store web addresses

Note: Methods of connecting to the Internet have the same principles but may vary depending on your particular communications equipment and ISP.

5.1 Loading Internet Explorer

Exercise 1

Load Internet Explorer.

Method

From the **Start** menu, select: **Programs**, **Internet Explorer** or click on: the 🔵 **Launch Internet Explorer Browser** icon on the **Taskbar**.

> If you are not already connected to the Internet, a connection dialogue box will be displayed. Key in your **User name** and **Password** and click on: **Connect**. Passwords are used to prevent unauthorised access. Always choose one that is not easy for others to guess.
>
> When you are connected, the 🖥 icon appears on the **Taskbar**. To disconnect, right-click on the icon and select: **Disconnect**.

Either method will result in the Internet Explorer window being displayed (Figure 3.16).

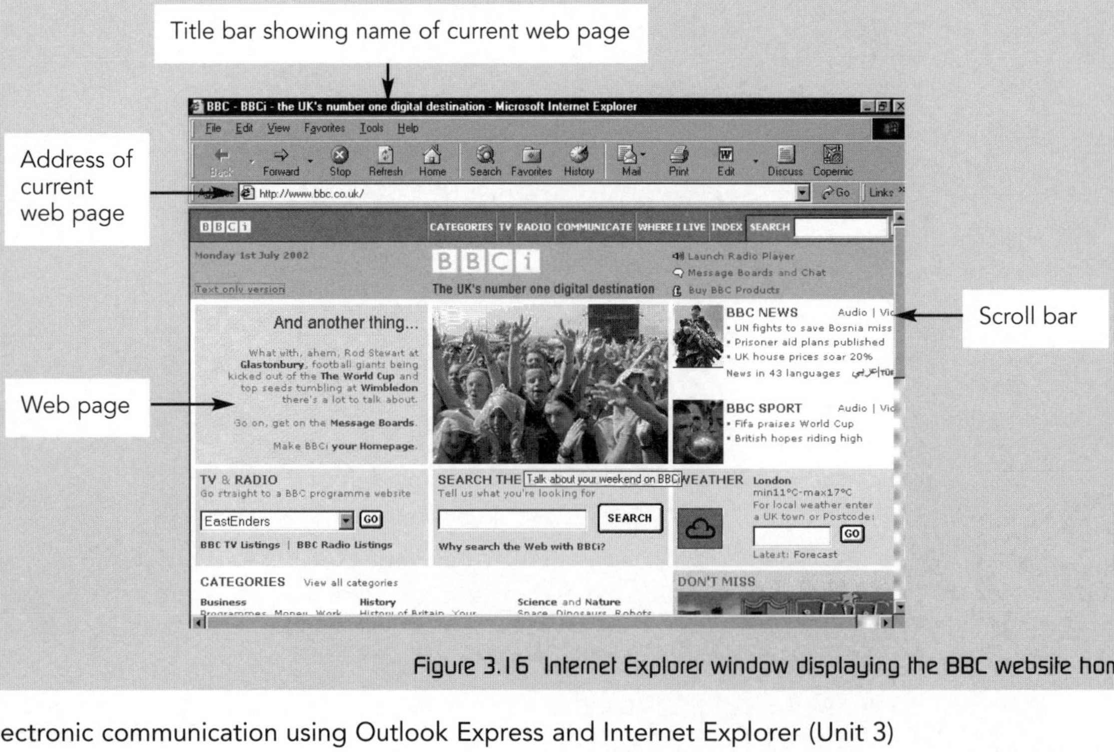

Figure 3.16 Internet Explorer window displaying the BBC website home page

Note: The web page displayed (known as your *home page*) is determined by the set up of your computer. Toolbar buttons are labelled in Figure 3.17.

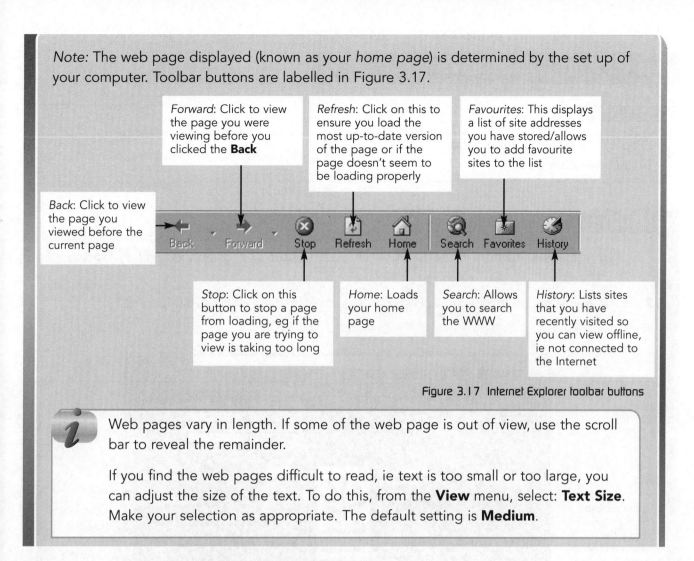

Forward: Click to view the page you were viewing before you clicked the **Back**

Refresh: Click on this to ensure you load the most up-to-date version of the page or if the page doesn't seem to be loading properly

Favourites: This displays a list of site addresses you have stored/allows you to add favourite sites to the list

Back: Click to view the page you viewed before the current page

Stop: Click on this button to stop a page from loading, eg if the page you are trying to view is taking too long

Home: Loads your home page

Search: Allows you to search the WWW

History: Lists sites that you have recently visited so you can view offline, ie not connected to the Internet

Figure 3.17 Internet Explorer toolbar buttons

i Web pages vary in length. If some of the web page is out of view, use the scroll bar to reveal the remainder.

If you find the web pages difficult to read, ie text is too small or too large, you can adjust the size of the text. To do this, from the **View** menu, select: **Text Size**. Make your selection as appropriate. The default setting is **Medium**.

5.2 What is a web address?

A *website* is a collection of pages on the web owned by an individual or organisation. The first page of a website is the *home page.* Every web page has a unique address. This is known as a **URL** (Uniform Resource Locator). It usually begins with 'http://www.' (http stands for *HyperText Transfer Protocol* and tells the web browser that it is looking for a web page). Most modern browsers have 'http://' stored so you can usually ignore the http part and start at 'www'. Here are some addresses to examine (the first accesses the page displayed in Figure 3.16):

http://www.bbc.co.uk
http://www.f1-live.com
http://www.nhm.ac.uk

The text after the www shows the *domain name* (the organisation's name), eg BBC, f1 (Formula 1) and nhm (Natural History Museum); the type of site, eg .co and .com are commercial companies, .ac is an academic community; and the country, eg uk is United Kingdom.

Note: The dots are important in a web address and the address must be spelt correctly, with the correct upper and lower case letters. Sometimes addresses are longer because they include the pathname (an exact location within the website), eg:

www.bbc.co.uk/weather/worldweather/europe/index.shtml

Exercise 2

Display the following web page:
http://www.nhm.ac.uk

Method

1 Key in the web address in the address bar, press: **Enter** *or* click on the **Go to** button.

2 The home page of the Natural History Museum website is displayed (Figure 3.18).

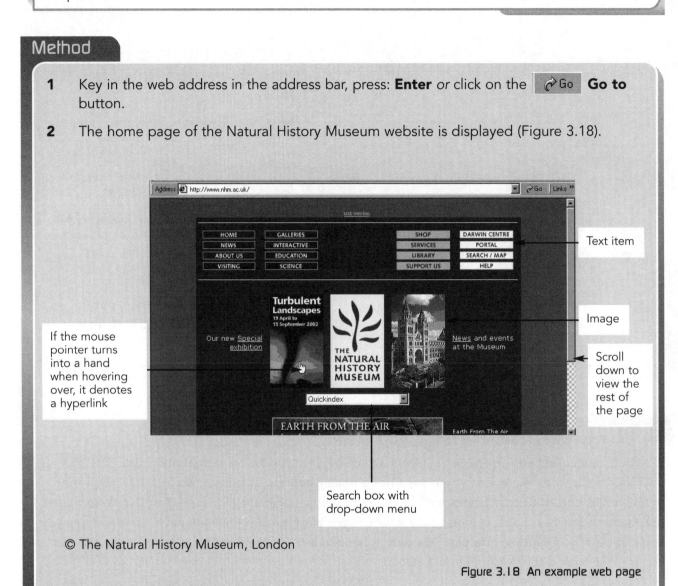

© The Natural History Museum, London

Figure 3.18 An example web page

5.4 Using hyperlinks

Web pages have links (called *hyperlinks*) that you can click on to take you to other places within the current page, current site or to other websites. Links can take the form of underlined text, text in a different colour or they can be image links. When you hover over a link the mouse pointer (usually) turns into a hand. The home page of the Natural History Museum site (displayed in Figure 3.18) has text and image links.

Exercise 3

Follow one of the links on the Natural History Museum home page to find out specific information, eg what galleries are there? What is new?

1 Click on the link. Another page of the site is displayed. Notice that the address and Title bar have changed to reflect that you are viewing another page.

2 Collect the information you are looking for.

Return to the original page by clicking on the ⟵ Back **Back** button. *Note:* If you click on the down arrow of the **Back** button, if you have visited several pages, you can go back several pages at once. You will notice that the previously viewed pages may load quicker because your computer has temporarily stored their contents.

5.5 Searching for information

There are many ways that you can find specific information on the web. Two common ones include:

- If you know the web address of the site where you can find the information, go straight to the site by keying in the address and use the site's search box (if it has one) or use hyperlinks to navigate through the site.

- Using a chosen search engine. There are many search engine sites. You will find that a particular search engine usually finds what you are looking for and is easy to use. Popular search engines include:

http://www.google.co.uk
http://www.altavista.com
http://www.ask.co.uk

5.6 Using a website's local search box

Exercise 4

Access the Britannica Encyclopaedia site http://www.britannica.com. You want to look up a type of monkey but you are not sure what type it is.

Method

1 Access the Britannica website.

2 In the **Search box**, key in: **monkey**, and press: **Go** (Figure 3.19).

The Web's Best Search
Featuring the *Encyclopædia Britannica*, the Web magazines, and more.

All Britannica.com ▼

Monkey   Go

Figure 3.19 Entering search into site search box

Reproduced with permission from Encyclopaedia Britannica

3 A search will be made to find the appropriate information on the Britannica site.

4 After a short delay, the results will appear on screen (Figure 3.20).

5 You have now remembered that it is 'squirrel monkey' that you need information about.

Encyclopedia Articles   *premium service*

The search results below are from
Encyclopædia Britannica. Click to see results
from *Britannica's*
Concise Encyclopedia or *Student Encyclopedia*.

monkey

in general, any of nearly 200
species of tailed primate,
with the exception of lemurs,
tarsiers, and lorises. The
presence of a tail (even if
only a tiny nub), along with their narrow-chested
bodies ...

rhesus monkey

(species Macaca mulatta),
sand-coloured macaque
native to forests of South and
Southeast Asia. The rhesus
monkey is about 4764 cm
(1725 inches) long, excluding
the furry, 2030-centimetre
tail, and ...

squirrel monkey

most abundant primate of riverside forests in the
Guianas and the Amazon River basin, distinguished
by a circle of black, hairless skin around the nose and
mouth set against an expressive white face. ...

Figure 3.20 Results for 'monkey' search

Reproduced with permission from Encyclopaedia Britannica

5.7 Using a search engine and its search box

Exercise 5

Find sites where you can look up train times using the Google search engine.

1 Access the Google website (http://www.google.co.uk).

2 Key **train times** into the **Search** box, click in the: **pages from the UK** button and enter it by clicking on **Google Search** (Figure 3.21). *Note:* If you click on: **I'm Feeling Lucky**, you will be taken straight to what Google believes is the most relevant site.

Reproduced with permission from Google

Figure 3.21 Using a search engine

3 My search resulted in the following (Figure 3.22).

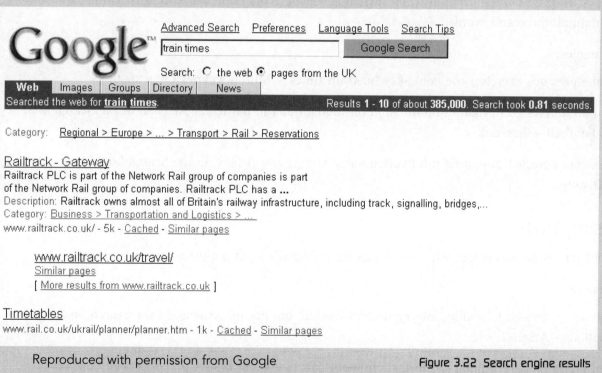

Reproduced with permission from Google

Figure 3.22 Search engine results

4 Click on a site link to find out if it is useful to you.

5 Click on: the **Back** button (or the **Back** button arrow) to return to the Google search results.

5.8 Refining searches

As you can see from the previous exercises, searches can result in a huge number of possibly useful sites. You will be glad to know that you can refine your searches so that the results are more relevant. This is achieved by using what are termed logical operators, ie AND, NOT (or their equivalents AND, +, &; NOT, -) and OR. Different search engines have slightly different rules about how you enter searches with logical operators.

Using AND

Use AND or one of the symbols when searching for more than one word. Results will list sites that contain all the search words.

Examples:

In the previous exercise, you could key in: **train times + Milton Keynes Central.**

You are interested in finding information on football and in particular Arsenal. In the Search box, key in: **Football + Arsenal.**

You are interested in finding information about Oscars and Disney. In the Search box, key in: **Oscars + Disney.**

Using NOT

Use NOT or the minus sign when searching for information but omitting certain information.

Examples:

You are interested in finding information on football but not on Arsenal. In the Search box, key in: **Football - Arsenal.**

You are interested in finding information about Oscars but not Disney. In the Search box, key in: **Oscars - Disney.**

Using OR

You are interested in finding information about cameras. You could key in: **Camera OR photography,** since both of these might find useful information.

For some search engines, quotation marks can be used to group words together, eg 'motor racing' may find more confined results than motor racing.

As you can see, you may need to follow several links before you arrive at the information you are searching for, but refining searches can help speed up the process.

Exercise 8

Try out some other searches with logical operators. Note the different search format requirements and which methods give the most relevant results.

5.9 Saving a web page as a file

Exercise 9

Save one of the web pages you have visited as a file.

Method

1   Load the web page by keying in the address in the **Address** box.

2   From the **File** menu, select: **Save As**.

3   The **Save As** dialogue box is displayed.

4   Select the location where you want to save the web page and key in a filename.

5   In the **Save as type** section, select from the list (Figure 3.23).

6   Click on: **Save**.

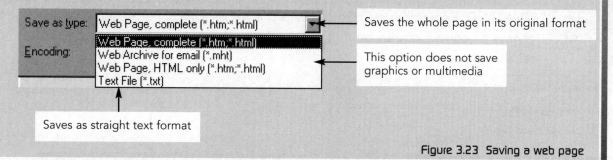

Figure 3.23 Saving a web page

5.10 Printing a web page

Exercise 10

Print one of the web pages you have visited.

1 From the **File** menu, select: **Print** or click on: the **Print** button.

2 The **Print** dialogue box is displayed (Figure 3.24).

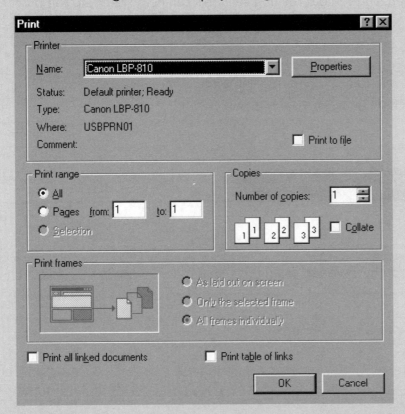

Figure 3.24 Printing

3 Make selections as appropriate.

4 If the web page is divided into frames, enter your choices in the **Print Frames** section.

5 Click on: **OK**.

 WARNING: Remember anyone can set up a website and information may not always be correct or may be misleading. Try to check that information is from a reliable source.

5.11 Saving and printing an object on a web page

Sometimes you do not need to save or print the whole web page, but just a map or an image from it.

Exercise 11

Visit the BBC weather site, http://www.bbc.co.uk/weather. Save today's UK weather map and print it.

1 Access the site.

2 Follow the links for **UK**.

3 Right-click on: the weather map graphic.

4 From the pop-up menu, select: **Save Picture As** (Figure 3.25).

Figure 3.25 Saving a graphic

5 The **Save Picture** dialogue box is displayed.

6 In the **Save in:** box, select a location.

7 In the **File name** box, key in: a filename.

8 Click on: **Save**.

9 Once the file is saved, you will be able to open it and print it in the normal way.

5.12 Saving a list of your favourite websites

When you find a site that you would like to visit again, or a site that you visit often, it is a good idea to save the address of the site to make it easier to re-visit in the future. These sites are then known as *Favorites*. *Note:* These are known as *Bookmarks* in Netscape (the main alternative web browser).

Exercise 12

Save and access a site of your choice in your **Favorites** list.

Method

1   With the home page of the site displayed, from the **Favorites** menu, select: **Add to Favorites**.

2   The **Add Favorite** dialogue box is displayed.

3   A default name already appears in the **Name** box. Change the name if you want to.

4   Click on: **OK**.

Accessing Favorites

Method

From the **Favorites** menu, click on: the website name.

5.13 Exiting Internet Explorer and disconnecting

Exercise 13

Exit Internet Explorer.

Method

From the **File** menu, select: **Close**.

Note: Check that your computer has automatically disconnected from the Internet (is the **connected** icon still displayed on the **Taskbar**?). If it is, right-click on this icon and select: **Disconnect**. Forgetting to disconnect can prove expensive.

Using the web practice

Practice 1

Access the Internet and find the following information:

1   What events are on in Bristol this month? Pick one that might interest you. Save the page and add it to your favorites.

2   Three hotels in Bristol. Save and print a graphic from a web page of one of them. Add one of their websites to your favorites.

3   A road map of the route and average time taken to drive to Bristol from your region. Save and print a copy of the page with the map.

4   Does Bristol have an airport? If so where is it located? Save and print a page with a map and directions, if available.

Practice 2

Add some more websites to your favorites. Here are some addresses that you may find useful:

All Recipes	www.allrecipes.com
Angela Bessant's website	www.bessant.co.uk
Art Guide	www.artguide.org
BBC Health	www.bbc.co.uk/health
BBC News	news.bbc.co.uk
Britannica	www.britannica.com
Coronation Street	www.coronationstreet.co.uk
Dictionary.com	www.dictionary.com
Do It Yourself.com	doityourself.com
EastEnders	www.bbc.co.uk/eastenders
Football 365	www.football365.com
Information Britain	www.information-britain.co.uk
International Movie Database	www.imdb.com
ITN Online	www.itn.co.uk
Multimap	www.multimap.com
National Gallery	www.nationalgallery.org.uk
Scoot Cinema Guide	www.scoot.co.uk/cinemafinder
Scrabble	www.mattelscrabble.com/en/home.html
The Guardian	www.newsunlimited.co.uk
The History Channel UK	www.historychannel.com
The Mirror	www.mirror.co.uk
The Times	www.the-times.co.uk

Action	Keyboard	Mouse	Right-mouse menu	Menu
Address Book, open		Click: the **Addresses** **Address Book** button		**Tools, Address Book**
Add address automatically when message is received				**Tools, Options, Send tab, Automatically put people I reply to in my address book**
Delete address	Open Address Book. Select the address			
	Delete	Click: the **Delete** **Delete** button	**Delete**	**File, Delete**
Attach files to messages		Click: the **Attach** **Attach File** button		**Insert, File Attachment**
Attachment, delete	Double-click the message with the attachment so that it appears in its own window. Select attachment			
	Delete	Click: the **Delete** **Delete** button		
Attachments, save	Select the attachment			
			Save As	**File, Save Attachments**
Copy messages	Key in the address in the **To:** box. Use **Cc:** box to send a 'carbon copy'			
Create message		Click: the **New Mail** **New Message** button		
Delete message	Select message			
	Delete	Click: the **Delete** **Delete** button	**Delete**	**Edit, Delete**
Delete text	Select text			
	Delete			
Exit Outlook Express		Click: the **X Close** button		**File, Exit**
Folders, create new				**File, New, Folder**
Forward a message	**Ctrl + F**	Click: the **Forward** **Forward** button	**Forward**	**Message, Forward**
Help	**F1**			**Help, Contents and Index**
Load Outlook Express	In the Windows 98 desktop			
		Click: the **Launch Outlook Express** icon on the Taskbar		**Start, Programs, Outlook Express**

Action	Keyboard	Mouse	Right-mouse menu	Menu
Open received messages		Click: **Inbox** in left-hand window Click: the message (to view in Preview) *or* Double-click: the message (to view in own window)		
Print messages	(With transaction details and message visible in its own window)			
	Ctrl + P	Click: the 🖨 **Print** button		**File**, **Print**
Print attachment			**Print**	
	If saved, print from its application			
Reply to message	**Ctrl + R**	Click: the 📧 **Reply** button	**Reply to Sender**	
Send message using Address Book	With a new message displayed, double-click in the **To:** box Click on: the recipient's name and then on the **To:** button			
Spellcheck	**F7**			**Tools**, **Spelling**
Transmit/ receive messages		Click: the 📧 Send/Recv **Send and Receive** button		**Tools**, **Send and Receive**
View attachments	(With message in its own window – attachment visible)			
		Double-click: the attachment		

Using the web quick reference for New CLAIT (Internet Explorer)

Action	Keyboard	Mouse	Right-mouse menu	Menu
Access a website	Key in the web address in the address box			
Exit Internet Explorer		Click: the ⊠ **Close** button		**File**, **Close**
Favorites, add to open	**Ctrl + D**	Click: the ⭐ Favorites **Favorites** button	**Add to Favorites**	**Favorites**, **Add to Favorites**
Help	**F1**			**Help**, **Contents and Index**
Hyperlink, follow		Click: the hyperlink		
Load Internet Explorer	In the Windows 98 desktop			
		Click: the 🌐 **Launch Internet Explorer Browser** icon on the **Taskbar**		**Start**, **Programs**, **Internet Explorer**

Action	Keyboard	Mouse	Right-mouse menu	Menu
Page Setup				**File**, **Page Setup**
Print	**Ctrl + P**	Click: the [Print] **Print** button	**Print**	**File**, **Print**
Return to previous page		Click: the [Back] **Back** button		
Save web page	**Ctrl + S**			**File**, **Save As**
Save an image on a web page			**Save Picture As**	
Searching, using common logical operators	Use **Search** button *or* a Search Engine Use AND, +, &, or NOT, -, or use OR			

Keyboard shortcuts for Internet Explorer

These can be very useful to reduce time online.

Alt + Home	Displays your home page
Esc	Stops download
Ctrl + D	Adds the current page to Favorites
Ctrl + N	Opens a new browser window (this is useful if you have a heavily hyperlinked page that you want to keep going back to to follow the links)
F5	Refreshes page
Ctrl + P	Prints the current page
Ctrl + S	Saves the current page

Hints and tips

Common errors made when completing CLAIT assignments include:

- Not entering e-mail addresses correctly.
- Entering RE or FW when composing new messages, replying and forwarding messages. Remember Outlook will enter these for you when necessary.
- Omitting to attach the attachment.
- Attaching the incorrect attachment.
- Data entry errors. Always check carefully.
- You must use the CC: box when copying messages. BCC or adding the address to the To: box is unacceptable.
- Not deleting e-mail addresses when requested.
- Not storing e-mail addresses when requested.
- Not producing the correct printouts.

Electronic communications: sample full practice assignment

Before you begin this assignment, you will need the following:

1   A prepared e-mail message, which has been sent to you as follows:

Subject:	European tour
Message:	Here is the image required for all documents relating to the forthcoming European tour. The cost of the tour has now been calculated and will be £278 inclusive per person.
Signature:	Events Manager
Attachment:	bridge.gif

2   An e-mail address from which this message is sent. Candidates will be required to reply to this address, store it in the Address Book and send a new message to it. The address (its nickname or alias) must be identical on each of the above occasions.

3   The image file **bridge.gif** for the message attachment from the CD-ROM.

4   Two further e-mail addresses. OCR supplies two dummy addresses as follows:

hr@progress-media.co.uk
training@progress-media.co.uk

You will need to ensure that:

1   The Address Book has been cleared of any addresses used in this assignment (for actual CLAIT assignments it should be entirely cleared).

2   The Favorites has been cleared of any sites used during the assessment (for actual CLAIT assignments it should be entirely cleared).

3   Any 'history' and 'auto-completion' facilities of Windows Explorer are disabled.

Scenario

You work as an administrative assistant in a European company. You are currently gathering information for a brochure containing information on a forthcoming European tour.

The events manager has sent you an e-mail message containing an image for all European tour documents.

1   Open your mailbox and read the message entitled **European tour**.
Add the sender's e-mail address to your Address Book.
Print a copy of the attached file, **bridge.gif**.

You need to inform the Human Resources Department about inserting the image onto all European tour documents.

2   Prepare to forward the message **European tour** and its attachment to
hr@progress-media.co.uk adding the following text:
I am forwarding the attached image for the documents that you are preparing for the tour.

Add your name and centre number to the end of your message.
Check your message for errors and, making sure the system saves outgoing messages, forward the e-mail message including the attachment.
You should acknowledge receipt of the image.

3 Prepare a reply to the Events Manager with the following message:

Thank you for the image. I believe that all documents will be ready by next Friday.
Add your name and centre number to the end of the message.
Check your message for errors and, making sure your system saves outgoing messages, send the reply.

You need to manage your mailbox to reduce storage demands.

4 Save the attachment **bridge.gif** separately from the mailbox and delete the message **European tour**.

Your manager needs to add information about the exchange rate for the pound against the euro and has asked you to look up the current UK pound/euro exchange rate.

5 Use a web-based search engine to search for web pages that give the European exchange rates. Follow links to find a specific page that displays the current rate for the UK pound. Bookmark the page and print a copy.

The Events Manager has been advised that the graphic design team require some additional assistance in producing some of the material to take with them on the tour. She requires information on consultancy rates for graphic designers. A graph of this data can be found on the company's website.

6 Access the company's website at:
www.progress-media.co.uk
Follow the links to the Search page. Use the local search facility to locate a page on the site that displays a graph of **consultancy rates for graphic designers**.
Bookmark the page and print a copy.
Save the graph as **graphic rates.gif**.

Prepare a new e-mail message to the Events Manager using the e-mail address recalled from your Address Book.

7 Give the message the subject heading: **Graphic Designer rates**.
Use the following message:
Here is a graph of the consultancy rates for graphic designers that you requested. I hope you find it useful.
Locate and attach the file **graphic rates.gif** saved at Step 6.
Add your name and centre number to the end of your message.
Make sure a copy of your message will be sent to the Training Department at:
training@progress-media.co.uk
Check your message for errors and, making sure your system saves outgoing messages, send the message and attachment.

8 Locate the copies of the messages you have sent and print a copy of each message. Make sure header details (To, From, Date, Subject) are shown. Make sure attachment details are shown where appropriate (Steps 2 and 7).

9 Access the bookmark facility and ask your tutor to check the stored URLs.

10 Exit the software securely.

Electronic communication using Outlook Express and Internet Explorer (Unit 3)

Spreadsheets using Excel (Unit 4)

 ## Getting started

In this section you will become familiar with spreadsheet terminology and Excel. You will discover the advantages of using a spreadsheet application. You will learn how to:

- load Excel
- enter text and numeric data
- enter simple formulae
- print the spreadsheet
- close the spreadsheet file

- understand the parts of the Excel window
- change column width
- save the spreadsheet
- print the spreadsheet showing formulae
- exit Excel

1.1 What is a spreadsheet application?

A spreadsheet has some aspects of a filing system and some of a calculator. It consists of a large area, or grid, in which you enter data and text and in which calculations are carried out. The application performs calculations as instructed by you. You can edit spreadsheets and, when changes are made, new values are recalculated automatically. Spreadsheets are very fast, accurate and flexible. You can print them or parts of them and save them to disk to edit later. Spreadsheets are used for various tasks, including accounting to produce budgets, balance sheets and payrolls, and in scientific analysis and 'What if' scenarios. Microsoft Excel is a spreadsheet application. You will learn about and appreciate the advantages of spreadsheet applications as you progress through this chapter.

1.2 Loading Excel

Exercise 1

Load Excel.

Method

Load Excel in the same way as other Office 2000 applications, this time selecting:

☒ Microsoft Excel   from the **Programs** menu

or

Click on: the ☒ **Excel** shortcut icon (if you have one).

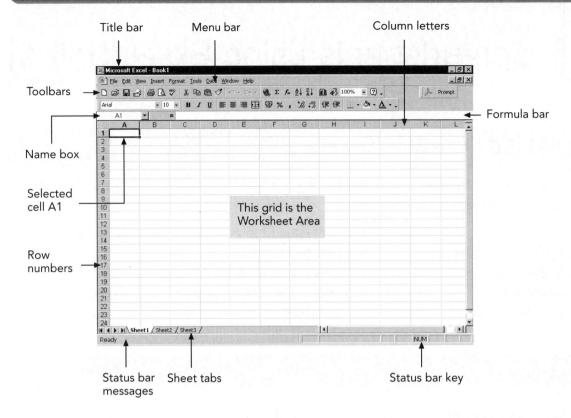

Figure 4.1 The application window

The **Title bar** and **Menu bar** are at the top of the application window.

The **Menu bar** has a set of *drop-down* menus that provide access to all of Excel's features.

The **Toolbar** is a row of buttons and selection boxes that, in most cases, provide shortcuts to the menu options or quick ways of entering values. (In Figure 4.1 the *Standard* and *Formatting* toolbars are shown.)

The **Formula bar** displays the data you enter into your worksheet.

The **Name box** displays the active cell reference.

The **Sheet tabs** allow you to move from one sheet to the next. (You can have more than one spreadsheet in an Excel document. Together these sheets are known as a *Workbook.*)

The **Status bar**, located at the bottom of the window, displays messages about current events as you work on the spreadsheet.

The **Status bar key** shows NUM (by default). This denotes that the **Num Lock** key on your keyboard is on, enabling you to use the number keys 0 to 9 (at the right of the keyboard) to enter numbers more quickly. If you want to use the movement keys instead, press: the **Num Lock** key to turn **Num Lock** off.

The Worksheet Area

This is the area between the Formula bar and the Status bar where your document (spreadsheet) is displayed. It consists of cells, each with their own cell reference, eg A1, B7, F9.

- Rows go across and are labelled 1, 2, 3, 4 ...
- Columns go down and are labelled A, B, C, D ...

Figure 4.2 shows the position of cell C6.

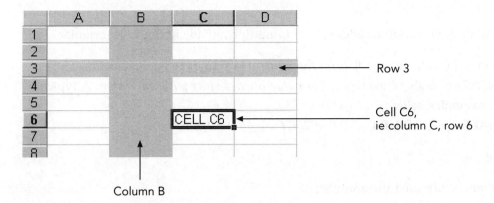

Figure 4.2 Cell references

Practise:

Moving around the spreadsheet:

1 Moving around your document using the scroll bars (Figure 4.3).

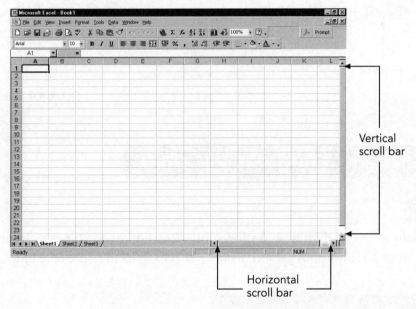

Figure 4.3 Scroll bars

2 Using navigation keys, **Page Up** and **Page Down**, to move up and down a page at a time.

3 Moving the cell selector with the arrow keys.

4 Using the **Go To** command in the **Edit** menu. Enter the cell address, eg C5 in the **Reference** box and click on: **OK.**

5 Pointing to a cell with the mouse and clicking.

6 Pressing: **Ctrl + Home** takes you to the top of your spreadsheet. **Ctrl + End** will take you to the last cell with data entered on your spreadsheet (when you have entered data).

1.4 Spreadsheet contents

You can enter:

- text
- numeric data
- formulae.

Text entries are used for titles, headings and any notes. They are entries that you do not want to manipulate arithmetically.

Numeric data consists of numbers you want to add, subtract, multiply, divide and use in formulae.

Formulae are used to calculate the value of a cell from the contents of other cells. For instance, formulae may be used to calculate totals or averages. *Formulae always start with an = sign.* A typical formula could look like the examples below:

    =A1+A2   =SUM(A1:A6)   =B6-B4   =C2*C7   =A2/B9

    =A2*B6+A4 =C2/D2-F8

The following operators (symbols) are used in formulae:

    +(ADD)   -(SUBTRACT)   *(MULTIPLY)   /(DIVIDE)

	A	B	C	D
1		MON	TUES	WED	← Text
2	TEA	10	14	30
3	COFFEE	66	55	9	← Numeric data
4	TOTALS	=B2+B3	=C2+C3	=D2+D3

Formula

Figure 4.4 Types of spreadsheet entry

1.5 Inserting text and numeric data

Exercise 2

The spreadsheet below (Figure 4.5) shows the sales figures for three different cosmetic companies over a four-month period. Enter the data into the spreadsheet.

	A	B	C	D
1	MONTH	ESSENZ	LIVENUP	STARS
2	JAN	490	210	130
3	FEB	608	419	400
4	MAR	309	318	534
5	APR	600	521	470

Figure 4.5 Spreadsheet data

Method

1   Move to cell A1 and key in **MONTH**.

2   Move to cell B1 and key in **ESSENZ**.

3   Move to cell C1 and key in **LIVENUP**.

4   Complete the spreadsheet in this way until it looks like Figure 4.5.

Sometimes you need to enter data that is too long to display in full in the cell. (The default is about nine numeric characters.) You can adjust the column width to display cell entries in full. All entries must be displayed in full for New CLAIT.

To widen a column

1 Position the cursor at the column border (see below); a double arrow appears.

2 Drag the right-hand edge of the column border (next to the column letter) to the right.

or

Double-click on the column border to fit the widest entry.

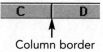

Column border

This topic is covered in more detail in Section 3.

1.6 Entering simple formulae

Exercise 3

Enter simple formulae to add up cell contents.
Remember: Formulae must always begin with the = sign.

Method

1 Move to cell A6 and key in **TOTAL**.

2 We want to add up the sales figures for ESSENZ. These are displayed in cells B2, B3, B4 and B5. Move to cell B6 (where you want the answer to appear).

 Notice as you key in that the formula appears on the Formula bar. It may be too long to fit the cell but you can ignore this. Cell references can be in upper or lower case.

Key in: **=B2+B3+B4+B5** and press: **Enter**. The answer 2007 appears in cell B6.

3 Add up the sales figures for LIVENUP in the same way by keying in: **=C2+C3+C4+C5** and press: **Enter**. The answer 1468 appears in cell C6.

 In the early stages of learning how to construct formulae it is worth checking that the answer is as expected by working out the result for yourself. Of course once you are confident, let the spreadsheet application do things for you! However, it is still worth having a rough idea of what the answer should be, just in case you have mis-keyed an entry.

Your spreadsheet will now look like Figure 4.6.

	A	B	C	D
1	MONTH	ESSENZ	LIVENUP	STARS
2	JAN	490	210	130
3	FEB	608	419	400
4	MAR	309	318	534
5	APR	600	521	470
6	TOTAL	2007	1468	

Figure 4.6 Totalling column B and column C

Using the built-in SUM function

On a large business spreadsheet, you might need to add a huge number of cell contents and specifying each cell reference would not be practical. A quicker way to add up figures is by using one of Excel's built-in *functions*, SUM, to work out the formula as follows:

To produce a TOTAL for STARS:

1   Move to cell D6 (where you want the answer to appear).

2   Key in =SUM(D2:D5) and press: Enter.

> The colon between the cell references in the formula above means 'to include all the cells in between D2 and D5'. To speed things up, Excel has many functions including SUM (used for adding) and AVERAGE (used to calculate the average value for a range of cells), ie instead of keying in, for example
>
> **=A1+B1+C1+D1/4** you can use **=AVERAGE(A1:D1)**
>
> *Note:* You do not need to use SUM in the formula when subtracting, multiplying or dividing. For instance, the formula for subtracting the contents of cell A6 from those in cell D4 would be **=D4-A6**.

Your spreadsheet will now look like Figure 4.7.

	A	B	C	D
1	MONTH	ESSENZ	LIVENUP	STARS
2	JAN	490	210	130
3	FEB	608	419	400
4	MAR	309	318	534
5	APR	600	521	470
6	TOTAL	2007	1468	1534

Figure 4.7 Totalling column D

Practise using the SUM function:

1   Delete the Totals of ESSENZ (cell B6) and LIVENUP (cell C6) by selecting them and pressing: **Delete**.

2   Add the Totals again, this time using the SUM function, in cell B6 **=SUM(B2:B5)** and in cell C6 **=SUM(C2:C5)**.

Using the AutoSum button

There is an even quicker way to add cell values using the toolbar button **AutoSum**.

To practise this, let's add up the totals for the three cosmetic companies for each month.

1   Move to cell E1 and key in **SALES**.

2   Move to cell E2, the cell where you want the total sales for JAN to appear.

3   Click on: the Σ **AutoSum** button. You will notice that a dotted line has appeared around cells B2 to D2.

In this example, Excel has automatically chosen the correct cells to add. Sometimes it chooses the wrong ones. If this happens you will need to select the cells you want. Click on the cell you want to start with, holding down the left mouse and dragging the dotted line across the correct cells. Be careful that you don't drag too far and include the cell where you want the answer to appear by mistake. The answer cell cannot be included in the formula. If you try to include the cell reference where you want the answer to appear in a formula, an error message will be displayed. Follow the instructions given in the error message.

4   Press: **Enter**.

5   The answer 830 appears in cell E2.

6   Use this method to calculate the sales totals for FEB, MAR and APR.

When adding sales for MAR, you will notice that Excel has mistakenly decided that you now want to add the figures from above the cell and has placed the dotted line around cells E2 and E3. Move the highlight by clicking the first cell you want to add (B4) and dragging across to D4. Watch out for this.

If you have done everything correctly, the totals will be as in Figure 4.8.

FEB   in cell E3   Total = 1427
MAR   in cell E4   Total = 1161
APR   in cell E5   Total = 1591

	A	B	C	D	E
1	MONTH	ESSENZ	LIVENUP	STARS	SALES
2	JAN	490	210	130	830
3	FEB	608	419	400	1427
4	MAR	309	318	534	1161
5	APR	600	521	470	1591
6	TOTAL	2007	1468	1534	

Figure 4.8 Sales figures for JAN, FEB, MAR and APR

1.7 Saving the spreadsheet

Exercise 4

Save the spreadsheet.

Method

1   From the **File** menu, select: **Save As**. The **Save As** dialogue box appears (Figure 4.9).

2   Select the location where you want to save your file and key in **Sales** in the **File name** box.

3   Click on: **Save**.

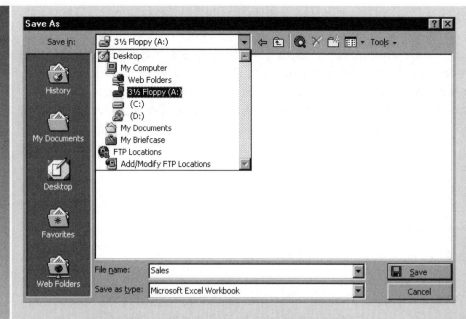

Figure 4.9 The Save As dialogue box

1.8 Printing spreadsheets

Exercise 5

Print the spreadsheet.

Method

Note: If you are working in a shared printer situation, it is a good idea to add your initials in a cell a few rows below the bottom row of cell entries (so that you will recognise your printout).

Previewing a spreadsheet before printing

It is always wise to preview your spreadsheet before printing so you are sure that it will print exactly what you want. This will save paper as well as effort.

1   Click on: the ▯ **Print Preview** button.

2   Click on: the **Zoom** option to see your spreadsheet contents. Click on: **Zoom** again to return to default view.

3   If you are happy with the **Print Preview**, click on: **Print**. (You can change default options here if necessary.)

4   Click on: **OK**.

Should you need to exit Print Preview at step 3, press: **Esc** *or* click on: **Close** to return to the spreadsheet.

Always examine your printout very carefully to check that all data is showing in full; you may have overlooked something, or your default printer may be set up so that you need to leave additional space on your spreadsheet.

Printing in landscape

By default the spreadsheet will print a portrait display (the narrow edge at the top of the page). If you prefer, or if your spreadsheet does not fit across the page, you can change the display to landscape.

Note: Dotted lines appear on the spreadsheet to denote a page break.

Portrait	
	Landscape

To do this from **Print Preview**, click on: **Setup**:

1   Click on: the **Page** tab, then on: the **Landscape** option button.

2   Click on: **OK**.

If not using Print Preview:

1   From the **File** menu, select: **Page Setup**.

2   Click on: the **Page** tab, then on: the **Landscape** option button.

3   Click on: **Print**.

1.9 Printing formulae

Exercise 6

Print a copy of the spreadsheet showing the formulae used.

It is useful to have a printout of the formulae used on your spreadsheet so you can cross-reference for accuracy. This is required for the CLAIT assessment.

Method

To show formulae on your spreadsheet

1   With your spreadsheet on screen, from the **Tools** menu, select: **Options**.

2   Click on: the **View** tab (if not already selected); the **Options** dialogue box appears. Click on: the **Formulas** check box so that a tick appears in this box. Click on: **OK** (Figure 4.10).

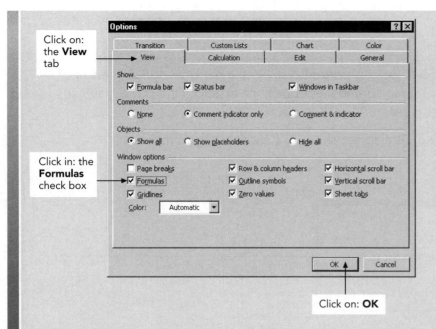

Click on:
the **View**
tab

Click in: the
Formulas
check box

Click on: **OK**

Figure 4.10 Showing formulae

3 Notice that the columns have widened to accommodate the formulae.

 Do not reduce the column widths because when you take the 'show formulas' off the cell widths will need altering again. For a quicker way to show formulae, press: **Ctrl** + ` (to the left of the number one key).

4 Check that the spreadsheet will fit on one page by using **Print Preview** (as above).

5 If it fits, print as before.

6 If it does not fit, check that it is in landscape by following the instructions above.

7 Check that all the formulae are displayed in full. If they are not, you will need to widen the cells as appropriate and reprint.

 In **Page Setup** in the **Scaling** section, there is also an option **Fit to page**. This ensures that the whole spreadsheet (although reduced in size) will fit on one page. *Note*: You will still need to widen cells that are not displaying their entire contents.

Exercise 7

Change the spreadsheet so that numbers are displayed instead of formulae.

Removing showing formulae

Method

1 From the **Tools** menu, select: **Options**.

2 Click on: the **View** tab (if not already selected); click in: the **Formulas** check box so that the tick is removed. Click on: **OK**.

A quick way to change back to values display – press: **Ctrl +`**.

1.10 Closing a spreadsheet file

Exercise 8

Close the spreadsheet file.

Method

From the **File** menu, select: **Close**. *Note:* You may be asked if you want to save changes, click on: **Yes**.

1.11 Exiting Excel

Exercise 9

Exit Excel.

Method

Click on: the ⊠ **Close** button in the top right-hand corner.

Spreadsheets practice 1

 In the following exercises, some of the numeric data has decimal places, ie figures after the decimal point (the decimal point is entered using the full stop key (but no spaces after it)). When there is one number to the right of the decimal point, the number has one decimal place. When there are two numbers after the decimal point, the number has two decimal places. If there is no decimal point, the number is a whole number (also known as an *integer*). You will be working with formatting decimal places in Section 3.

Note: When entering numbers with decimal places and trailing zeros, eg 12.30, this may appear on the spreadsheet as 12.3 (the trailing 0 is missing). You need not be concerned about this at this stage.

Practice 1

1 Create a new spreadsheet.

2 Enter the following data, leaving the **TOTAL** column blank.

DEPT SALES						
DEPT	OVERHEADS	MARK UP	MON	TUE	WED	TOTAL
FRUIT	6	0.17	44	68	22	
VEG	4	0.15	55	88	21	
FISH	10	0.12	52.5	16	28	
CHILLED	7	0.1	12	72	14	
DAIRY	6	0.13	65	32	43	
DRINKS	2.5	0.25	19	31	41.5	

3 Enter your name, centre number and today's date a few lines below the data.

4 The TOTAL for each department is calculated by adding the figures for **MON**, **TUE** and **WED**.

Insert a formula to calculate the **TOTAL** for **FRUIT**.

5 Save your spreadsheet report with the filename **P1 sec1 shop** and print one copy. Make sure that all the data is displayed in full.

6 Print a copy showing the formula used. Make sure the formula is displayed in full.

7 Close the spreadsheet file and exit Excel.

Practice 2

1 Create a new spreadsheet.

2 Enter the following data, leaving the **TOTAL** column blank.

GOODS						
PRODUCT	WEEK1	WEEK2	WEEK3	COST	CARRIAGE	TOTAL
BACKPACK	328	627	321	32.5	22.5	
HOLDALL	198	562	1211	45.2	25.25	
WHEELBAG	231	125	324	17.99	35.5	
BRIEFCASE	362	321	375	40	15.55	
PILOT	732	268	432	39.75	50	
ATTACHE	120	112	39	12.99	32.5	
BINDER	560	270	110	6	9.5	

3 Enter your name, centre number and today's date a few lines below the data.

4 The **TOTAL** for each product is calculated by adding the figures for **WEEK1**, **WEEK2** and **WEEK3**.

Insert a formula to calculate the **TOTAL** for **BACKPACK**.

5 Save your spreadsheet report with the filename **P2 sec1 travel** and print one copy. Make sure that all the data is displayed in full.

6 Print a copy showing the formula used. Make sure the formula is displayed in full.

7 Close the spreadsheet file and exit Excel.

In this section you will learn how to:

- reload a saved file
- change entries made to your spreadsheet
- delete a row or column
- copy or replicate entries and formulae
- insert a new row or column
- recalculate data
- save the spreadsheet using a new filename

2.1 Reloading a saved file

Exercise 1

Reload the spreadsheet **Sales** saved in Section 1.

Method

1 With Excel loaded, click on: the 📂 **Open** button; the **Open** dialogue box appears (Figure 4.11).

2 Select the location where your file is stored by clicking on: the down arrow.

3 Click on: the filename **Sales**.

4 Click on: **Open**.

Figure 4.11 Opening a saved file

Exercise 2

Some of the original data in the spreadsheet **Sales** has been found to be incorrect:

The Sales figures for ESSENZ should be **520** in **JAN** and **250** in **MAR**.

We need to change these entries.

Method

1   Move to cell B2 and key in: **520** and press: **Enter**.

2   Move to cell B4 and key in: **250** and press: **Enter**.

 Notice that the original figures are overwritten. Look what has happened to the Total for ESSENZ. You will see that the formula has been recalculated to give a new Total. The Sales figures for JAN and MAR in column E have also been updated to reflect the changes made. This will usually happen. When you change cell contents within a spreadsheet, all the formulae referring to that cell will be recalculated automatically.

Your spreadsheet will now look like Figure 4.12.

	A	B	C	D	E
1	MONTH	ESSENZ	LIVENUP	STARS	SALES
2	JAN	520	210	130	860
3	FEB	608	419	400	1427
4	MAR	250	318	534	1102
5	APR	600	521	470	1591
6	TOTAL	1978	1468	1534	

Figure 4.12 Updated spreadsheet

2.3 Deleting a row or column

Exercise 3

It has been decided that the figures for FEB are not required. Delete this row. Close up space, do not leave a blank row.

Method

1   Click on: the box to the left of the row to be deleted, ie row 3. Row 3 is highlighted (Figure 4.13).

Click here →

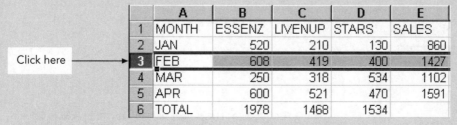

Figure 4.13 Selecting a row

2   Right-click on: the selected row; a pop-up menu appears (Figure 4.14).

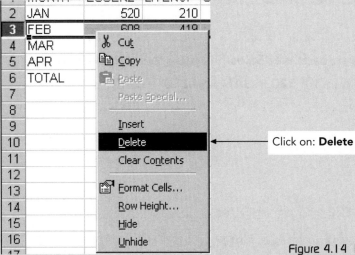

Click on: **Delete**

Figure 4.14 Right-clicking displays a pop-up menu

3   Click on: **Delete**. The spreadsheet contents move up to occupy the empty space and the figures are recalculated to reflect the change (Figure 4.15).

	A	B	C	D	E
1	MONTH	ESSENZ	LIVENUP	STARS	SALES
2	JAN	520	210	130	860
3	MAR	250	318	534	1102
4	APR	600	521	470	1591
5	TOTAL	1370	1049	1134	

Figure 4.15 Spreadsheet after deletion of the FEB row

 When you are asked to delete rows or columns, it is necessary to delete the whole row/column as shown in the method above. Do not just clear the contents by pressing (thus leaving an empty row/column). If you are familiar with Excel, do not use Excel's **Hide** facility. This simply hides, ie it does not delete, the row or column.

Exercise 4

The figures for LIVENUP are no longer required. Delete this column.

Method

1   Click in: the box at the top of the column to be deleted, ie C; column C is highlighted.

2   Right-click on: the selection; a pop-up menu appears.

3   Click on: **Delete**.

The spreadsheet now looks like Figure 4.16.

	A	B	C	D
1	MONTH	ESSENZ	STARS	SALES
2	JAN	520	130	650
3	MAR	250	534	784
4	APR	600	470	1070
5	TOTAL	1370	1134	

Figure 4.16 Spreadsheet after deletion of the LIVENUP column

Exercise 5

Replicate the formula used to calculate the TOTAL for STARS so that the TOTAL for SALES is also calculated.

Method

1 Move to the cell in which the formula you want to copy is stored. In this case C5.

2 Point the mouse at the bottom right of this cell until a black cross + appears then, holding down the left mouse, drag across cell D5 (where you want the formula copied to). Release the mouse.

The spreadsheet now looks like Figure 4.17.

	A	B	C	D
1	MONTH	ESSENZ	STARS	SALES
2	JAN	520	130	650
3	MAR	250	534	784
4	APR	600	470	1070
5	TOTAL	1370	1134	2504

Figure 4.17 Spreadsheet after replication of formula

If you make an error performing this procedure, Click on: the ↶ **Undo** button and try again. You can not only replicate formulae in this way but also copy other spreadsheet entries.

Relative and absolute cell references

When replicating formulae, the cell references change to reflect their new position. (You can check this by looking at the formula that you have just replicated.) A relative cell reference will change relatively to its position on the spreadsheet. By contrast, a cell reference can be made absolute. This means that it will not change even if it is replicated or moved to another part of the spreadsheet. You can copy entries that do not contain formulae using the method above. This results in exact copies of the initial cell entry into the destination cells.

Exercise 6

Adding a new column

Insert a new column headed JUST4U after ESSENZ and before STARS. Enter the following information:

JAN, 720.15 **MAR, 630.25** **APR, 938.5**

1 Click in: the box at the top of the column after where the new column is to appear, ie column C; column C is highlighted (Figure 4.18).

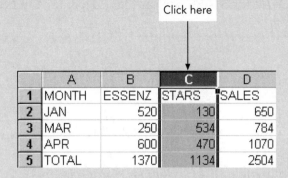

Figure 4.18 Selecting a column

2 Right-click on: the selection; a pop-up menu appears. Click on: **Insert** (Figure 4.19). An empty column appears.

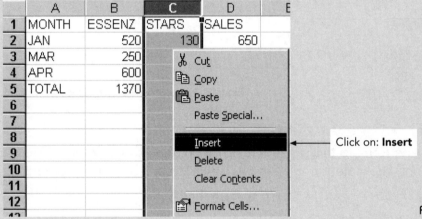

Figure 4.19 Inserting a column

3 Enter the new text and data shown above.

The spreadsheet now looks like Figure 4.20.

	A	B	C	D	E
1	MONTH	ESSENZ	JUST4U	STARS	SALES
2	JAN	520	720.15	130	1370.15
3	MAR	250	630.25	534	1414.25
4	APR	600	938.5	470	2008.5
5	TOTAL	1370		1134	4792.9

Figure 4.20 Spreadsheet after addition of JUST4U column and data

Calculate the Total for JUST4U, using one of the quicker methods you have learnt. The Total is 2288.9.

Adding a new row

It has been decided to re-insert the figures for FEB. Insert a new row for FEB with the following information: **ESSENZ 608**, **JUST4U 99.60**, **STARS 400**.

1   Click in: the box to the left of the row below where you want the new row to appear, ie row 3. Row 3 is highlighted (Figure 4.21).

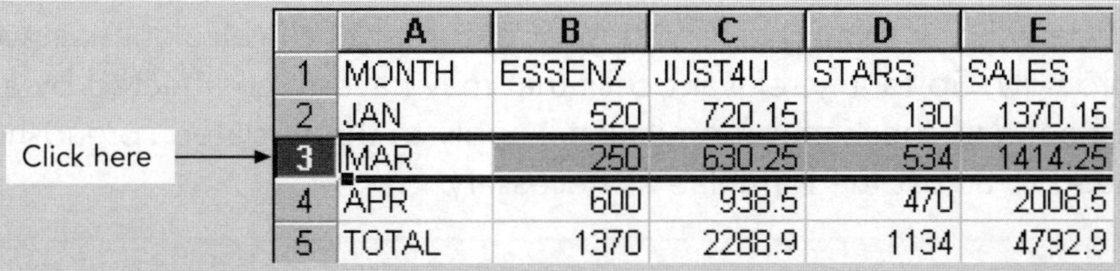

Click here →

	A	B	C	D	E
1	MONTH	ESSENZ	JUST4U	STARS	SALES
2	JAN	520	720.15	130	1370.15
3	MAR	250	630.25	534	1414.25
4	APR	600	938.5	470	2008.5
5	TOTAL	1370	2288.9	1134	4792.9

Figure 4.21   Adding a new row

2   Right-click on: the highlighted row; a pop-up menu appears (Figure 4.22). Click on: **Insert**. An empty row appears.

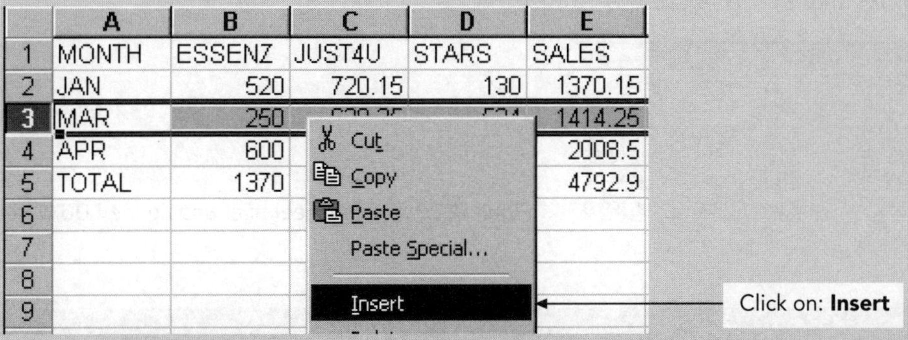

	A	B	C	D	E
1	MONTH	ESSENZ	JUST4U	STARS	SALES
2	JAN	520	720.15	130	1370.15
3	MAR	250			1414.25
4	APR	600	✄ Cut		2008.5
5	TOTAL	1370	▤ Copy		4792.9
6			▤ Paste		
7			Paste Special...		
8					
9			Insert		

Click on: **Insert**

Figure 4.22 Inserting a row

3   Enter the new text and data shown above.

Replicate the formula from cell E2 to produce a Total in cell E3 for FEB SALES. The total is 1107.6.

2.6 Adding a new column or row to create new values

Exercise 8

Insert a new column for LOOKS after STARS and before the SALES column (see above Section 2.5).

Enter the following data:

JAN, 654.43   FEB, 821.12   MAR, 500.3   APR, 320.55

Replicate the formula from D6 to give a Total value in cell E6 for LOOKS.

Note: In Excel 2000, these figures (although at the end of the existing SUM cell range) are automatically included in the Sales column figures. This did not happen in earlier versions of Excel. Look out for this as you may not always want Excel to include new data in formulae.

When adding, deleting or editing cells you must ensure that all calculations have been updated accordingly. Go to any relevant cells that may have been affected by a change to the spreadsheet and check that formulae still apply to the updated spreadsheet. If not you will need to adjust the formulae as necessary.

Method

Follow the method in Section 2.5.

The spreadsheet now looks like Figure 4.23.

	A	B	C	D	E	F
1	MONTH	ESSENZ	JUST4U	STARS	LOOKS	SALES
2	JAN	520	720.15	130	654.43	2024.58
3	FEB	608	99.6	400	821.12	1928.72
4	MAR	250	630.25	534	500.3	1914.55
5	APR	600	938.5	470	320.55	2329.05
6	TOTAL	1978	2388.5	1534	2296.4	8196.9

Figure 4.23 Spreadsheet after adding the LOOKS column

2.7 Save your spreadsheet as Sales1

Saving your spreadsheet with a new filename will ensure that the original version is not overwritten. You will now have two spreadsheets, **Sales** (the original) and **Sales1** (the updated spreadsheet).

2.8 Print one copy of your spreadsheet, Sales1

2.9 Close the file and exit Excel

Practice 3

1   Load Excel.

2   Reload the spreadsheet **P1 sec1 shop** saved in Section 1.

3   In the **TOTAL** column, replicate the formula in the **FRUIT** row to show totals for all departments.

4   Resave using the original filename and print one copy of the spreadsheet.

5   Insert a new column entitled **PROFIT** between the columns **DEPT** and **OVERHEADS**.

6   **PROFIT** is calculated by multiplying the **TOTAL** figure by the **MARK UP** and subtracting the **OVERHEADS**.

Insert a formula to calculate the **PROFIT** for **FRUIT**. Replicate this formula to show the **PROFIT** for each department.

Some changes need to be made to the spreadsheet.

7   Delete the entire row for **DIARY**.

8   Make the following amendments to the spreadsheet:

   a The **MARK UP** for **FISH** should be **0.10**.
   b The **OVERHEADS** for **VEG** should be **2.5**.
   c The **WED** sales for **VEG** should be **36**.
   d **CHILLED** should be **FROZEN**.

Make sure the **TOTAL** and **PROFIT** have updated as a result of these changes.

9   Save the spreadsheet as **P3 sec2 shop**.

10 **a** Print one copy showing the data and one copy showing the formulae used.
   b Ensure all data and formulae are showing in full on the printouts.

11 Close the spreadsheet file and exit Excel.

Practice 4

1   Load Excel.

2   Reload the spreadsheet **P2 sec1 travel** saved in Section 1.

3   In the **TOTAL** column, replicate the formula in the **BACKPACK** row to show totals for all departments.

4   Resave using the original filename and print one copy of the spreadsheet.

5   Insert a new column entitled **TOTAL COST** between the columns **WEEK3** and **COST**.

6   **TOTAL COST** is calculated by multiplying the **TOTAL** figure by the **COST** and adding the **CARRIAGE**.

Insert a formula to calculate the **TOTAL COST** for **BACKPACK**.

7 Replicate this formula to show the **TOTAL COST** for each item.

Some changes need to be made to the spreadsheet.

8 Delete the entire row for **PILOT**.

9 Make the following amendments to the spreadsheet:

    a The **COST** for **HOLDALL** should be **32.5**.
    b The **CARRIAGE** for **BINDER** should be **6.5**.
    c The **WEEK3** orders for **BRIEFCASE** should be **430**.
    d **WHEELBAG** should be **TROLLEY**.

10 Make sure the **TOTAL COST** and **TOTAL** have updated as a result of these changes.

11 Save the spreadsheet as **P4 sec2 travel**.

12 **a** Print one copy showing the data and one copy showing the formulae used.
    b Ensure all data and formulae are showing in full on the printouts.

13 Close the spreadsheet file and exit Excel.

3 Using display features

In this section you will learn how to:

- left and right align text and numeric data
- use integer format and decimal format to display numbers
- display in currency format

Reload the spreadsheet **Sales1** saved at the end of Section 2.

3.1 Left and right justifying text

 When data is first entered, text is placed on the left of the cell and numbers line up on the right. Three toolbar buttons can be used to apply a new alignment to a selected range.

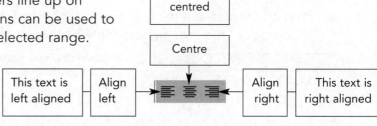

To align cell contents

1 Select the cells to be realigned.
2 Click on: the appropriate toolbar button.

Exercise 1

Display the headings: **MONTH**, **ESSENZ**, **JUST4U**, **STARS**, **LOOKS** and **SALES** so that **MONTH** is left justified and **ESSENZ**, **JUST4U**, **STARS**, **LOOKS** and **SALES** are right justified.

Method

The heading **MONTH** is already left justified. To right justify the other headings:

1 Select cells **B1** to **F1** (Figure 4.24).

	A	B	C	D	E	F
1	MONTH	ESSENZ	JUST4U	STARS	LOOKS	SALES
2	JAN	520	720.15	130	654.43	2024.58
3	FEB	608	99.6	400	821.12	1928.72

Figure 4.24 Cells selected to right justify

2 Click on: the **Align Right** toolbar button.

3.2 Changing column width

Exercise 2

Change the heading **SALES** so that it becomes **MONTHLY SALES**.

1   Move to cell F1.

2   Click the cursor in front of the **S** of **SALES** (Figure 4.25) on the formula bar and key in: **MONTHLY** and a space. Press: **Enter**.

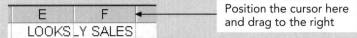

	A	B	C	D	E	F
1	MONTH	ESSENZ	JUST4U	STARS	LOOKS	SALES
2	JAN	520	720.15	130	654.43	2024.58

Figure 4.25 Positioning the cursor to alter a heading

3   The entry is now too long to fit the cell. There are several ways to widen the column:

 Click on: the **Undo** toolbar button after trying each method so that you can practise.

a   Position the cursor at the column border; a double arrow appears. Drag the right-hand edge of the column border (next to the column letter) to the right (Figure 4.26).

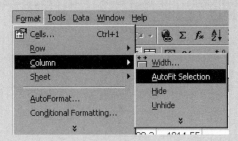

Position the cursor here and drag to the right

Figure 4.26 Changing column width

b   Position the cursor as above and double-click the mouse (this action widens to fit the longest entry exactly).

c   With the cell selected, from the **Format** menu, select: **Column**, **Width**. Key in a new width (ie the number of characters in the cell).

d   With the cell selected, from the **Format** menu, select: **Column**, **AutoFit Selection** (Figure 4.27).

Format	Tools	Data	Window	Help
Cells...	Ctrl+1			
Row	▶			
Column	▶	Width...		
Sheet	▶	AutoFit Selection		
		Hide		
AutoFormat...		Unhide		
Conditional Formatting...				

Figure 4.27 Widening a column using the menus

 If a cell is filled with ####### characters, the column is not wide enough to display the numeric value held in that cell. Widen the cell, as above, to display the cell contents.

Exercise 3

Enter a column headed **AVERAGE SALES** after the MONTHLY SALES column. Right justify this heading and widen the cell to display this heading in full.

In cell G2, enter a formula to work out the AVERAGE SALES for JAN, ie MONTHLY SALES divided by 4 (as there are 4 companies). The formula is: =F2/4.

Replicate this formula to cells G3, G4, G5 and G6.

The spreadsheet will now look like Figure 4.28.

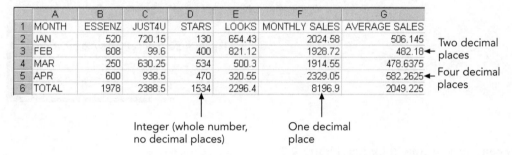

	A	B	C	D	E	F	G
1	MONTH	ESSENZ	JUST4U	STARS	LOOKS	MONTHLY SALES	AVERAGE SALES
2	JAN	520	720.15	130	654.43	2024.58	506.145
3	FEB	608	99.6	400	821.12	1928.72	482.18
4	MAR	250	630.25	534	500.3	1914.55	478.6375
5	APR	600	938.5	470	320.55	2329.05	582.2625
6	TOTAL	1978	2388.5	1534	2296.4	8196.9	2049.225

Two decimal places

Four decimal places

Integer (whole number, no decimal places)

One decimal place

Figure 4.28 Spreadsheet with the Average Sales column added

Exercise 4

Display the numeric data in the AVERAGE SALES column as integers (no decimal places).

Method

1   Select the column entries, ie cells G2 to G6.

2   Right-click: the highlighted area; a pop-up menu appears (Figure 4.29).

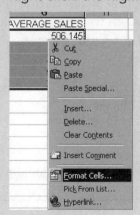

Figure 4.29 Formatting cells

3   From the menu, select: **Format Cells**; the **Format Cells** dialogue box is displayed (Figure 4.30).

4   Click on: the **Number** tab.

5   In the **Category** box, click on: **Number**.

6   In the **Decimal places** box, use the down arrow to set to zero (0).

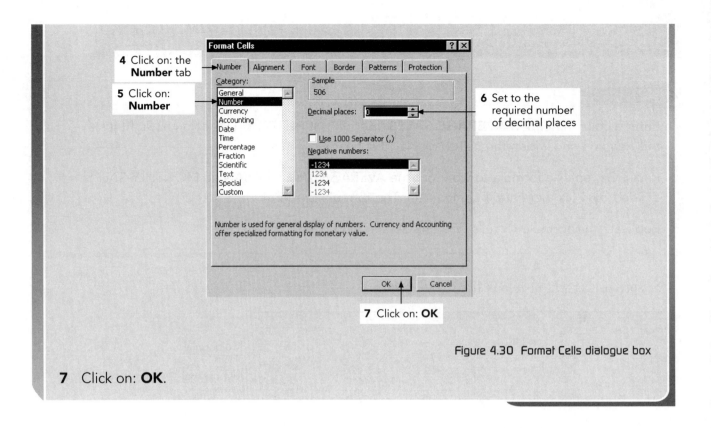

4 Click on: the **Number** tab

5 Click on: **Number**

6 Set to the required number of decimal places

7 Click on: **OK**

Figure 4.30 Format Cells dialogue box

7 Click on: **OK**.

The AVERAGE SALES column will now look like Figure 4.31.

G
AVERAGE SALES
506
482
479
582
2049

Figure 4.31 Average Sales figures displayed as integers

 Notice that the figure for MAR, which was 478.6375, is now 479. Excel will display figures rounded up to the nearest whole number when the number after the decimal point is 5 or greater than 5. Although it displays as a whole number, when performing calculations Excel works on the original entry. Therefore if you were to work out the result on a calculator using the displayed figures, there would be a slight difference in the answer (ie Excel would be more accurate).

Note: With the cells selected, you can also use the toolbar buttons [icon] **Increase Decimal/Decrease Decimal** to change the number of decimal places.

Follow the instructions above to display the numeric data in the **LOOKS** column to two decimal places, ie two places after the decimal point.

The LOOKS column should now look like Figure 4.32.

E
LOOKS
654.43
821.12
500.30
320.55
2296.40

Figure 4.32 LOOKS figures displayed with 2 decimal places

Spreadsheets using Excel (Unit 4)

3.4 Displaying in currency format

Exercise 5

Display the numeric data in the TOTAL row in currency format (displaying a £ sign) to two decimal places.

Method

1 Select: the row entries, ie cells B6 to G6.

2 Right-click: the highlighted area; a pop-up menu appears.

3 From the menu, select: **Format Cells**; the **Format Cells** dialogue box is displayed.

4 Click on: the **Number** tab.

5 In the **Category** box, click on: **Currency**.

6 In the **Decimal places** box, use the down arrow to set to **2**.

7 In the **Symbol** box, use the down arrow to select the **£** sign. *Note:* You should not add the £ sign manually.

 Although it is normal to show currency with two decimal places, ie £13.57 to indicate 13 pounds and 57 pence, when working with spreadsheets none, one or more than two decimal places can also be displayed. Set this in the **Decimal places** box.

When you want to format currency to two decimal places and a £ sign, you can also use the 🔢 **Currency** button.

3.5 Save the spreadsheet

Save the spreadsheet as **Sales2**, print a copy showing the data and another showing the formulae.

3.6 Close the spreadsheet file and exit Excel

Spreadsheet practice 3

Practice 5

1 Load Excel.

2 Reload the spreadsheet **P3 sec2 shop** saved in Practice 3, Section 2.

3 Apply alignment as follows:

    a The column heading **DEPT SALES** and all row labels (eg **FRUIT**, **VEG**, etc) should be left-aligned.

    b The other column headings (eg **PROFIT**, **OVERHEADS**, **MARK UP**, etc) should be right-aligned.

    c All numeric values should be right-aligned.

4 Format the data as follows:

    a The figures for **MON**, **TUE** and **WED** should be displayed in integer format (to zero decimal places).

    b The figures for **OVERHEADS**, **MARK UP** and **TOTAL** should be displayed to two decimal places.

    c The **PROFIT** data only should be displayed with a £ sign and to two decimal places.

5 Save your spreadsheet using the filename **P5 sec3 shop**.

6 Print one copy showing figures, not formulae. Make sure that all data is displayed in full.

7 Print the spreadsheet with all the formulae showing. Make sure that all formulae are displayed in full.

8 Close the spreadsheet file and exit Excel.

Practice 6

1 Load Excel.

2 Reload the spreadsheet **P4 sec2 travel** saved in Practice 4, Section 2.

3 Apply alignment as follows:

    a The column heading **GOODS** and all row labels (eg **BACKPACK**, **HOLDALL**, etc) should be right-aligned.

    b The other column headings (eg **WEEK1**, **WEEK2**, etc) should be left-aligned.

    c All numeric values should be right-aligned.

4 Format the data as follows:

    a The figures for **CARRIAGE** and **TOTAL** should be displayed in integer format (to zero decimal places).

    b The figures for **COST** should be displayed to two decimal places.

    c The **TOTAL COST** data *only* should be displayed with a £ sign and to one decimal place.

5 Save your spreadsheet using the filename **P6 sec3 travel**.

6 Print one copy showing figures, not formulae. Make sure that all data is displayed in full.

7 Print the spreadsheet with all the formulae showing. Make sure that all formulae are displayed in full.

8 Close the spreadsheet file and exit Excel.

Action	Keyboard	Mouse	Right-mouse menu	Menu
Align cell entries	Select cells to align			
		Click: the relevant button: ≡ ≡ ≡	**Format Cells**	**F**ormat, C**e**lls
			Select the **Alignment** tab Select from the **Horizontal:** drop-down menu as appropriate	
Capitals (blocked)	**Caps Lock** (press again to remove)			
Close a file	**Ctrl + W**	Click: the ✖ **Close** button		**F**ile, **C**lose
Columns, changing width of		Drag the column border C ✛ D to fit the widest entry	Select the column(s) by clicking (and dragging) on the column ref box (at top of column)	
			Column Width Key in the width you want	**F**ormat, **C**olumn, **W**idth Key in the width you want or **F**ormat, **C**olumn, **A**utoFit **Selection**
Columns, deleting	Select the column you want to delete by clicking on the column ref box (at top of column)			
	Delete		**Delete**	**E**dit, **D**elete
Columns, inserting	Select the column following the one where you want the new column to appear – by clicking on the column ref box (at top of column)			
			Insert	**I**nsert, **C**olumns
Copy (replicate) formulae	Select cell with formula to be copied Drag the mouse from bottom right corner of cell over cells to copy to, release mouse			
Currency symbols		Click: the 💷 **Currency** button for UK currency		**F**ormat, C**e**lls, **Number**, **C**ategory, **Currency**. Select number of decimal places
Decimal places		Click: the .00 **Increase Decimal** button to increase the number of decimal places Click: the .00 **Decrease Decimal** button to decrease the number of decimal places	**Format Cells** Select the **Number** tab Click: **Number** in the **Category:** menu Select the number of decimal places you need	**F**ormat, C**e**lls
Enter formulae	Click: in the cell where you want text to appear Key in: = followed by the formula Press: **Enter**			
Enter numeric data	Click: in the cell where you want text to appear Key in: the data Press: **Enter**			
Enter text	Click: in the cell where you want text to appear Key in: the text Press: **Enter**			

Action	Keyboard	Mouse	Right-mouse menu	Menu
Exit Excel		Click: the **X** **Close** button		**File**, **Exit**
Fit to page				**File**, **Page Setup**, **Fit to (1) Page(s) wide**
Formulae, functions	Click on the cell where the result is required Use: =**SUM(cell ref:cell ref)** for adding a range of cells *or* Click: **Σ AutoSum** button Click and drag over the cell range Press: **Enter**			
Formulae, operators	+ add - subtract * multiply / divide			
Formulae, showing	**Ctrl + `**			**Tools**, **Options**, **View** Under **Window options**, select **Formulas** so that a tick appears
Formulae, printing	Ensure the formulae are showing			
				File, **Page Setup**, **Page tab**, **Landscape** *or* **File**, **Page Setup**, **Page tab** Under **Scaling**, select **Fit to 1 page wide by 1 page tall**
Help	**F1**			**Help** **Microsoft Excel Help**
	Shift + F1			**Help**, **What's This?**
Integers (whole numbers)		Click: the **.00 +.0 Decrease Decimal** button until you have reduced the number of decimal places to zero	**Format Cells** Select the **Number** tab Click: **Number** in the **Category** menu Change the number of decimal places to zero	**Format**, **Cells**
Loading Excel	In the Windows 98 desktop			
		Double-click: the **Excel** shortcut icon		**Start**, **Programs**, **Microsoft Excel**
Moving around	Use the cursor keys	Click where you want to move to		
Move to top of document	**Ctrl + Home**			
Move to end of document	**Ctrl + End**			
New file	**Ctrl + N**	Click: the **New** button		**File**, **New**
Open an existing file	**Ctrl + O**	Click: the **Open** button		**File**, **Open**
	Select: the drive required Select: the filename Click: **Open**			
Page Setup	From the **File** menu, select: **Page Setup** Choose from **Margins**, **Paper Size**, **Paper Source**, **Layout**			

Action	Keyboard	Mouse	Right-mouse menu	Menu
Print file	**Ctrl + P** Select the options you need Press: **Enter**	Click: the 🖨 **Print** button		**File**, **Print** Select the options you need and click: **OK**
Printing in Landscape	From the **File** menu, select: **Page Setup** Click: the **Page** tab Select: **Landscape** Click: **OK**			
Print Preview		Click: the 🔍 **Print Preview** button		**File**, **Print Preview**
Replicate (copy) formulae	Select: the cell with the formula to be copied Drag the mouse from the bottom right corner of the cell over the cells to copy to Release mouse			
Restore deleted input	**Ctrl + Z**	Click: the ↺ **Undo** button		**Edit**, **Undo**
Rows, adding	Select the row by clicking in the row ref box (at side of row) below the one where you want the new row to appear			
			Insert	**Insert**, **Rows**
Rows, deleting	Select the row by clicking in the row ref box (at side of row) below the one that you want to delete			
			Delete	**Edit**, **Delete**
Save	**Ctrl + S**	Click: the 💾 **Save** button		**File**, **Save**
	If you have not already saved the file you will be prompted to specify the directory and to name the file If you have already done this, then Excel will automatically save it			
Save using a different name or to a different directory				**File**, **Save As**
	Select the appropriate drive and change the filename if relevant Click: **Save**			
Selecting cells	Click and drag across cells			
Removing selection	Click in any white space			
Undo	**Ctrl + Z**	Click: the ↺ **Undo** button		**Edit**, **Undo**
Zoom		Click: the 100% ▾ **Zoom** button		**View**, **Zoom**

Hints and tips

Using AutoFill

If the cell contains a number, date or time period that can extend in a series, by dragging the fill handle of a cell you can copy that cell to other cells in the same row or column. The values are incremented. For example, if the cell contains MONDAY, you can quickly fill in other cells in a row or column with TUESDAY, WEDNESDAY and so on.

1 Key in and enter the first label or, if numeric, key in and enter the first two numbers.

2 Select the cell(s) containing the label or numbers you entered.

3 Move the mouse over the bottom right corner of the selected cell(s).

4 Press and hold down the left mouse and drag over the cells you want to include in the series.

5 Release the mouse.

You must not have a cell active whilst trying to format it.

When deleting columns/rows, you should not delete contents only, ie you should not leave a blank row after a deletion.

Do you have the correct number of printouts? Is the data showing in full as requested? On the printout showing formula, check that the formulae are displayed in full.

Check that any amendments have changed calculations accordingly.

Check your work carefully. All numeric data must be 100% correct in spreadsheet assignments.

Spreadsheets: sample full practice assignment

Scenario

You are working as an Administrative Assistant for a car rental company. Your job is to produce routine customer invoices.

Produce a spreadsheet report showing the three-day rental costs including costs for surplus mileage for different classes of vehicles.

1 Create a new spreadsheet.

2 Enter the following data, leaving the **SURPLUS** column blank.

RENTAL COSTS						
CAR	COST	RATE	DAY1	DAY2	DAY3	SURPLUS
MINI	100	0.2	12	4	18	
ECONOMY	120	0.25	22	0	6	
COMPACT	140	0.27	10	12	45	
STANDARD	176	0.3	6.5	12	21	
PREMIUM	276	0.42	14	60	53	
LUXURY	316	0.62	10	23	0	
SPECIAL	356	0.79	8	1	5	

3 Enter your name, centre number and today's date a few lines below the data.

4 The **SURPLUS** for each car is calculated by adding the figures for **DAY1**, **DAY2** and **DAY3**.

    a Insert a formula to calculate the **SURPLUS** for **MINI**.
    b Replicate this formula to show the **SURPLUS** for each car.

5 Save your spreadsheet report with the filename **rentals** and print one copy, showing the figures not the formula. Make sure that all the data is displayed in full.

6 Insert a new column entitled **TOTAL COST** between the columns **COST** and **RATE**.

7 **TOTAL COST** is calculated by multiplying the **SURPLUS** figure by the **RATE** and then adding the **COST**.

    a Insert a formula to calculate the **TOTAL COST** for **MINI**.
    b Replicate this formula to show the **TOTAL COST** for all cars.

8 Your Team Leader would like you to align as follows:

   a The column heading **CAR** and all row labels (eg **MINI**, **COMPACT**, etc) should be left-aligned.

   b The other column headings (**COST**, **TOTAL COST** etc) should be right-aligned.

   c All numeric values should be right-aligned.

9 Format the data as follows:

   a The surplus mileage figures for **DAY1**, **DAY2** and **DAY3** should be displayed in integer format (to zero decimal places).

   b The figures for **COST**, **RATE** and **SURPLUS** should be displayed to two decimal places.

   c The **TOTAL COST** figures data only should be displayed with a £ sign and to two decimal places.

Your Team Leader has noticed that there were some errors in the original data so you will need to make changes to the report.

10 Currently there are no cars in the **COMPACT** class. Delete this entire row.

11 Make the following amendments to the spreadsheet:

   a The **RATE** for **STANDARD** should be **0.4**.

   b The **COST** for **LUXURY** should be **330**.

   c The mileage figure for **PREMIUM** for **DAY2** should be **49**.

   d **SPECIAL** should read **SPORTS SPECIAL**.

Make sure that the **SURPLUS** and **TOTAL COST** have updated as a result of these changes.

12 Save the spreadsheet using the filename **car invoices**. Print one copy showing figures, not formulae. Make sure that all data is displayed in full.

13 Print the spreadsheet with all formulae showing. Make sure that all formulae are displayed in full.

14 Close the spreadsheet and exit the software securely.

Databases using Access (Unit 5)

1 Getting started

In this section you will practise and learn how to:

- understand database applications basics
- understand the parts of the document window
- enter new records
- amend data
- print data in table format
- close the database file
- load Access
- open an existing database
- delete records
- replace specified data
- save the database data
- exit Access

Note: The exercises in this section use the Access datafiles **Fitness**, **Car sales** and **Holidays** on the CD-ROM. It is advisable to copy these files to your own storage medium before you begin (details of how to do this are given in the Appendix).

1.1 Understanding database applications basics

A database application allows you to store data in an organised record format. It is sometimes known as an 'electronic filing system' and is structured so that it can be used to retrieve, sort and search for data quickly and in many different ways. Database files can be saved to disk and printed. Computerised databases have vast storage capacity to store records such as tax details of UK citizens and stock control in supermarkets. Smaller databases may be used for storing details of your personal CD collection, for example. Using a computerised database is much faster than using a paper database, in which, for instance, filing cards are stored on a manual card index system. *The Phone Book* is an example of a paper database in which records are listed in alphabetical order of name. It is now possible to find telephone numbers on the Internet – this method uses a computerised database. Directory Enquiries accesses telephone numbers quickly because operators have access to computerised databases. Databases are used extensively by many organisations and businesses.

Access is a database application. It is very powerful with numerous helpful features. Some of these include searching, sorting, querying, reporting and outputting specified data in various ways (eg reports and forms). Some of these features are also available in spreadsheet programs, such as Excel. For New CLAIT it is acceptable to use Excel for this unit. However, knowledge of Access will be very useful generally and if you want to progress to CLAIT Plus. In this chapter, you will use only features necessary to edit, sort, search and print using simple databases. Different facets of Access will be explained as and when you meet them. Creating a database from scratch is not a requirement for New CLAIT.

Common database terms

Common database terms (general to all types of database applications) include:

File A file is a collection of related records.

Record A collection of information for each item in a file is called a record.

Field A record is divided into separate categories, known as fields. There are different types of field. The common ones are:

Alphabetic (in Access called *Text*) fields. These contain text that is manipulated alphabetically.

Numeric (in Access called *Number*) fields. These recognise numbers and sort in ascending or descending numerical order. *Note:* In Access DATE/TIME and CURRENCY fields can also be used as number fields where appropriate. The format of such fields is determined when the database is designed. For example, a date format could be 10/02/03, or 10 February 2003, or 10-Feb-02, depending on the database design. It does not matter which format you use to enter the date since Access will always follow the format set. When working with currency you should use only the numeric value, ie no £ symbol or commas. Access will automatically format it.

Alphanumeric (in Access called *Text*) fields. These contain numbers and text that do not need to be sorted in number order, telephone numbers, for example.

An Access database file contains database *objects*. We will be using two database objects – *Tables* and *Queries*. We will meet all the above terms as we progress through this chapter.

1.2 Loading Access and an existing database

Exercise 1

Load Access and the database file **Fitness**.

Method

1   Load Access in the same way as loading other programs in the Microsoft Office suite:

From the **Programs** menu, select: 🅰 Microsoft Access

The Access window appears, and you will notice that there are many similarities with the Word window, for example Title bar, Menu bar and Standard toolbar, which are all used in the same way as when using other Office applications.

2   On loading Access, a dialogue box also appears (Figure 5.1).

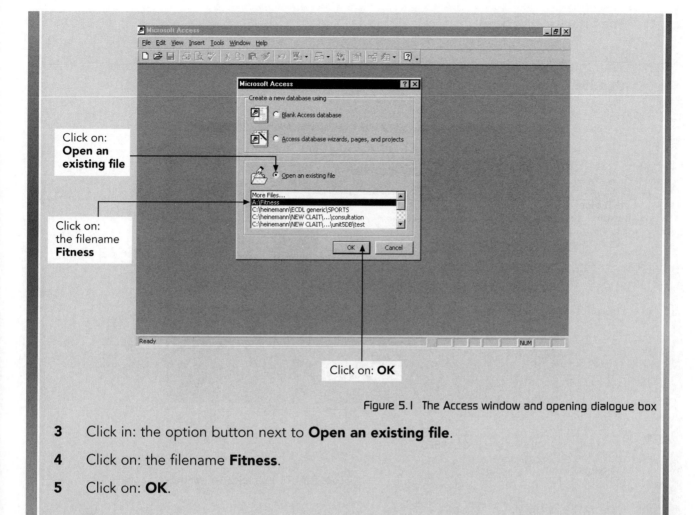

Click on:
Open an existing file

Click on:
the filename
Fitness

Click on: **OK**

Figure 5.1 The Access window and opening dialogue box

3   Click in: the option button next to **Open an existing file**.

4   Click on: the filename **Fitness**.

5   Click on: **OK**.

 The most recently used files will display in the box. If you do not see the file **Fitness**, click on **More Files** and locate the file as in previous chapters.

1.3 Accessing the database table

Exercise 2

Load the database table **CLASSES**.

Method

The window in Figure 5.2 enables you to access all *objects* of the database. For New CLAIT, you will only be working with the objects, *Tables* and *Queries*.

The overall database filename is **Fitness**. Within this file there can be many objects, such as tables and queries that have their own individual names. In this case (Figure 5.2) the **Tables** button is selected (it looks as if it is pressed in) and the table attached to this database is named **CLASSES**. A table is used to store records, each record consisting of fields. We will access this table next. In Section 2 we will query the database in order to extract specified records only.

1   The **Fitness: Database** window is displayed (Figure 5.2).

2   With the **Tables** button selected in the **Objects** section, double-click on the table **CLASSES**.

Click on: the **Tables** button

Double-click on: **CLASSES**

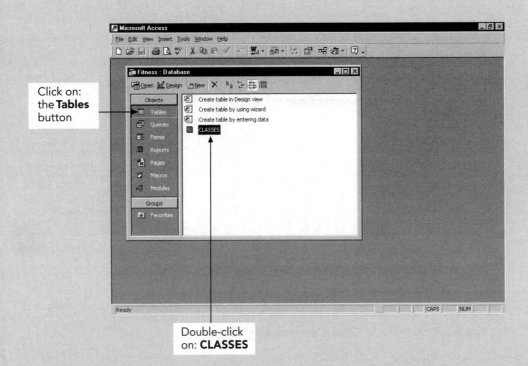

Figure 5.2   Fitness:Database window/Loading a table

3   The table is displayed (Figure 5.3).

Field names: there are 7 fields in this database

Records: there are 16 records in this database

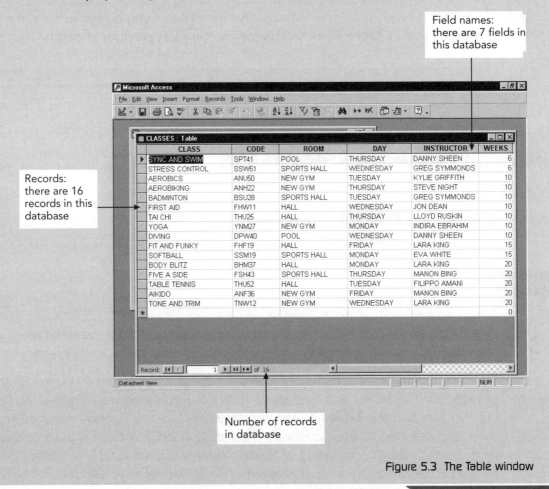

Number of records in database

Figure 5.3   The Table window

Refer to Figure 5.3 and locate the following on your screen display:

1 Field names

There are seven fields in each record of this database. They are CLASS, CODE, ROOM, DAY, INSTRUCTOR, WEEKS, START DATE (you may need to use the scroll bar to view them all).

CLASS, ROOM, DAY and INSTRUCTOR are alphabetic (in Access *Text*) fields. CODE is an alphanumeric (in Access *Text*) field. WEEKS is a numeric (in Access *Number*) field. START DATE is a numeric (in Access *Date*) field.

2 Records

One row of data represents one record. Therefore this database has 16 records. The number of records is displayed at the bottom of the table window.

1.5 Moving around the database table

Exercise 4

Practise moving around the database.

Method

There are several ways to move around:

- Use the arrow keys.
- Use the **Tab** key.
- Click anywhere on the table.
- Use the navigation buttons at the bottom of the table (Figure 5.4).

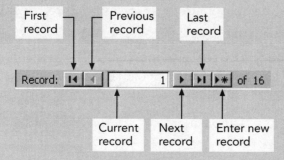

Figure 5.4 Navigation buttons

Exercise 5

Enter the following new records to the database:

CLASS	CODE	ROOM	DAY	INSTRUCTOR	WEEKS	START DATE
TENNIS	THM21	SPORTS HALL	MONDAY	EVA WHITE	10	16/09/02
JUDO	JNT40	NEW GYM	TUESDAY	MANON BING	15	10/9/02
FENCING	FSM31	SPORTS HALL	MONDAY	KYLIE GRIFFITH	20	9/09/02

Method

1 Move the cursor to the last empty row using one of the methods in Section 1.5 (Figure 5.5). Notice that the record number now shows 17.

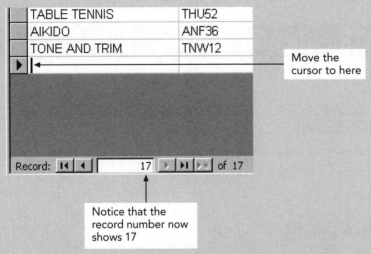

Move the cursor to here

Notice that the record number now shows 17

Figure 5.5 Adding a new record

2 Press: the **Caps Lock** key so that you are consistently using upper case letters to conform with the rest of the database entries.

3 Key in the data for each record in the appropriate fields, pressing **Enter** or **Tab** after each entry.

4 Proofread on screen. Notice that the START DATE of the FENCING class automatically changes to display 09 instead of 9 and 2002 instead of 02. (The database date field has been designed for this to happen.)

5 You should now have 19 records in the database.

Always check your work very carefully. It is very important that data is entered accurately. If it is not, results of searches (in the next section) will not work properly. Accuracy is essential for CLAIT assignments. When adding/amending always use the same case as the rest of the entries for the database fields. In New CLAIT it is essential that all data is displayed in full on printouts. Check the database on screen to see if any columns need widening. To widen a column:

1 With the table displayed, in the field headings row position the mouse on the line between the field headings. The pointer changes to a double arrow.

2 Hold down the left mouse button and drag to the right until the data is displayed in full.

3 Release the mouse button.

1.7 Deleting records

Exercise 6

FIRST AID on **WEDNESDAY** in the **HALL** has been cancelled. Delete this record.

Method

1 Click the row selection box to the far left of the record (Figure 5.6).

Click in this box to select the **FIRST AID** record

Figure 5.6 Selecting a record

2 An arrow appears in the box; the entire record is highlighted.

3 Right-click anywhere on the selection.

4 A pop-up menu appears (Figure 5.7).

Figure 5.7 Deleting a record

5 Select: **Delete Record**.

6 You will be asked to confirm that you want to delete this record; click on: **Yes**.

Notice how the other records move up. It is important that you delete the record and not just the contents of the record since this would leave a blank row. Check to see the new number of records at the bottom of the table. It should now display 18.

1.8 Amending data

Exercise 7

Some of the data needs amending. Make amendments as follows:

1   The **CODE** for **SOFTBALL** should be **SSM26** and the **WEEKS** should be **12**.

2   **BADMINTON** should take place in the **NEW GYM**.

Method

1   Position the cursor in the place where you need to make the amendment.

2   Delete the incorrect data by pressing: **Delete** or the ← **Del** (Backspace) key.

3   Key in the correct data.

1.9 Replacing data

Exercise 8

In the **ROOM** field, use the codes as follows to replace the existing data:

POOL = P   SPORTS HALL = SH
NEW GYM = NG   HALL = H

Method

1   Select the **ROOM** field column by clicking on the name at the top of the column.

2   From the **Edit** menu, select: **Replace**.

3   The **Find and Replace** dialogue box is displayed (Figure 5.8).

4   Ensure the **Replace** tab is selected.

5   In the **Find What** box, key in **POOL**.

6   In the **Replace With** box, key in **P**.

7   Check that the **Look In** box displays the field that you want to amend, ie in this case **ROOM**.

8   Click on: **Replace All**.

9   You will be asked to confirm; click on: **Yes**.

10   Continue with the other codes.

11   When you have completed all the replacements, click on: the **Close** button of the **Find and Replace** box.

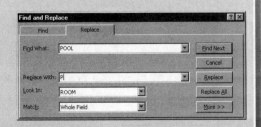

Figure 5.8 Find and Replace dialogue box

Using **Search and Replace** is extremely time-saving when you have a large number of records. You can also use **Search** to locate records in a large database to save having manually to scroll through all the records.

1.10 Printing the data in table format

Exercise 9

Print all the data in table format.

Method

(*Note*: It is best if the table fits on one page. This method shows how to do this.)

1 From the **File** menu, select: **Print Preview**.

2 From this you will see that the table is being split over two pages in portrait display. (Use the arrows at the bottom to view other pages.)

3 Click on: **Close** to return to the table.

4 To change to landscape display, from the **File** menu, select: **Page Setup**.

5 Click on: the **Page** tab and then in the **Landscape** option button. Click on: **OK** (Figure 5.9).

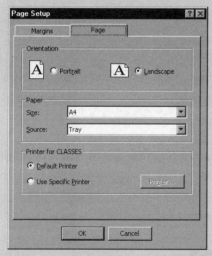

Figure 5.9 Changing to landscape display

6 Now check **Print Preview** again. It should now fit on one page. (The arrows at the bottom of the screen are greyed out.)

7 Return to the table, then from the **File** menu, select: **Print**.

8 The **Print** dialogue box is displayed.

9 Click on: **OK**.

10 Proofread your printout to ensure data is accurate and that all amendments have been made.

To make it easier to check through, you can sort the data. For a quick method to sort, see the quick reference at the end of this chapter.

1.11 Saving the database table

Exercise 10

Save the database table.

Method

1 Click on: the ☒ **Close** button at the top right of the **Table** window.

2 The updated data is saved automatically. (*Note:* This is unlike most Office applications where you are reminded to save data.)

1.12 Saving and closing the database

Exercise 11

Save the database file **Fitness**.

Method

From the **File** menu, select **Close**.

 The components of the database file are automatically saved together. Each individual part, such as the table **CLASSES**, has been saved as we have progressed through the exercises. If any parts are not saved, you will be prompted to save before closing.

1.13 Exiting Access

Exercise 12

Exit Access.

Method

From the **File** menu, select: **Exit**.

Databases practice 1

Note: For the following two exercises you will need to access the Access files **Car sales** and **Holidays** on the CD-ROM.

Practice 1

1 Open the database **Car sales**.

2 Add the following new records to the database as follows:

    a **CARTERS** garage now has a **VAUXHALL CORSA**, colour is **RED**. It has **2** previous owners and is priced at **3495**. The MOT is due on **16/2/03**.

    b **BROMLEYS** garage now has a **FORD KA**, colour is **RED**. It has **1** previous owner and is priced at **2995**. The MOT is due on **2/1/03**.

    c **DAVID PIKE** garage now has a **FORD PUMA**, colour is **SILVER**. It has **1** previous owner and is priced at **6500**. The MOT is due on **12/5/03**.

3 The **LANDROVER DISCOVERY** at **SMYTHES** has been sold. Delete this record.

4 Make the following amendments and save the data:

    a The **NISSAN MICRA** at **BROMLEYS** is **GREEN** and has been reduced to **2995**.

    b At **DAVID PIKE** garage, the **SILVER FORD FIESTA's** MOT due date is **21/6/03**.

5 It has been decided to use codes in the **MAKE** field. Replace the existing entries as follows:

FORD = FD
RENAULT = RT
VAUXHALL = VX
NISSAN = NS
LANDROVER = LR

6 Print all the data in table format.

7 Close the database and exit Access.

Practice 2

Remember: When working with currency, use the numeric value only, ie no £ symbols or commas. Access will automatically format the entry.

1 Open the database **Holidays**.

2 Add the following new records to the database:

    a 3 nights, **HOTEL** accommodation in **BONN, GERMANY**. The code is **GB237** and the departure date is **13 March 2002**. The cost is **250**.

    b 2 nights, **APARTMENT** accommodation in **ST MALO, FRANCE**. The code is **FS388** and the departure date is **15 April 2002**. The cost is **162**.

    c 14 nights, **HOTEL** accommodation in **PERTH, AUSTRALIA**. The code is **AP589** and the departure date is **16 June 2002**. The cost is **1450**.

3 The **APARTMENT** accommodation in **PERTH, AUSTRALIA** costing **1199** should not have been entered. Delete this record.

4 Make the following amendments and save the data:

a The departure date of the **APARTMENT** holiday code **GB455** in **BONN, GERMANY** should be **16 January 2002**.

b The **HOTEL** accommodation in **ANTIBES**, code **FA541** should cost **350**.

5 It has been decided to use codes in the **COUNTRY** field. Replace the existing entries as follows:

FRANCE = FR
GERMANY = GE
SWITZERLAND = SW
AUSTRALIA = AU
BULGARIA = BU

6 Print all the data in table format.

7 Close the database and exit Access.

2 Manipulating data

In this section you will practise and learn how to:

- create and save queries
- select data on two criteria
- sort data numerically/alphabetically
- present only selected fields
- select data on one criterion
- print queries
- sort by date

A database can be *sorted* into a certain order to match the task that you are carrying out, eg alphabetical order of surname or numeric order of account balance. There are two methods to sort the database. For quick table sorting, see the quick reference guide. For CLAIT assignments, you are usually asked to sort selected data and save it. In order to do this without overwriting any other data sort, you will need to create a query.

What is a query?

Once you have stored information in your database, you will want to query (question) the database to extract information, in other words *search* the database for specific information, eg all people who work on Fridays or all orders over £100. This section explains how to create and sort queries in Access.

2.1 Creating and saving a query, selecting data on one criterion

Exercise 1

Using the file **Fitness** saved in Section 1, set up the following database query:

1   Select all the classes that take place on **TUESDAY**.

2   Sort the data in ascending order of **WEEKS**.

3   Display all fields.

Method

1   Load Access and the database file **Fitness** saved at the end of Section 1.

2   In the **Objects** section of the **Fitness:Database** window, click on the: **Queries** button.

3   Double-click on: **Create query in Design view** (Figure 5.10).

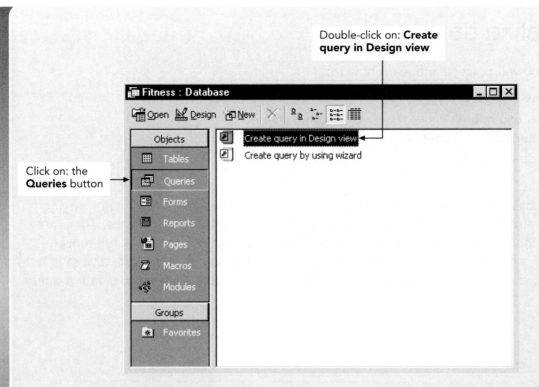

Double-click on: **Create query in Design view**

Click on: the **Queries** button

Figure 5.10 Creating a query

4 The **Show Table** box appears with the Table **CLASSES** selected (Figure 5.11).

5 Click on: **Add**, then on: **Close**.

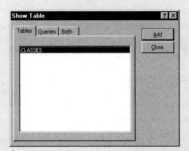

Figure 5.11 Show Table box

6 The **Query – Design View** window is displayed (Figure 5.12).

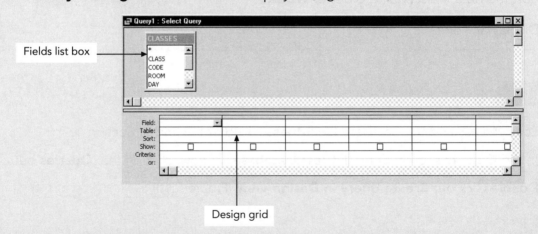

Fields list box

Design grid

Figure 5.12 Query Design

7 The fields of the **CLASSES** table are displayed in a Fields List box. Place the fields in the Design Grid as follows:

a In the **Design Grid**, in the **Field** row, click in: the first field column.

b Click on: the down arrow.

c Click on: the name of the field that you want to appear, ie **CLASS** (*Note:* **CLASS** not **CLASSES** since **CLASSES** is the name of the table, not a field name.)

d Click in: the next field column; click on: the down arrow.

e Click on: the name of the next field you want to appear, ie **CODE**.

f Repeat steps (d) to (e) until all the fields are on the grid (as in the **Field** row of Figure 5.13).

There are other ways to place the fields in the Design Grid:

1 Double-click on: the field name that you want in the Design Grid.

2 Drag the field name on to the Design Grid.

8 In the field **DAY** column, click in: the **Criteria** row, then key in: **TUESDAY**.

9 In the field **WEEKS** column, click in: the **Sort** row, then click on: the down arrow, then on: **Ascending** (Figure 5.13).

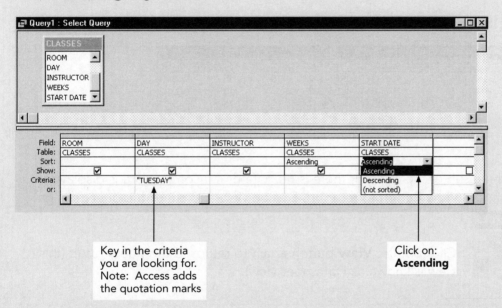

Key in the criteria you are looking for. Note: Access adds the quotation marks

Click on: **Ascending**

Figure 5.13 Entering criteria and sorting

When sorting you can choose to sort in **Ascending** (alphabetic A–Z, or numeric lowest to highest, dates earliest to most recent) or **Descending** (alphabetic Z–A, or numeric highest to lowest, dates most recent to earliest). Although this chapter contains descending alphabetic sorts, alphabetic sorts for New CLAIT are always in ascending order, ie A–Z.

10 To save the query, from the **File** menu, select: **Save As**. Replace the default name **Query1** by deleting it and keying in the query name **Tues weeks ascending**. Click on: **OK** (Figure 5.14).

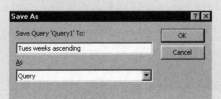

Figure 5.14 Saving the sorted query

11 Close the query window by clicking on: the **Close** button in the right-hand corner of the Design window.

12 You are returned to the **Fitness:Database** window.

13 To view the results of the query, double-click on: the query name (Figure 5.15).

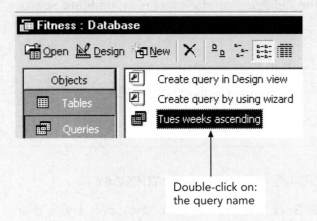

Double-click on:
the query name

Figure 5.15 Viewing the Query results

14 The query result should look like Figure 5.16.

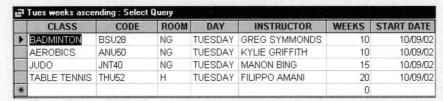

CLASS	CODE	ROOM	DAY	INSTRUCTOR	WEEKS	START DATE
BADMINTON	BSU28	NG	TUESDAY	GREG SYMMONDS	10	10/09/02
AEROBICS	ANU50	NG	TUESDAY	KYLIE GRIFFITH	10	10/09/02
JUDO	JNT40	NG	TUESDAY	MANON BING	15	10/09/02
TABLE TENNIS	THU52	H	TUESDAY	FILIPPO AMANI	20	10/09/02
*					0	

Figure 5.16 Result of query

Scan the result of the query. If there is no data or if incorrect data is displayed, click on: the **View** button to return to Design view and check the query design.

Click on: the **View** button again to return to the query result (this view is known as Datasheet view).

15 Click on: the **Close button** in the top right-hand corner of this window to return to the **Fitness:Database** window.

2.2 Printing a query

Exercise 2

Print the query saved as **Tues weeks ascending**.

Method

1 In the **Fitness:Database** window, click on: the **Queries** button.

2 Double-click on: **Tues weeks ascending**.

3 From the **File** menu, use **Print Preview** and **Page Setup** to print in landscape.

4 From the **File** menu, select: **Print**.

5 Click on: **OK**.

2.3 Creating and saving a query, selecting data on two criteria

Exercise 3

Set up the following database query:

1 Select all classes that take place in the **SPORTS HALL** that run for **10 WEEKS or more than 10 weeks**.

2 Sort the data into descending numerical order of **WEEKS**.

3 Display all fields.

> (greater than) symbol is obtained by holding down the **Shift** key and pressing the full stop key.

< (less than) symbol is obtained by holding down the **Shift** key and pressing the comma key.

The following symbols are used in queries:

=	is equal to
>	greater than (or more recent than in the case of a date)
<	less than (or before in the case of a date)
>=	greater than or equal to
<=	less than or equal to
<>	not equal to

Working with dates

Before 10 February 2001	<10 February 2001 (*Note:* You can use an abbreviated version of the date and it will change to the set format, eg 10/02/01.)
After 10 February 2001	>10 February 2001
10 February 2001 or after	>=10 February 2001
10 February 2001 or before	<=10 February 2001
10 February 2001 to 20 February 2001 inclusive	>9 February 2001 and <21 February 2001
	or
	>=10 February 2001 and <=20 February 2001
	or
	Between 10 February 2001 and 20 February 2001

In this instance, as we have already created a query, **Tues weeks ascending**, we can use this as the basis for this query.

You could create a completely new query for this if you wanted to, but this would only duplicate effort.

Method

1 From the **Fitness:Database** window, click on: the **Queries** button, double-click on: the query **Tues weeks ascending**, then on: the **View** button to switch to Design view.

2 Delete the entry you keyed in for the original query, ie **TUESDAY** and the sort order, ie **Ascending** so that the original query data is cleared.

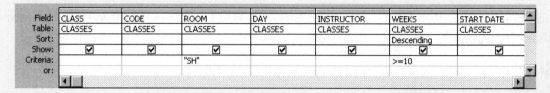

Field:	CLASS	CODE	ROOM	DAY	INSTRUCTOR	WEEKS	START DATE
Table:	CLASSES	CLASSES	CLASSES	CLASSES	CLASSES	CLASSES	CLASSES
Sort:						Descending	
Show:	☑	☑	☑	☑	☑	☑	☑
Criteria:			"SH"			>=10	
or:							

Figure 5.17 Selecting more than one criterion

3 In the field **ROOM** column and the **Criteria** row, key in **SH** and press: **Enter**.

4 In the field **WEEKS** column and the **Criteria** row, key in **>=10** and press: **Enter**.

5 In the field **WEEKS** column, click in: the **Sort** row, then click on: the down arrow, then on: **Descending**.

6 Save the query as **SH 10 or more** and print.

2.4 Sorting by date

Exercise 4

Set up the following database query:

1 Select all classes that start **before 12/9/02** and run for **12 weeks or less**.

2 Sort the data into descending **START DATE** order.

3 Display all fields.

Method

1 Set up the query following one of the methods above. (For the **START DATE** criterion, key in **<12/9/02**.)

2 Save the query with a relevant descriptive name and print.

Exercise 5

Access the query saved in Exercise 4. Sort the query in ascending order of CLASS. Produce a printout displaying only the following fields:

CLASS, **INSTRUCTOR** and **START DATE**

Method

1   Access the query and display it in Design view.

2   Delete the **START DATE** sort by clicking on the down arrow in the START DATE **Sort** box and selecting: **(not sorted)**.

3   Select the requested **CLASS** sort.

4   In the **Show** row, remove the ticks, by clicking on them, in the fields that you do not want to display (Figure 5.18).

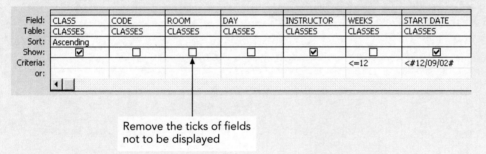

Field:	CLASS	CODE	ROOM	DAY	INSTRUCTOR	WEEKS	START DATE
Table:	CLASSES	CLASSES	CLASSES	CLASSES	CLASSES	CLASSES	CLASSES
Sort:	Ascending						
Show:	☑	☐	☐	☐	☑	☐	☑
Criteria:						<=12	<#12/09/02#
or:							

Remove the ticks of fields not to be displayed

Figure 5.18 Showing selected fields only

5   Save the query with a new name and print.

- You will notice that only the fields with ticks appear on the printout.
- *Remember:* It is always a good idea to check that your query is showing the correct result, so always view it before printing. If it is not showing what you think you have asked for, return to Design view by clicking the View toolbar button and checking the details you have entered.
- You can sort and search within the same query.
- When creating queries, Access adds quotation marks (in Design view) to the criteria you key in. You do not need to worry about this.
- If you are presenting selected fields, you do not need to enter all the database fields in the Design Grid. However, you will need to enter those that you are sorting or searching even if you do not need to display them.
- When working with tables and queries, in order to view all fields you can resize the field columns by dragging the field name row using the mouse (as shown on page 164). Always check that the data is still displayed in full.

1 Hover the mouse over the line between the field names.

2 A double-arrow appears.

3 Hold down the left mouse button and drag to the left.

4 Release the mouse button.

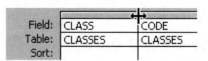

Table   Query

Common errors

- Misspelling the criterion so that it does not find an exact match (this can also be due to a spelling error in the data in the database). Always proofread carefully.
- Making the criterion plural, ie **MONDAYS** instead of **MONDAY**. The query will not find **MONDAYS** as this is not what was entered in the database and therefore is not an exact match.
- Leaving spaces where they should not be.

2.6 Exit Access

Databases practice 2

Practice 3

1 Open the database **Car sales** saved in Practice 1, Section 1.

2 Set up the following database query:

    a Find all vehicles at **DAVID PIKE** garage.

    b Sort the selected records in alphabetical order of **MODEL**.

    c Display all fields.

    d Save the query.

    Print the query results in table format.

3 Set up the following database query:

    a Select all **RED** vehicles that have had **2** or fewer previous owners.

    b Sort the selected records into descending order of price.

    c Display only the fields **GARAGE**, **COLOUR**, **PREVIOUS OWNERS** and **PRICE**.

    d Save the query.

    Print the query results in table format.

4 Set up the following database query:

    a Select all vehicles with a price of less than **3500**.

    b Sort the records into ascending order of MOT due date.

    c Display only the fields **MAKE**, **MODEL** and **MOT DUE**.

    d Save the query.

    Print the query results in table format.

5 Close the file and exit Access with all the data saved.

Practice 4

1 Open the database **Holidays** saved in Practice 2, Section 1.

2 Set up the following database query:

    a Find all holidays in **AUSTRALIA**.

    b Sort the selected records into descending order of **DEPARTURE DATE**.

    c Display all fields.

    d Save the query.

    Print the query results in table format.

3 Set up the following database query:

    a Select all **APARTMENT** accommodation with a departure date before **16 April 2002**.

    b Sort the selected records into alphabetical order of location.

c Display only the fields **LOCATION**, **CODE** and **DEPARTURE DATE**.

d Save the query.

Print the query results in table format.

4 Set up the following database query:

a Select all holidays of less than **7** nights costing more than **200**.

b Sort the records into ascending departure date order.

c Display only the fields **COUNTRY**, **ACCOMMODATION** and **NO OF NIGHTS**.

d Save the query.

Print the query results in table format.

5 Close the file and exit Access with all the data saved.

Note: Since Access is a little different from other Office applications, this quick reference guide follows a different format from others in the book.

Adding a record	**1** Position the cursor in the row under the last record and enter the information **2** Close the table **3** Data is saved automatically when you close the **Table** window
Closing the database	From the **File** menu, select: **Close** IMPORTANT: *Always close the database file properly*
Creating queries, sorting them, specifying simple criteria and printing queries	**1** If the database is not already open, open it so that the **Database** window is displayed **2** Click on: the **Queries** tab **3** Double-click: **Create query in Design view** **4** Select table. Click on: **Add** and then on: **Close** **5** The fields of the table are now displayed in a list box in the **Query** window **6** Place the fields that you need for your query in the field row of the query grid
Deleting an entire record	**1** Select the record by clicking in: the left window border next to the first field of that record **2** Press: **Delete** **3** Click on: **OK** to save the change
Editing records in a table	**1** Open the Table if it is not already open. (In the **Database** window, click on: the **Tables** tab, and double-click on: the table name) **2** Click on: the entry you wish to edit and key in the new data
Loading Access	**Start** menu, **Programs**, **Microsoft Access**
Opening a database file	**1** In the Access opening dialog box, click in: **Open an existing file** option button **2** Locate the file **3** Click on: the filename **4** Click on: **OK**
Opening a table	**1** In the **Database** window, click on: the **Tables** button **2** Double-click on: the table name
Printing a table	**1** Open the table you want to print **2** From the **File** menu, select: **Print** **3** Click on: **OK**
Printing on landscape	**1** Open the table you want to print **2** From the **File** menu, select: **Page Setup** **3** Click on: the **Page** tab, click on: **Landscape**, **OK**
Printing specific fields	Use the **Show** row in the grid to choose whether or not to display a particular field in the query A tick in the **Show** box means that the field will show, no tick means that it will not show. Click to toggle between them
Printing a query	With the query result on screen, from the **File** menu, select: **Print**
Quick sorting records	**1** Open the table if it is not already open **2** Select the field that you wish to sort by clicking on: the **Field Name** at the top of the field column **3** Click on: the ⒜↓ **Sort Ascending** button or on: the ⒵↓ **Sort Descending** button
Saving a query	**1** When you have finished designing your query, save it by selecting: **Save as** from the **File** menu **2** Key in an appropriate query name **3** Click on: **OK**

	4 Close the **Query** window
	5 To see the results of your query, double-click on: the query name
Searching and replacing	**1** With the table open, select the field to search by clicking on: the **Field Name**
	2 From the **Edit** menu, select: **Replace**
	3 With the **Replace** tab selected, key in the data to find in the **Find What** box
	4 In the **Replace With** box, key in the replacement data
	5 Click on: **Replace All**
	6 Click on: **Yes**
	7 Click on: **Close**
Sorting a query	In the **Design** grid, click in: the **Sort** box in the appropriate field
	Select: **Ascending** or **Descending**
Specifying simple criteria	Use the **Criteria** row in the grid to specify the conditions in a specific field, eg **RED** in the **COLOUR** field

Hints and tips

Saving tables before and after amendments

When completing New CLAIT assignments, it can be very irritating if you spot that you have made an error(s) before making amendments and you now only have the amended table to work with. In such instances, the only answer is to retrace your steps, reversing the amendments so that you arrive back at the original table. This can be very tedious and produces a lot of errors.

To save your original table intact, follow the steps below:

1 With the table name selected in the **Database** window, click on: the **Copy** button.

2 Click on: the **Paste** button.

3 In the **Paste Table** box, key in the new table name; ensure **Structure and Data** is selected.

4 Click on: **OK**.

You will now have two exact copies of the same table. Make amendments to one of them, leaving the other intact.

Other tips

- Always proofread your work carefully. This is especially important with database work as one error could make sorting and searching incorrect.
- Be consistent with use of upper, lower, sentence or title case within fields.
- Ensure all data is displayed in full on printouts.
- Ensure records are fully deleted, ie do not leave a blank row by deleting the contents only.
- Have you made all the amendments requested?
- Have you replaced specified data?
- Always check that your query results are those expected.
- Are the queries sorted in the order requested?
- Do you have the correct number of printouts?

Databases: sample full practice assignment

Note: For this assignment you will need to use the Access database file, **Houses**, on the CD-ROM.

Scenario

You work as an Administrative Assistant for a large estate agent. Your job is to update the database of properties in the company's local offices as requested by the Office Manager.

Your Office Manager has asked you to amend and update the database of current properties for sale.

1 Open the database **Houses**.

Four new properties need to be added to the database.

2 Create records for the new properties as follows:

   a In the **MILTON KEYNES** Office there is a new property located in **WILLEN** that was registered on **19 September 2002**. The property ref is **M285** and the price is **199995**. The vendor's surname is **LUHRMANN** and there have been **0** viewings to date.

   b In the **MILTON KEYNES** Office there is a new property located in **FISHERMEAD** that was registered on **20 September 2002**. The property ref is **M790** and the price is **179999**. The vendor's surname is **JENSON** and there has been **1** viewing to date.

   c In the **OLNEY** Office there is a new property located in **PODINGTON** that was registered on **20 September 2002**. The property ref is **Y133** and the price is **69995**. The vendor's surname is **GALLWAY** and there have been **0** viewings to date.

   d In the **OLNEY** Office there is a new property located in **TURVEY** that was registered on **21 September 2002**. The property ref is **Y185** and the price is **78950**. The vendor's surname is **SMITH** and there have been **0** viewings to date.

3 Delete the record at the **MILTON KEYNES** office, vendor **GIULIANI**, property ref **M682**. This has been withdrawn.

4 It has been decided to use codes in the **OFFICE** field. Replace the existing entries as follows:

MILTON KEYNES	MK
BLETCHLEY	BY
WOLVERTON	WN
OLNEY	OL
STONY STRATFORD	SS
NEWPORT PAGNELL	NP

5 Two of the records need amending:

   a At the **WOLVERTON** office, property ref **W821**, the location should be **HODGE LEA**.

   b At the **MILTON KEYNES** office, the property with the vendor **JOHNSON** should be priced at **159995**.

   Make these changes and save the amended data.

6 Print all the data in table format.

Your Office Manager would like to find out about viewings.

7 Set up the following database query:

    a Select all properties that have had fewer than **3** viewings.

    b Sort the data in alphabetical order of **VENDOR**.

    c Display only the fields **LOCATION**, **VENDOR** and **VIEWINGS**.

    d Save the query.

Print the results of the query in table format.

A prospective buyer is looking for a property for sale in the Milton Keynes office. She has already secured finance up to 160000.

8 Set up the following database query:

    a Select all properties in the **MILTON KEYNES** office under **160000**.

    b Sort the data in ascending order of **DATE REGISTERED**.

    c Display only the fields **PROPERTY REF**, **PRICE** and **DATE REGISTERED**.

    d Save the query.

Print the results of the query in table format.

The Office Manager would like you to find information about recently registered properties in the WOLVERTON office.

9 Set up the following database query:

    a Select all properties registered since the beginning of **AUGUST** in **WOLVERTON**.

    b Sort the data in descending order of **PRICE**.

    c Display only the fields **LOCATION**, **VENDOR** and **PROPERTY REF**.

    d Save the query.

Print the results of the query in table format.

10 Close the file and exit the software with all the data saved.

Chapter 6 | Desktop publishing using Publisher (Unit 6)

1 Getting started

In this section you will learn how to:

- understand Publisher basics
- load Publisher
- create a master page for a single-page publication
  - set up a page layout
    - set page size/orientation
    - set margins
- save the master page
- close the publication
- exit Publisher

1.1 What is Publisher?

Publisher is a desktop publishing (DTP) application that enables the creation of professional-looking and interesting documents that integrate text and graphics, for example newsletters, flyers and brochures. Modern word processors such as Word can achieve similar results but these do not have the versatility of a dedicated DTP application, which includes control over the size and positioning of images and the flow of text. Publisher is at the budget-end of such applications, but still has many useful features.

1.2 Loading Publisher

Exercise 1

Load Publisher.

Method 1

1   In the Windows 98 desktop, click on: the **Start** button.

2   Select: **Programs** (by hovering the mouse over it), then click on: **Microsoft Publisher** (Figure 6.1).

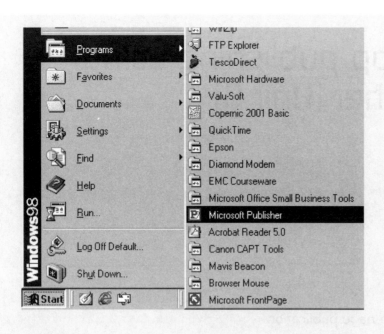

Figure 6.1 Loading Publisher

Method 2

(Use if you have a shortcut icon to Publisher on your desktop.)

In the Windows desktop, double-click on: the **Microsoft Publisher** shortcut icon.

Either method results in the Publisher window being displayed, with the **Microsoft Publisher Catalog** in the foreground (Figure 6.2). Note: If the **Microsoft Publisher Catalog** is not displayed, you will be taken automatically to a blank document.

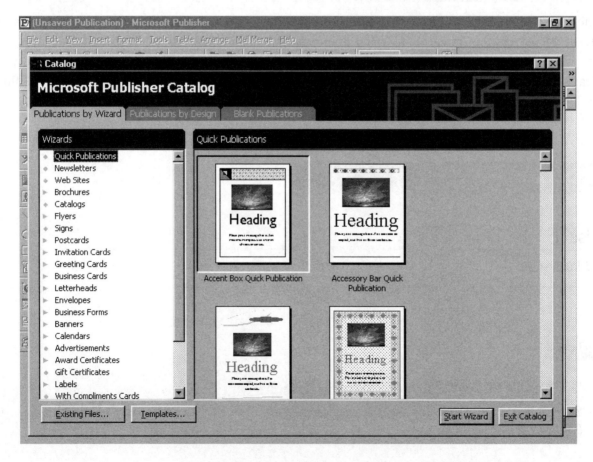

Figure 6.2 Publisher's opening window, displaying the Publisher Catalog in the foreground

The Microsoft Publisher Catalog enables you to produce publications using wizards, publications by design (ie using pre-designed templates) and a blank publication for you to do the design work yourself. For CLAIT, we will use the blank design option.

1.3 Selecting a blank publication

Exercise 2

Select a blank, full-page publication.

Method

1   In the **Microsoft Publisher Catalog** window, click on: the **Blank Publications** tab (Figure 6.3).

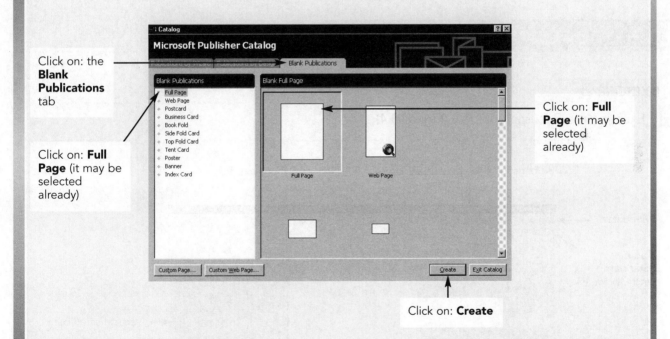

Click on: the **Blank Publications** tab

Click on: **Full Page** (it may be selected already)

Click on: **Full Page** (it may be selected already)

Click on: **Create**

Figure 6.3 Selecting Blank Publications

2   In the **Blank Publications** section, ensure **Full Page** is selected or in the **Blank Full Page** section, click on: **Full Page**.

3   Click on: **Create**.

4   The **Blank** page is displayed.

Note: If you prefer, in future when loading Publisher, you can hide the Microsoft Publisher Catalog at startup as follows:

1   From the **Tools** menu, select: **Options**.

2   Click on: the **General** tab.

3   Click in the option box next to **Use Catalog at startup** so the tick is removed.

4   Click on: **OK**.

You will then automatically start with a blank page.

> If the Quick Publication Wizard is displayed on the left-hand side, click on: the
> **▼ Hide Wizard** **Hide Wizard** button. So that this Wizard does not appear each
> time you open Publisher:
>
> **1** From the **Tools** menu, select: **Options**.
> **2** Click on: the **User Assistance** tab.
> **3** Click in: the option box next to **Use Quick Publication Wizard for Blank Publications** to remove the tick.
> **4** Click on: **OK**.

1.4 The Publisher window

Exercise 3

Examine the Publisher window (Figure 6.4).

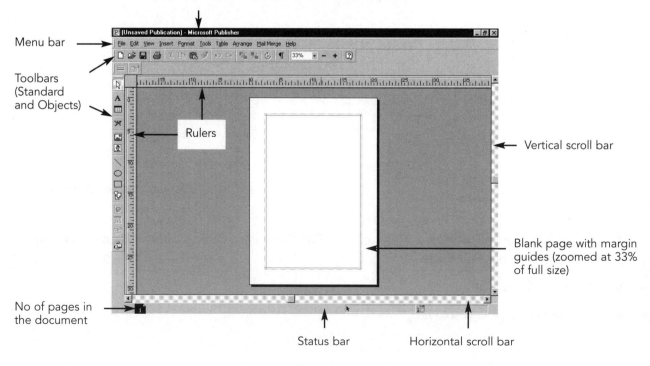

Figure 6.4 Publisher window

The Objects toolbar

The Objects toolbar is specific to Publisher. You will learn about the relevant toolbar buttons as you progress through this chapter.

1.5 Setting page size/orientation

Exercise 4

Set up a master page (template) for the page as follows:

Page size: A4
Orientation: Portrait

 A master page is a page that you design for your particular purpose so that it can be reused throughout a publication. This gives consistency to the publication as well as making it attractive and easier to read.

Method

1   From the **File** menu, select: **Page Setup**.

2   The **Page Setup** dialogue box is displayed (Figure 6.5).

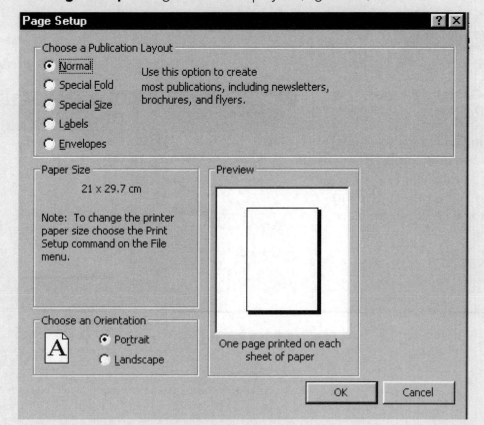

Figure 6.5 Page Setup

3 In the **Choose a Publication Layout** section, click in: the **Normal** option button.

4 Check that the paper size is 21 x 29.7 mm. This is A4 and is the default so should not need changing. If it does need changing, you will need to set this in the **File** menu, **Print Setup**.

5 In the **Choose an Orientation** section, click in: the **Portrait** option button.

Note: Portrait orientation has the narrowest side at the top (shown in Figure 6.5).

6 Click on: **OK**.

1.6 Setting margins

Exercise 5

Set up margins for the master page (template) as follows:

Top/bottom: 3 cm
Left/right: 2.5 cm

Method

1 From the **Arrange** menu, select: **Layout Guides** (Figure 6.6).

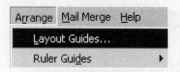

Figure 6.6 Selecting Layout Guides

2 The **Layout Guides** dialogue box is displayed (Figure 6.7).

3 In the **Margin Guides** section, enter the new margins in the relevant boxes by using the arrows next to the boxes, or by clicking in the boxes, deleting the contents and keying in the new values.

4 Click on: **OK**.

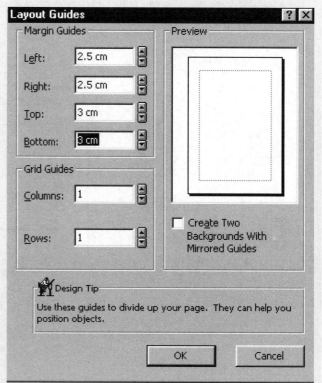

Figure 6.7 Setting margins

Desktop publishing using Publisher (Unit 6)

Exercise 6

Save the master page/template with the filename **chocolate**.

Method

1   From the **File** menu, select: **Save As**.

2   The **Save As** dialogue box is displayed (Figure 6.8).

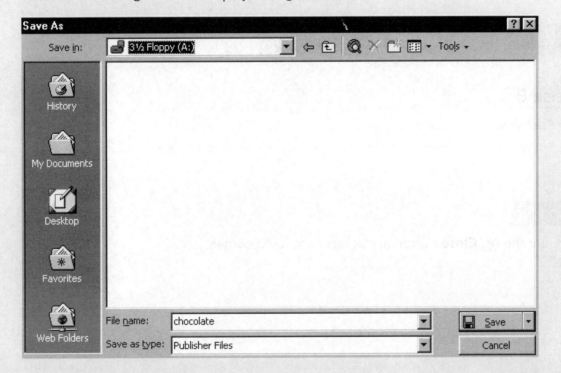

Figure 6.8 Save As dialogue box

3   In the **Save in** box, click on: the down arrow and click on: the location where you want to save the template. (If you are saving to a floppy disk, remember to have it inserted in the drive.)

4   Click in: the **File name** box and key in the filename **chocolate** (case does not matter).

5   Click on: **Save**.

 In the **Save as type** box drop-down menu, there is an option to save as a **Publisher Template**. Templates are stored in the Publisher **Templates** folder on the C Drive. Since you may be saving to the A Drive and are producing a single-page publication, in this instance we will not use the **Publisher Template** option. However, you should be aware of this option.

1.8 Closing a file

Exercise 7

Close the file **chocolate**.

Method

From the **File** menu, select: **Close**.

1.9 Exiting Publisher

Exercise 8

Exit Publisher.

Method

Click on: the ☒ **Close** button at the top right-hand corner.

Desktop publishing practice 1

Practice 1

1 Load Publisher and a new single-page publication.

2 Set up the master page as follows:

- page size: A4
- page orientation: Portrait
- top/bottom margins: 1.5 cm
- left/right margins: 2 cm

3 Save the master page/template with the name **prac1[your initials]**.

4 Close the file.

5 Exit Publisher.

Practice 2

1 Load Publisher and a new single-page publication.

2 Set up the master page as follows:

- page size: A4
- page orientation: Landscape
- top/bottom margins: 2.5 cm
- left/right margins: 1 cm

3 Save the master page/template with the name **prac2[your initials]**.

4 Close the file.

5 Exit Publisher.

2 | Importing

In this section you will learn how to:

- open an existing publication
- set column widths/spacing
- use serif and sans serif fonts
- import text files
- print

- create text areas/frames
- enter a heading
- change font size
- import images

Note: For the exercises in this section you will need to have access to the files **chocoholic** and **cake**. These are on the CD-ROM that accompanies this book. In the examples that follow, I have copied the files to a floppy disk.

2.1 | Opening an existing publication

Exercise 1

Open the publication **chocolate**, saved in Section 1.

Method

1   With Publisher loaded, from the **File** menu, select: **Open**.

2   The **Open Publication** dialogue box is displayed (Figure 6.9).

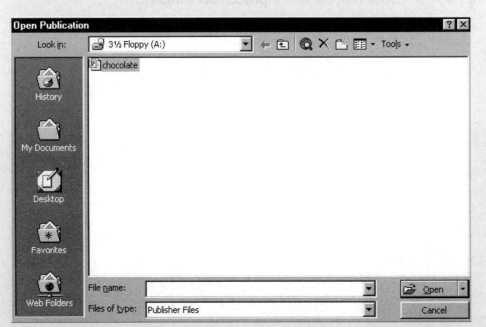

Figure 6.9 Opening an existing publication

3   In the **Look in** box, click on: the down arrow and select the publication's location.

4   Click on: the filename and then on **Open**.

2.2 Saving the publication with a different filename

Saving the publication with a different filename at this point will ensure that the template publication file is kept content free in case it is required at a later date. *Note:* You may have the (default) option switched on that pops up from time to time and asks you if you want to save. Since designing a Publisher page is so fluid, it is a good idea to save at regular intervals. This ensures when each part of the design is complete it is safely saved.

Method

Save the publication as **chocolate1** using the method in Section 1.7.

2.3 Creating text areas/frames

When entering text or graphics on the page, text or picture frames need to be created to hold the content. It is usual for text files to be produced in word processor applications, such as Word, and then imported into a frame in a DTP application.

Exercise 2

Set up the page in newsletter format, with a page-wide heading at the top of the page.

Method

1   Click on: the **A** **Text Frame Tool** on the **Objects** toolbar (at the left side of the window).

2   Move the cursor to the top left-hand corner of the margin guides.

3   Press down the left mouse button and drag down and to the right of the page to form a frame for the heading.

4   Release the mouse.

5   Reposition if necessary by dragging the frame handles, ie click in the frame to select it (if not already selected), hold down the left mouse button on a frame handle and drag the handle to the required position. Release the mouse.

Exercise 3

Set up a text frame below the heading frame.

Method

Follow the method above, but starting just below the left bottom corner of the heading frame.

Your page should now look similar to Figure 6.10. Notice that the Formatting toolbar displays text-formatting buttons when a text frame is selected.

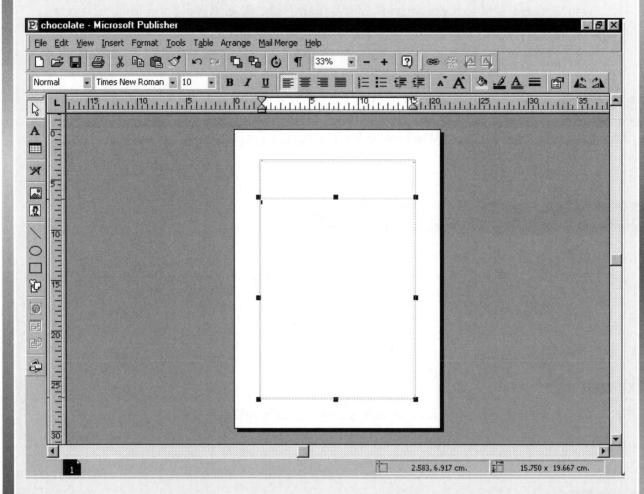

Figure 6.10 Text frames set

Exercise 4

Set the bottom frame to have 2 columns with a space of 1.5 cm between the columns.

Method

1   Select the bottom text frame by clicking in it.

2   From the **Format** menu, select: **Text Frame Properties**.

3   The **Text Frame Properties** dialogue box is displayed (Figure 6.11).

4   In the **Columns** section, **Number** box, change the number to **2** using the arrows.

5   In the **Spacing** box, key in **1.5 cm**.

6   Click on: **OK**.

7 The document will now look similar to Figure 6.12.

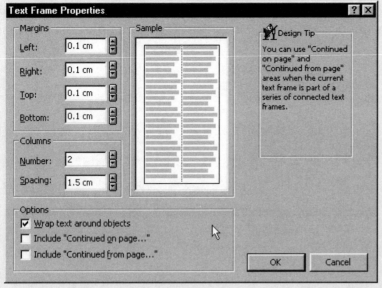

Figure 6.11 Setting columns

Figure 6.12 Columns created

2.4 Inserting text directly into a frame

Exercise 5

Insert the text **Chocolate News** directly into the heading frame.

Method

1 Click on the heading frame to select it.

2 Increase the Zoom so that you can see what you are keying in.

3 To do this: click on the down arrow of the **Zoom** box (Figure 6.13) and click on: **100%**.

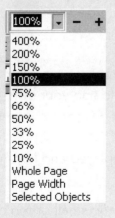

Figure 6.13 Changing the Zoom

4 Key in the text.

The height of fonts is measured in *points* (*pt*). The default point size is 12. Below are some sample point sizes:

6 pt

10 pt

12 pt

18 pt

28 pt

36 pt

44 pt

68 pt

Exercise 6

Increase the size of the heading text so that it extends across the page and centre it.

Method

1   Select the text by dragging the mouse over it:

   a   Click the cursor at the beginning of the text you are selecting, in this case the **C** of **Chocolate**.

   b   Hold down the left mouse button and drag the I-beam pointer across the heading so that it is highlighted.

   c   Release the mouse.

 There are many ways to select text. These are given in the quick reference at the end of this chapter. There is no right or wrong way. Experiment to find your own preferred method.

2   In the **Font Size** box (Figure 6.14), delete the size that is already displayed and key in a new size.

Note: You will notice that the sizes given in the drop-down list are either too small or too big in this instance. You will need to experiment to see what fits best, ensuring that the heading stays on one line. You can key in sizes with decimal places such as 40.1, 50.3 and so on.

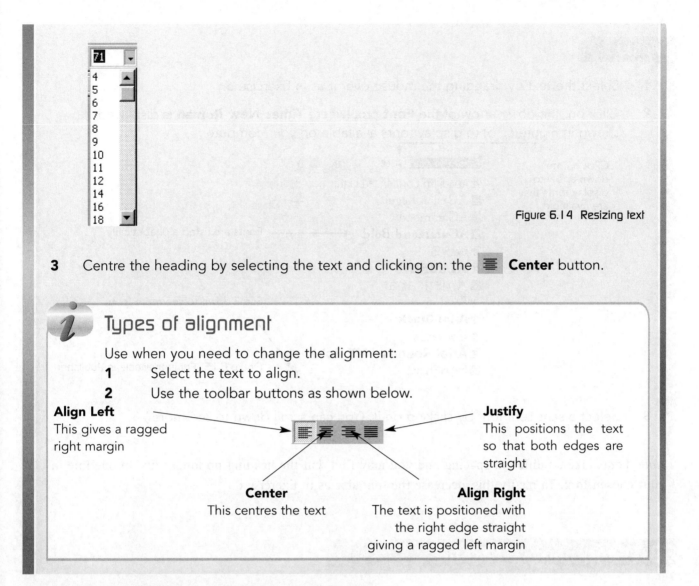

Figure 6.14 Resizing text

3 Centre the heading by selecting the text and clicking on: the ▤ **Center** button.

> ### ℹ Types of alignment
>
> Use when you need to change the alignment:
> **1** Select the text to align.
> **2** Use the toolbar buttons as shown below.
>
> **Align Left**
> This gives a ragged
> right margin
>
> **Justify**
> This positions the text
> so that both edges are
> straight
>
> **Center**
> This centres the text
>
> **Align Right**
> The text is positioned with
> the right edge straight
> giving a ragged left margin

2.6 Serif and sans serif fonts

The term *font* refers to the design of the characters. In Word there are numerous fonts to choose from. The default font is *Times New Roman*. This is a *serif* font. Serifs are small lines that stem from the upper and lower ends of characters. Serif fonts have such lines. *Sans serif* fonts do not have these lines. Examples:

Times New Roman is a serif font
Arial is a sans serif font

There are numerous fonts available but you may prefer to stick to **Times New Roman** and **Arial**.

Exercise 7

Change the heading to a sans serif font.

1 Select the text by dragging the mouse over it as in Exercise 6.

2 Click on: the down arrow of the **Font** box (where **Times New Roman** is displayed, shown in Figure 6.15) to display fonts available on your computer.

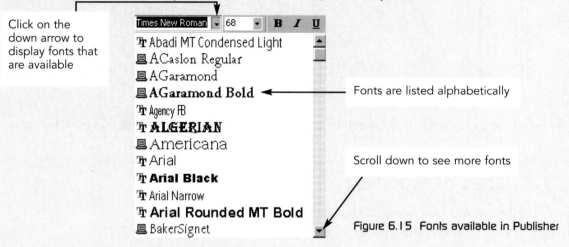

Click on the down arrow to display fonts that are available

Fonts are listed alphabetically

Scroll down to see more fonts

Figure 6.15 Fonts available in Publisher

3 Select a sans serif font by clicking on it. (You can scroll down to see more.)

Note: Fonts take up different spacing and you may find that the heading no longer fits on one line in your chosen font. To rectify this, decrease the font size as in Exercise 6.

2.7 Importing a text file

Exercise 8

Import the text file **chocoholic** into the 2-column text frame.

Method

1 Select the text frame by clicking in it.

Note: You may want to reduce the zoom for this exercise so that you can see both columns of the text frame clearly.

2 From the **Insert** menu, select: **Text File** (Figure 6.16).

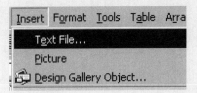

Figure 6.16 Importing a text file

3   The **Insert Text** dialogue box is displayed (Figure 6.17).

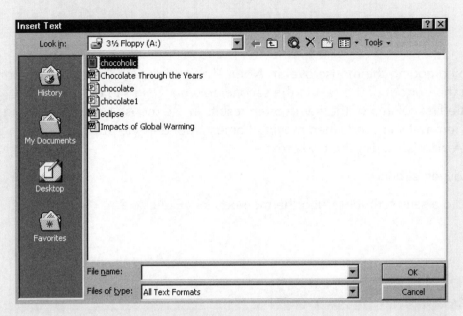

Figure 6.17 Insert Text dialogue box

4   In the **Look in:** box, click on the down arrow and select the location of the file to import.

5   Click on: the filename.

6   Click on: **OK**.

The text is inserted into the first column and may flow into the second column of the text box (Figure 6.18). This text is known as the body text. Any words that are not in the Publisher dictionary are underlined with a wavy line. You do not need to be concerned about this at this level.

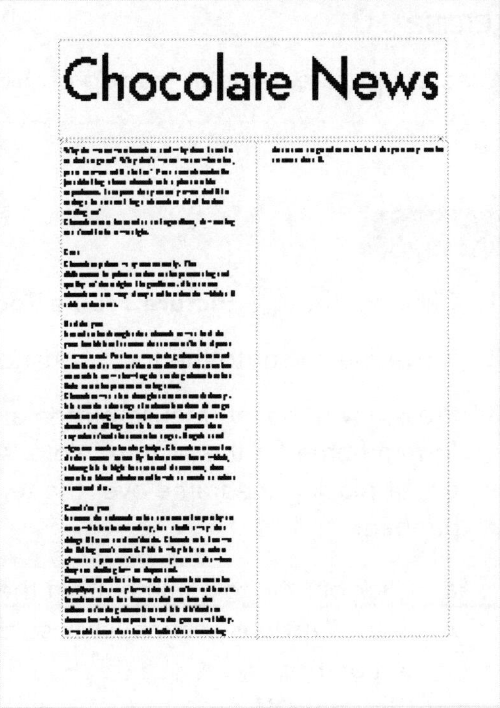

Chocolate News

Figure 6.18 Text imported into frame

2.8 Formatting body text

Exercise 9

Format the body text so that it is left-aligned and in a sans serif font.

Method

1   Select the text by dragging the mouse over it. *Note*: This is sometimes easier to perform if you drag from the bottom of the text in the second column. Trying to drag from the top left text in the first column of the frame often results in the mouse pointer changing to a mover (ie a removal van used when moving frames around in the publication). Pressing **Ctrl** + **A** will also select the body text.

2   The text is already left aligned.

3   Change the text to a sans serif font using the method as in Exercise 7.

2.9 Creating a picture frame

When importing an image into a publication, you need first to create a picture frame for it.

Exercise 10

Create a picture frame at the top of the first column.

Method

1   Click on: the ▣ **Picture Frame Tool** button on the **Objects** toolbar.

2   Move the cursor to the top left-hand corner of the first column.

3   Press down the left mouse button and drag down towards the bottom right of the page to form a frame for the picture. *Note*: A roughly square shape will fit in well. Do not worry about placing the frame over the text, as the text will move out of the way. If this does not happen:

   a   Click on: the text frame, from the **Format** menu, select: **Text Frame Properties**.
   b   In the **Options** section, click so that there is a tick in the **Wrap text around objects** option box.
   c   Click on: **OK**.

4   Release the mouse.

5   Reposition if necessary using the frame handles.

The publication will now look similar to Figure 6.19.

Chocolate News

Figure 6.19 Picture frame created

2.10 Importing an image

Exercise 11

Insert the image **cake** into the picture frame created above.

Method

1 Click in: the picture frame to select it.

2 From the **Insert** menu, select: **Picture**, **From File** (Figure 6.20).

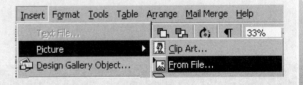

Figure 6.20 Inserting an image

3 The **Insert Picture** dialogue box is displayed (Figure 6.21).

4 In the **Look in** box, use the down arrow to select the location of the image file.

5 Click on: the filename (a preview of the file appears at the right).

6 Click on: **Insert**.

7 The image is inserted in the picture frame.

Note: You can change the size of the image by selecting the frame and dragging with the handles. Drag from a corner to maintain its proportions, ie not make the image too wide or too tall.

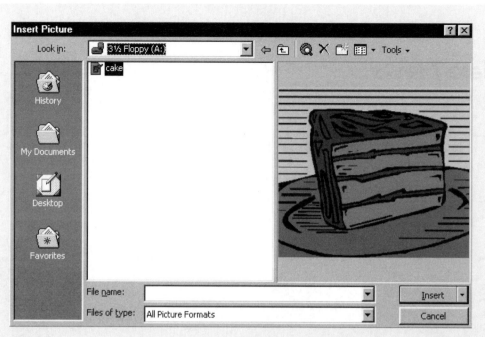

Figure 6.21 Insert Picture box

2.11 Saving the publication

Exercise 12

Save the publication with the existing filename **chocolate1**.

Method

Click on: the 🖫 **Save** button.

2.12 Printing

Exercise 13

Print one copy of the publication. Ensure it fits to one page.

 In desktop publishing the printouts at this stage are sometimes referred to as composite proofs. A composite proof shows all elements on the document arranged as specified. Composite proofs are used for checking and correcting.

1   From the **File** menu, select: **Print**.

2   The **Print** dialogue box is displayed (Figure 6.22).

3   Click on: **OK**.

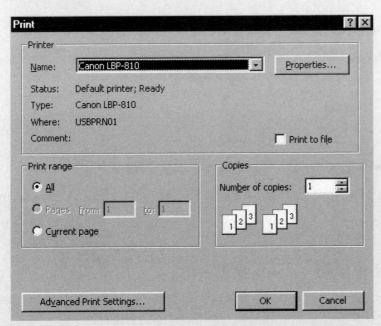

Figure 6.22 Print dialogue box

 For CLAIT assignments the printout should fit on one page. In this case it does. In the next section you will see how to determine if it fits on one page. Notice that the margin guides are not printed.

2.13 Close the publication and exit Publisher

Desktop publishing practice 2

Note: For these practice exercises you will need the following files. For Practice 3, **presentation.txt** and **speaker.gif**; for Practice 4, **global.txt** and **floods.gif**.

Practice 3

1 Load the master page/template, **prac1[your initials]**, created in Section 1, Practice 1.

2 Set up the page layout in newsletter format to include a page-wide heading above two columns of text.

column widths:	**equal**
space between columns:	**1.5 cm**

3 Enter the heading **Public Speaking** at the top of the page, using a **serif** font.

4 Increase the size of the heading text so that it extends across the full width of both columns.

5 Import the file **presentation** so that it begins at the top of the left-hand column, below the heading.

6 Format the body text to be **left-aligned** in a **sans serif** font.

7 Import the image **speaker**, and place it within the right-hand column at the top of the page, making sure it doesn't cover any text.

8 Save the publication with its original filename and print one composite proof copy. Make sure that it fits on one page.

9 Close the publication.

Practice 4

1 Load the master page/template, **prac2[your initials]**, created in Section 1, Practice 2.

2 Set up the page layout to include a page-wide heading above a column of text.

3 Enter the heading **GLOBAL WARMING** at the top of the page, using a **sans serif** font.

4 Increase the size of the heading text so that it extends across the full width of the frame below.

5 Import the file **global** so that it begins at the top left of the text frame below the heading.

6 Format the body text to be **justified** in a **serif** font.

7 Import the image **floods**, and place it at the top left-hand corner of the frame below the heading, making sure it doesn't cover any text.

8 Save the publication with its original filename and print one composite proof copy. Make sure that it fits on one page.

9 Close the publication.

Balancing page layout

In this section you will learn how to:

- use line and border features
- set paragraph spacing and first line indents
- resize text
- apply alignment and justification
- move/resize image
- balance columns

 This section contains exercises of skills that are common in DTP. If you look in a newspaper or brochure you will recognise DTP conventions such as first line indents, balancing columns, and justifying body text.

3.1 Using line features

Exercise 1

Open the publication **chocolate1** saved in Section 2. Insert a vertical line between the two columns.

Method

1 Open the publication in the normal way.

2 Click on: the ✎ **Line Tool** on the **Objects** toolbar.

3 Position the pointer (it has turned into a cross hair) where you want the line to begin. (You may want to zoom.)

4 Hold down the left mouse and the **Shift** key and drag the line downwards to the required length. The centre of the cross hair will be the end of the line.

5 Release the mouse.

 Some people find this quite difficult. Use the **Undo** button to remove the line and have another try. Continue practising until the line is well positioned. You can change the thickness of the line if you want to:

a Double-click on: the line.
b Make a selection from the Line dialogue box.

3.2 Adding borders

Exercise 2

Draw a single border around the two columns of text and the graphic to separate this section from the heading.

1   Click on the entire body text frame, ie including the two columns and the graphic, to
    select it. It will have handles all around.

2   From the **Format** menu, select: **Line/Border Style**, and click on a style to select it
    (Figure 6.23).

Figure 6.23 Adding a border

 Notice that you don't have to draw the border since it replaces the invisible
frame. If the image is overlapping the border, reduce its size (click on it to select
it, then drag inwards from a corner handle) until the frame is visible. Use the
Zoom to check the positioning of objects more precisely.

Your publication will now look similar to Figure 6.24.

Figure 6.24 Line and border added

Note: Before attempting the following exercises, ensure that you save the publication. Save it with the filename **chocolate2**. The following exercises involve manipulating the text and images and, should things go wrong, you will be able to revert back to your saved copy.

Exercise 3

Increase the size of the subheadings so that they are larger than the body text, but smaller than the page heading. The subheadings are: **Cost**, **Bad for you** and **Good for you**.

Method

1   Zoom in so that you can see the subheadings more clearly.

2   Select the first subheading.

3   Change the font size using the **Formatting** toolbar's **Font Size** box (as in Section 2.5).

4   With the altered heading still selected, click twice on: the ✎ **Format Painter** button.

5   Drag the mouse over the other subheadings in turn.

6   Press: **Esc** to turn the **Format Painter** off.

3.4 Moving the image and reducing its size

Exercise 4

Move the image so that it is further down the first column so that there is text both above and below it and reduce its size.

Method

1   Select the image by clicking on it.

2   With the pointer in its guise as a removal van, hold down the left mouse button over the image and drag it down the page.

3   Release the mouse.

4   Reduce the size of the image using its corner handles.

The publication may now look similar to Figure 6.25.

Note: Do not make the image too small or text will flow on either side of it. However you must make sure that it does not flow into any margin space, so ensure it is narrower than the line length.

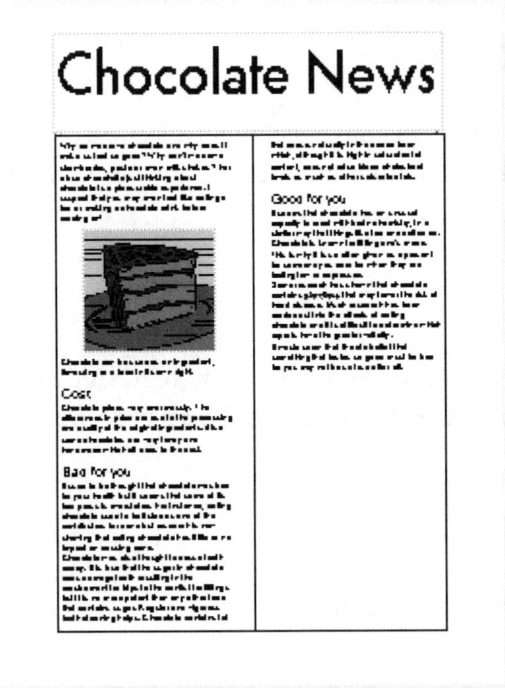

Figure 6.25 After repositioning the image and changing subheading size

3.5 Changing the justification of the body text

Exercise 5

Change the body text to be fully justified.

Method

1 Select the body text.
2 Click on: the **Justify** button.

3.6 Indenting first lines of paragraphs

Exercise 6

Indent the first lines of all paragraphs in the body text (not the subheadings).

Method

1 Select the first section of body text, ie in the first column directly below the main heading.
2 From the **Format** menu, select: **Indents and Lists** (Figure 6.26).

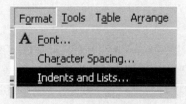

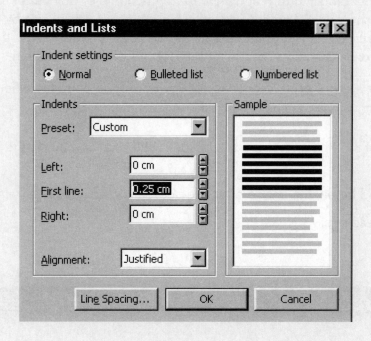

Figure 6.26 Indenting

3   The **Indents and Lists** dialogue box is displayed (Figure 6.27).

Figure 6.27 Indents and Lists dialogue box

4   In the **Indents** section, in the **First line** box, click on: the up arrow so that 0.25 is displayed.

5   Click on: **OK**.

6   Repeat for the other sections of body text.

Note: You may want to zoom in to check that all paragraphs are indented.

3.7 Balancing the text in columns

Exercise 7

Increase the size of the text so that the columns are balanced at the bottom of the page. Ensure that the heading, subheadings and body text are still different sizes.

Balancing columns is a requirement for the CLAIT assessment. The longest column must not be more than two lines longer than the other column(s). All text should still fit on one page.

Note: You will need to use your imagination for this since it may be necessary to adjust more than just the size of the text. I have listed some things that you might do in order to achieve the required results. However you must not alter margins and you must ensure that the text sizes of the different components retain their relative proportions, ie main heading largest size font, subheadings larger than body text. If things look wrong, use the **Undo** button.

1   Select the body text (not subheadings) in turn and increase by a couple of point sizes. If necessary, increase the point size again. Remember, you can increase the point size by single points and to decimal places. Check that the text has not flowed off the page. If it has there will be a   `A···` **Text in Overflow** symbol at the bottom of the last column.

Note: Sometimes you may see this symbol even if text has not flowed off the page (eg when there is a blank line(s) after the text), so always check carefully.

2   Reduce or increase the size of the image. (Ensure the image is still smaller than on the last printout.)

3   Increase the spaces above and below the image or above and below subheadings.

4   Increase the size of the subheadings.

3.8 Save the publication as chocolate3 and print one copy

3.9 Close the publication and exit Publisher

Practice 5

1 Load the file saved at Step 8 in Section 2, Practice 3.

2 Draw a vertical line between the two columns. Make sure the line does not overlap any text.

3 Increase the size of the subheadings **Nerves**, **Your Voice** and **Rehearsing** so that they are larger than the body text, but smaller than the page heading.

4 Make the image smaller and move it down the page so that there is text above and below it. Make sure the image does not extend into the margin space.

5 Change the body text to be **fully justified**.

6 Format the body text so that the first line of each paragraph is indented. Make sure the subheadings are not indented.

7 Increase the size of the text so that the columns are balanced at the bottom of the page. Make sure that the heading, subheadings and body text are still different sizes.

8 Save the publication with the name **Prac5[your initials]** and print one composite proof. Make sure the publication still fits on one page.

9 Close the publication and exit the software securely.

Practice 6

1 Load the file saved at Step 8 in Section 2, Practice 4.

2 Draw a border around the heading. Make sure the border does not overlap any text.

3 Increase the size of the subheadings **Temperatures** and **Ecosystems** so that they are larger than the body text, but smaller than the page heading.

4 Make the image larger and move it down the page so that there is text above, below and to the right of it. Make sure the image does not extend into the margin space.

5 Change the body text to be **left-aligned**.

6 Format the body text so that the first line of each paragraph is indented. Make sure the subheadings are not indented.

Note: When there is only one column set, text to the right of the graphic does not format with a first line indent.

7 If necessary, adjust the size of the text so that the text fits the page. Make sure that the heading, subheadings and body text are still different sizes.

8 Save the publication and print one composite proof. Make sure the publication still fits on one page.

9 Close the publication with the name **Prac6[your initials]** and exit the software securely.

Desktop publishing quick reference for New CLAIT (Publisher)

Action	Keyboard	Mouse	Right-mouse menu	Menu
Alignment	Select text to be aligned			
		Click: the relevant ▤▤▤▤ alignment button		
Borders, add	Select frame			
				Format, **Line/Border** Style
Close a file		Click: the ☒ **Close** button.		**F**ile, **C**lose
Columns, set widths/spacing	Select the text frame			
				Format, **Text Frame Prop**e**rties**, **Columns**, **Spacing**
Exit Publisher	**Alt** + **F4**	Click: the ☒ **Close** button		**F**ile, E**x**it
First line indents	Select the text to indent			
				Format, **I**ndents and Lists, **First** line
Font, change type	Select the text you want to change			
		Click: the ▾ down arrow next to the **Font** box Select: the font you require		**Fo**rmat, **Font**
Font, size	Select the text you want to change			
		Click: the ▾ down arrow next to the **Font Size** box Select: the font size you require		**Fo**rmat, **Font**
				Select: the required size from the **Size** menu
Help	**F1** **Shift** + **F1**			**Help** **Microsoft Publisher Help**
Image, resizing, moving	Select the image and use the handles to resize (use a corner handle to keep its proportions) Select the image. When the pointer changes to a removal van icon, hold down the left mouse and drag to the new position			
Import, images				**Insert, Picture, From File**
Import, text files				**Insert, Text File**
Line, add		Click: the ╲ **Line Tool** on the **Objects** toolbar		
Loading Publisher	In the Windows 98 desktop			
			Start, **Programs**, **Microsoft Publisher**	Double-click: the **Publisher** shortcut icon
Margins, set				**Arrange, Layout Guides**
Open an existing publication	**Ctrl** + **O**	Click: the ☞ **Open** button		**F**ile, **O**pen
	Select the appropriate folder and filename Click: **Open**			

Action	Keyboard	Mouse	Right-mouse menu	Menu
Page size/ orientation, set				**File**, **Page Setup**
Picture areas/ frames, create		Click: the 🖼 **Picture Frame Tool** on the **Objects** toolbar		
		Hold down the left mouse and drag out a frame		
Print				**File**, **Print**
Redo		Click: the ⤳ **Redo** button		**Edit**, make selection
Re-save document	**Ctrl + S**	Click: the 💾 **Save** button		**File**, **Save**
Save using a different name or to a different folder or drive				**File**, **Save As**
	Select the appropriate drive and folder, change the filename if relevant Click: **Save**			
Text areas/ frames, create		Click: the **A** **Text Frame Tool** on the **Objects** toolbar		
		Hold down the left mouse and drag out a frame		
Resize, move	Select the frame and use the handles to resize			
	Select the frame. When the pointer changes to a removal van icon, hold down the left mouse and drag to the new position			
Undo	**Ctrl + Z**	Click: the ↰ **Undo** button		**Edit**, make selection

Selecting text

Selecting what	Action
All text in selected frame	**Ctrl + A**
One word	Double-click on word
Any block of text	Click cursor at start of text, hold down: **Shift**. Click cursor at end of text and click
Deselect text	Click in any white space

Hints and tips

Common errors made when completing New CLAIT assignments include:

- Not importing the image file as specified.
- Importing incorrect files.
- Setting margins and spaces between columns incorrectly.
- Not using the correct serif and sans serif fonts where requested.
- Not aligning as specified.
- Not fitting to one page.
- Forgetting to add borders/lines.
- After balancing columns, not ensuring that the sizes of text are still different as specified, eg heading largest size, subheadings larger size than body text.
- Indenting the subheadings at the same time as the body text.
- Not balancing columns correctly – longest column should be no more than two lines short of the bottom margin and the second column should be no more than two lines short of the first column.

Check your work thoroughly. Have you done everything asked?

Desktop publishing: sample full practice assignment

Note: For this assignment you will need the files **meanings.txt** and **surfer.gif**. These can be found on the CD-ROM.

Scenario

You work as an administrative assistant for an IT training company. You have been asked to produce a publication that can be handed out at the introductory session for beginners in Information Technology.

1 Load Publisher and a new single-page publication.

2 Set up the master page as follows:
page size:	**A4**
page orientation:	**Portrait**
top/bottom margins:	**1 cm**
left/right margins:	**2 cm**

3 Save the master page/template.

4 Set up the page layout in newsletter format to include a page-wide heading above two columns of text.
column widths:	**equal**
space between columns:	**1.5 cm**

5 Enter the heading **WORDS IN CONTEXT** at the top of the page, using a **sans serif** font.

6 Increase the size of the heading text so that it extends across the full width of both columns.

7 Import the file **meanings** so that it begins at the top of the left-hand column, below the heading.

8 Format the body text to be **left-aligned** in a **serif** font.

9 Import the image **surfer**, and place it within the left-hand column at the top of the page, making sure it doesn't cover any text.

10 Print one composite proof copy. Make sure that it fits on one page.

11 Draw a line between the heading separating it from the graphic and columns of text. Make sure the line does not overlap any text.

12 Increase the size of the subheadings **Context**, **Window** and **Surfing** so that they are larger than the body text, but smaller than the page heading.

13 Make the image smaller and move it down the page so that there is text above and below it. Make sure the image does not extend into the margin space.

14 Change the body text to be **fully justified**.

15 Format the body text so that the first line of each paragraph is indented. Make sure the subheadings are not indented.

16 Increase the size of the text so that the columns are balanced at the bottom of the page. Make sure that the heading, subheadings and body text are still different sizes.

17 Save the publication and print one composite proof. Make sure the publication still fits on one page.

18 Close the publication and exit the software securely.

Graphs and charts using Excel (Unit 7)

Types of graphical representation

In this section you will learn about different ways of representing data using graphs and charts.

In this chapter we will be using the spreadsheet application Excel to produce graphs and charts. When you have created a spreadsheet, there are many different ways of graphically displaying its data. You will need to be aware of four of these: pie charts, bar charts, line graphs and comparative charts. The charts and graphs can display all the spreadsheet data or selected parts only. If data is changed in the spreadsheet, the graphs and charts will update accordingly to reflect the new data.

 Excel uses the word *chart* and not *graph* for all its graphical displays. In the UK we tend to differentiate between charts and graphs. Throughout this chapter the word chart, ie pie chart, column chart and bar chart, is used except when working with lines when the word graph is used, ie line graph.

1.1 Pie chart

A pie chart consists of a circle divided into a number of segments. In the example below (Figure 7.1), there are three segments, representing eye colours blue, brown and green in Tutor Group A. The largest segment is brown and it tells us that 44% of Tutor Group A have brown eyes, the next largest is green with 30%, and the smallest is blue with 26%. There is a legend (key) to show us which colour or shade represents which eye colour.

EYE COLOUR TUTOR GROUP A ←——————— Chart title

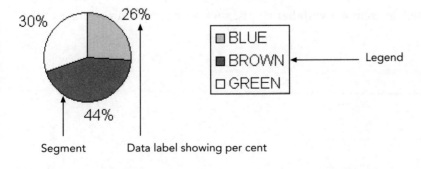

Segment   Data label showing per cent

Figure 7.1 Pie chart

Chart title   The chart title should be descriptive and clear.

Data labels   On a pie chart you can show percentage values or actual values. You can show the legend labels next to the segments instead of a legend.

Legend	A legend is a key showing the different colours/shades that correspond to the data represented in the pie chart.
Segment	The pie chart is made up of segments that represent different data types.

1.2 Bar chart

A bar chart uses bars to represent values. These can be vertical columns (as shown in Figure 7.2) or horizontal bars. (*Note:* For CLAIT assignments use vertical columns, known as a **Column** chart, not a **Bar** chart as in Excel.) The chart has two axes, the *x* (horizontal) axis and the *y* (vertical) axis. The *x* axis usually represents data that does not change, such as days of the week. The *y* axis usually represents values that fluctuate, such as monetary values or temperatures. This type of chart is useful for showing comparisons.

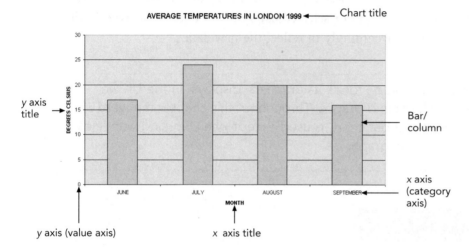

Figure 7.2 Bar chart

The bar chart (Figure 7.2) shows the comparison of average temperatures in London. The tallest bar, July, shows the overall hottest average temperature. The shortest bar, September, shows that this was the coolest month of those shown.

1.3 Line graph

A line graph shows trends in data at equal intervals. Points on the graph are joined together to form a continuous line. Line graphs have properties in common with bar charts, such as *x* and *y* axes and axes titles.

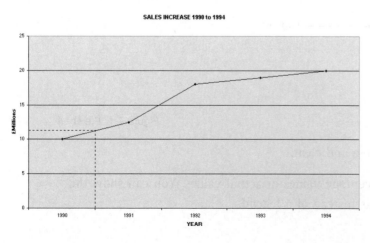

Figure 7.3 Line graph

The line graph (Figure 7.3) shows that the trend is up as the line is going up and not down. Sales have been increasing steadily since 1990. I have drawn a line from the x axis, at the end of 1990, to the plotted line, and then drawn a line to the y axis. Where this line joins the y axis, the value can be read, just over £11 million. This was the value of sales at the end of 1990.

1.4 Comparative chart/graph

A comparative chart is used to compare sets of data. The display shows two or more columns (if a comparative bar chart, Figure 7.4) or two or more lines (if a comparative line graph, Figure 7.5) of the same item.

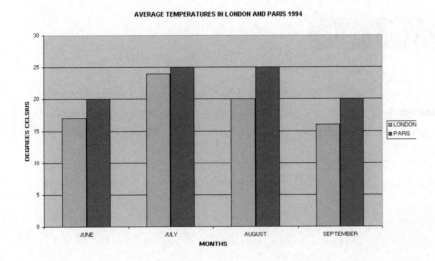

Figure 7.4 Comparative bar chart

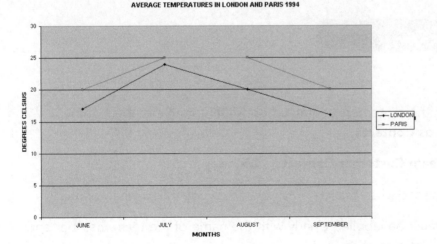

Figure 7.5 Comparative line graph

Section 1: checklist

Explain the following:

1 pie chart

2 bar chart

3 line graph

4 comparative graph/chart

5 legend

6 x axis

7 y axis.

2 Creating pie charts

In this section you will practise and learn how to:

- select a single data set
- create a pie chart
- save a chart
- print a chart
- close a chart

Note: The exercises in this section use the Excel datafile **Customers** on the CD-ROM. It is advisable to copy this file to your own storage medium before you begin (details of how to do this are given in the Appendix).

2.1 Accessing the data to chart

Exercise 1

Load Excel and the datafile **Customers**. (This file contains data on the number of existing customers that have been contacted by each member of a telesales team during one week.)

Method

Follow the methods in Chapter 4.

2.2 Creating a pie chart

Exercise 2

Produce a pie chart displaying the customers contacted on **MON** for all members of the telesales team. Save the chart as **Contacts**.

1   Give the chart the title: **Team Customer Contacts – Monday**.

2   Ensure that each sector is shaded so that data can be clearly identified when printed.

3   Each sector of the chart must be labelled clearly with the name of the team member and the number or percentage of customers.

Method

1   Examine the spreadsheet and select the range of cells (the *single data set*) that make up this data, ie A2 to B6 (Figure 7.6).

	A	B	C	D	E	F	G
1	Operator	Mon	Tue	Wed	Thu	Fri	Sat
2	Greg	15	16	12	10	4	27
3	Polly	12	22	10	3	12	30
4	Adjoa	21	17	14	10	19	22
5	Aidan	12	23	29	27	26	34
6	Jack	20	10	12	21	30	31

Figure 7.6 Data selected for charting

2   Click on: the **Chart Wizard** button.

3   **Step 1 of 4 Chart Wizard** dialogue box appears: **Chart Type** (Figure 7.7).

    a   The **Standard Types** tab is selected. In the **Chart type** box, click on: **Pie**.

    b   In the **Chart sub-type** box, click on: the top left pie type as shown. This is usually already selected as the default setting.

    c   Click on: **Next**.

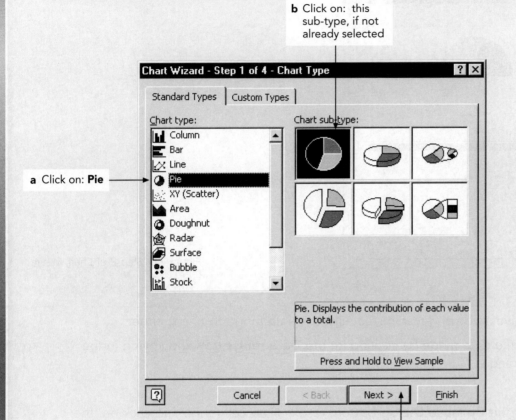

Figure 7.7 Step I of Chart Wizard

> There are many different types of pie charts that you can choose. For the purposes of New CLAIT, the simple pie type (chosen here in Figure 7.7) is a good choice. If you are not printing to a colour printer you may need to choose a pie chart that displays in black and white. The following methods ensure that the sectors of the pie chart are shaded so that they are easily identified. Always check that this is the case. To do this, click on: the **Custom Types** tab and then on **B&W Pie** (black and white pie chart). However, you can create a colour chart and then later select **B&W** for the printout.
>
> To view other pie chart samples, with the **Standard Types** tab selected, click and hold the mouse on: **Press and hold to view sample**. Try experimenting with the different types.

4   Step 2 Chart Wizard dialogue box appears: **Chart Source Data** (Figure 7.8).

There is a preview of the pie chart together with a legend (key representing the different segments of the pie). With the **Data Range** tab selected, the data range selected is shown as:

=Sheet1$A$2:$B$6

Ignoring the $ signs, this represents Sheet1, cells A2 to B6.

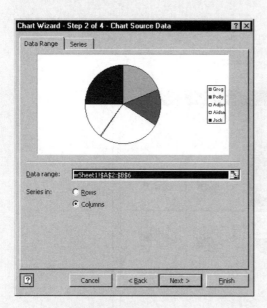

Figure 7.8 Step 2 of Chart Wizard

 If you have made an error in selecting the data range to chart, *either*:

change the data range by clicking in: the **Data range** box and keying in the correct range

or

click on: the **Collapse Dialog** button, reselect the cell range and click on: the **Collapse Dialog** button again.

Collapse Dialog
button

In this example we have the data series in columns. You will need to click in the **Rows** option button if the data series is in rows.
Should you need to go back a Step, after Step 1 of Chart Wizard, click on: **Back**.

In some circumstances, Excel will automatically make assumptions about what is a data range and will try to include, for example, years (ie 1993, 1994, 1995), since they are numerical. In such cases you will need to carry out steps (a) and (b) (above) to overwrite Excel's assumptions. Then click on: the **Series** tab. In the **Category (X) axis labels**, click on: the **Collapse Dialog** button and select the cell range for year labels. Click on: the **Collapse Dialog** button again. You can also overcome this problem by setting the years as text entries. To do this, *either*:

Select the cells containing the years. Then from the **Format** menu, select: **Cells**. The **Format Cells** box is displayed. With the **Number** tab selected, select: **Text**. Click on: **OK**.

or

Key in an apostrophe before keying in the first date in the range, ie '1993.

5 Click on: **Next**.

6 **Step 3 Chart Wizard** dialogue box appears: **Chart Options** (Figure 7.9).

   a With the **Titles** tab selected, click in: the **Chart title** box and key in: **Team Customer Contacts – Monday**.

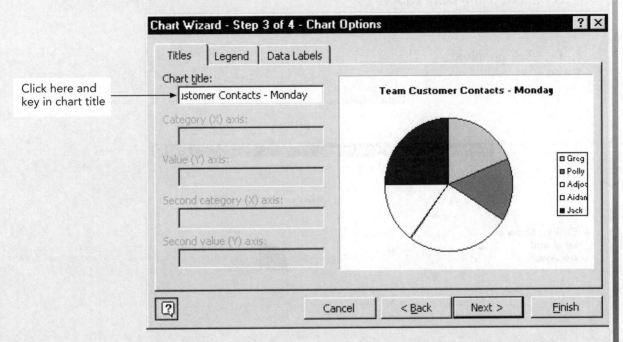

Figure 7.9 Step 3 of Chart Wizard

 In some cases you may not be able to see all the title as it will scroll out of the visible section. In such cases, do not press **Enter** as this will result in moving to the next step of Chart Wizard. If you do press **Enter**, click on: **Back**.

   b Click on: the **Legend** tab.

   c Click in: the **Show legend** tick box to remove the tick.

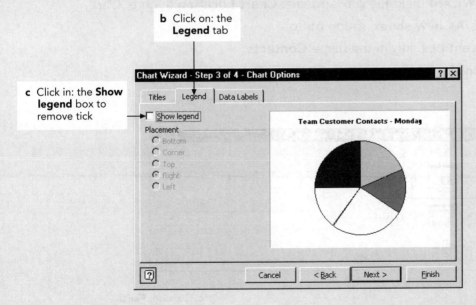

Figure 7.10 Removing a legend

You have been asked to show labels for each of the segments, together with a number or percentage, not a legend. Having segment data labels and a legend duplicates information and will make the chart appear cluttered.

d Click on: the **Data Labels** tab.

e Click in: the **Show label and percent** option button.

f Click on: **Next**.

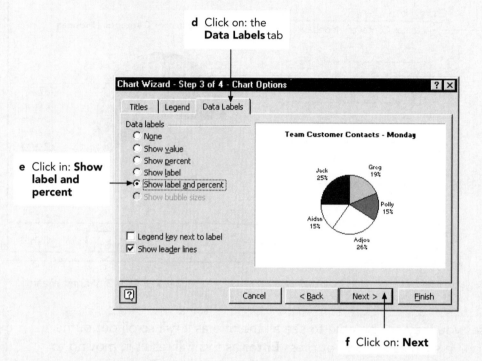

Figure 7.11 Showing labels

 You will notice that labels and choices appear on the chart preview as you work. If you make an error, carry out the instruction again. Notice other data labelling options.

7 **Step 4 Chart Wizard** dialogue box appears: **Chart Location** (Figure 7.12).

a Click in: the **As new sheet** option button.

b In the adjacent box, key in the name **Contacts**.

c Click on: **Finish**.

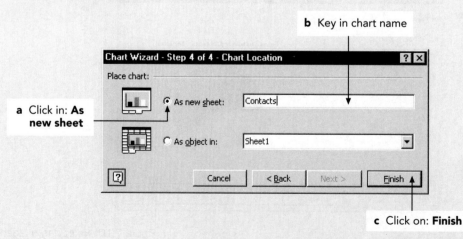

Figure 7.12 Step 4 of Chart Wizard

The chart will be located with the spreadsheet file whichever option you choose. Saving **As new sheet** is a good idea when you have a series of charts to plot from the same data. The sheet tabs and navigation arrows (shown below), at the bottom left of the Excel window, allow navigation between the sheets containing charts and the data spreadsheets. Click on the relevant sheet tab to view it.

The completed pie chart is displayed as shown in Figure 7.13.

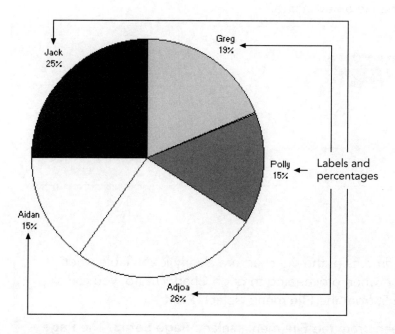

Figure 7.13 Completed pie chart

Should you need to make any changes, with the chart displayed on screen, right-click in the chart area to bring up the menu shown. You will notice that the menu items in the second section, ie below **Format Chart Area**, correspond to the dialogue boxes of **Chart Wizard**. Choose from these options: ⎯⎯⎯⎯⎯⎯⎯→

2.3 Saving the chart

Exercise 3

Save the datafile with its existing filename **Customers**.

Method

Click on: the **Save** button.

 You can use this quick saving method since the original datafile **Customers** (an Excel spreadsheet file) already exists. When you save the spreadsheet file the chart is saved with it. When you want to keep the original datafile intact, you need to save using the **File** menu, **Save As** and give the file a new name.

2.4 Printing the chart

Exercise 4

Print one copy of the pie chart.

Method

Note: Steps 1 to 4 ensure that the segments of the pie chart are clearly identifiable when printed. If you have chosen a B&W pie when proceeding through Chart Wizard, you can skip these steps and, instead, before step 5, from the **File** menu, select: **Print**.

1   With the chart displayed on screen, from the **File** menu, select: **Page Setup**. The **Page Setup** dialogue box appears (Figure 7.14).

2   Click on: the **Chart** tab.

Click on: the **Chart** tab

Click in: **Print in black and white** box so that a tick is displayed

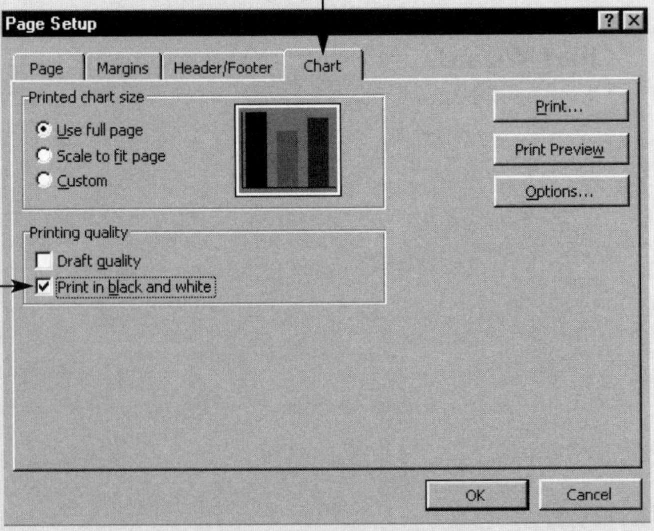

Figure 7.14 Page Setup dialogue box

3   Click in: the **Print in black and white** box so that a tick appears.

4   Click on: **Print**.

5   The **Print** dialogue box appears (Figure 7.15).

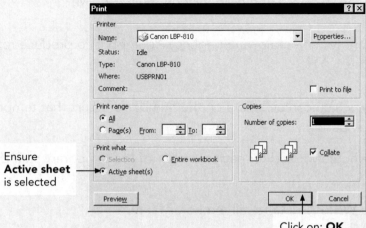

Ensure
Active sheet
is selected

Click on: **OK**

Figure 7.15 Print dialogue box

6   In the **Print what** section, ensure that the **Active sheet** option button is selected.

7   Click on: **OK**.

    By default the chart will print in landscape format.

2.5 Closing the datafile

Exercise 5

Close the datafile.

Method

From the **File** menu, select: **Close**.

    You can close with the display on either the chart or the spreadsheet containing the
data. *Remember:* The chart and the data sheet will be saved together with the same
filename.

Graphs and charts practice 1

Practice 1

Note: For this practice you will need the Excel file **Temp agency** on the CD-ROM.

You work as an Administrative Assistant for an employment agency. Your job is to produce reports on temporary staff for the Team Leader.

1   Open the datafile **Temp agency**, which contains data on the number of hours that temporary employees worked over a 5-week period.

 The first report will compare the hours worked for each member of the temporary staff during **WEEK1**, using a pie chart.

2   Create a pie chart to display the **WEEK1** data for all temporary staff.

 a Give the chart the heading: **WEEK1 Hours Worked**.
 b Ensure that each sector is shaded in such a way that the data can be clearly identified when printed.
 c Each sector of the chart must be labelled clearly with the name of the team member and percentage of hours worked.

3   Save the file using the name **hours**.

4   Print one copy of the pie chart.

5   Close the datafile.

Practice 2

Note: For this practice you will need the Excel file **books** on the CD-ROM.

You work as an Administrative Assistant for a bookstore. Your job is to produce reports on book sales for the Store Manager.

1   Open the datafile **books**, which contains data on the number of books sold in the past 6 days.

2   The first report will compare the books sold for each type on **MON**, using a pie chart.

3   Create a pie chart to display the **MON** data for all types of book.

 a Give the chart the heading: **Monday Sales**.
 b Ensure that each sector is shaded in such a way that the data can be clearly identified when printed.
 c Each sector of the chart must be labelled clearly with the number of books sold.
 d A legend should be shown to indicate the book types.

4   Save the file using the name **book sales**.

5   Print one copy of the pie chart.

6   Close the datafile.

3 Creating bar charts

In this section you will practise and learn how to:

- select a subset of a single data set
- create a bar chart
- set upper and lower limits for axes

3.1 Creating a bar chart

Exercise 1

Produce a bar chart showing the data for **Greg** from **Mon** to **Thu**.

1 Display the days along the x axis.

2 Give the bar chart the heading: **Greg Contacts Mon to Thu**.

3 Give the x axis the title **Day**.

4 Give the y axis the title **Contacts**.

Method

1 Load Excel and the datafile **Customers** saved in Section 2.

2 Ensure that the spreadsheet data is displayed. If not, click on the appropriate sheet tab, ie **Sheet1**, at the bottom of the screen.

3 Select the relevant data to chart (this is a *subset* of the data for **Greg** since it does not include all the data for **Greg**), ie **B1 to E2** (Figure 7.16).

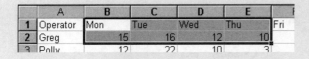

	A	B	C	D	E	F
1	Operator	Mon	Tue	Wed	Thu	Fri
2	Greg	15	16	12	10	
3	Polly	12	22	10	3	

Figure 7.16 Selecting a subset of data

4 Click on: the [chart icon] **Chart Wizard** button. **Step 1 of 4 Chart Wizard** dialogue box appears: **Chart Type**.

    a With the **Standard Types** tab selected, click on: **Column**. (This is the default.)

 Notice that in Excel **bar** charts have horizontal bars. We are therefore choosing **Column** instead of **Bar** as the column option is the more common way that bar charts are represented, ie with the bars vertical rather than horizontal.

    b In the **Chart sub-type** box, click on: the top left chart. (This is the default so may already be selected.)

    c Click on: **Next**.

Practise experimenting with the different chart types.

5 **Step 2 Chart Wizard** dialogue box appears: **Chart Source Data**.

6 Click on: **Next**.

7 **Step 3 Chart Wizard** dialogue box appears: **Chart Options**.

   a Select the **Titles** tab (if not already selected), click in: the **Chart title** box and key in: **Greg Contacts Mon to Thu**.

   b Click in the **Category (x) axis** box and key in: **Day**.

   c Click in the **Value (y) axis** box and key in: **Contacts**.

   d Click on: the **Legend** tab.

   e Click in: the **Show legend** tick box to remove the tick.

   f Click on: **Next**.

8 **Step 4 Chart Wizard** dialogue box appears: **Chart Location**.

   a Click on: **As new sheet** option button and key in the name **Greg**.

   b Click on: **Finish**.

The completed bar chart is displayed as shown (Figure 7.17).

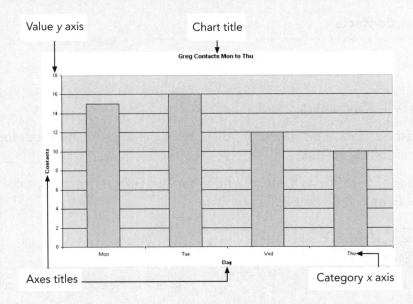

Figure 7.17 Bar chart

3.2 Setting upper and lower limits for axes

Exercise 2

Set the y axis to display the range 2 to 22.

Method

Referring back to Figure 7.17, you will see that the y axis is displaying 0 to 18. To alter this:

1 With the chart displayed, double-click on the **Value Axis** (the y axis).

2 The **Format Axis** dialogue box is displayed (Figure 7.18).

3 Click on: the **Scale** tab.

4 Click in: the **Minimum** box and key in: **2**.

5 Click in: the **Maximum** box and key in: **22**.

6 Click on: **OK**.

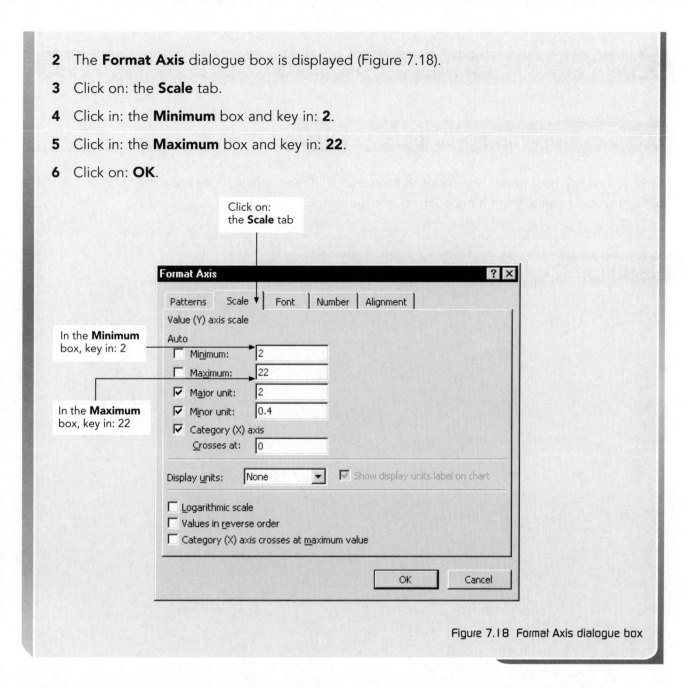

Figure 7.18 Format Axis dialogue box

The bar chart will now look like Figure 7.19.

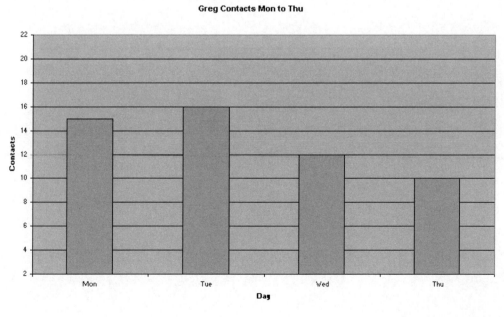

Fig 7.19 Chart with *y* axis set as specified

3.3 Save the chart named Greg within the datafile Customers

3.4 Print the chart as in Section 2.4

Note: You do not need to print this chart in black and white since the bars do not need to be distinguishable because there is only one set of data.

3.5 Close the datafile as in Section 2.5

Graphs and charts practice 2

Practice 3

The Team Leader has asked you to produce a bar chart showing the data for **Kym** from **WEEK1** to **WEEK4**.

1 Load the datafile **hours** saved in Practice 1, Section 2.

2 Produce a bar chart showing the data for **KYM** from **WEEK1** to **WEEK4**.

    a Display the weeks along the *x* axis.
    b Set the *y* axis to display the range **5** to **25**.
    c Give the bar chart the heading **Kym Hours – Week1 to Week4**.
    d Give the *x* axis the title **Weeks**.
    e Give the *y* axis the title **No of hours**.

3 Save the chart with the name **Kym** and the file with the name **Kym hours**.

4 Print one copy of the bar chart.

5 Close the datafile.

Practice 4

The Store Manager has asked you to produce a bar chart showing the data for the **Classics** genre from **Monday** to **Thursday**.

1 Load the datafile **book sales** saved in Practice 2, Section 2.

2 Produce a bar chart showing the data for **CLASSICS** from **MON** to **THU**.

    a Display the days along the *x* axis.
    b Set the *y* axis to display the range **25** to **225**.
    c Give the bar chart the heading: **Sales of Classics – Mon to Thu**.
    d Give the *x* axis the title **Day**.
    e Give the *y* axis the title **Number Sold**.

3 Save the file using the name **classics**.

4 Print one copy of the bar chart.

5 Close the datafile.

4 Creating line graphs

In this section you will practise and learn how to create line graphs.

4.1 Creating a line graph

Exercise 1

Produce a line graph showing the customer contacts on **Mon** for all the team *except* **Jack**.

1 Display the names of the team members along the x axis.

2 Give the line graph the heading: **CUSTOMER CONTACTS (EXCEPT JACK) – MON**.

3 Give the x axis the title **Team Members**.

4 Give the y axis the title **Contacts**.

Method

1 Load Excel and the datafile **Customers**.

2 Ensure that the spreadsheet data is displayed.

3 Select the relevant data to chart, ie A2 to B5.

4 Click on: the 📊 **Chart Wizard** button.

5 **Step 1 of 4 Chart Wizard** dialogue box appears: **Chart type**.

    a   With the **Standard Types** tab selected, click on: **Line**.
    b   In the **Chart sub-type** box, click on: the top left chart.
    c   Click on: **Next**.

6 **Step 2 Chart Wizard** dialogue box appears: **Chart Source Data**. Click on: **Next**.

7 **Step 3 Chart Wizard** dialogue box appears: **Chart Options**.

    a   Select the **Titles** tab, click in: the **Chart title** box and key in: **CUSTOMER CONTACTS (EXCEPT JACK) – MON**.
    b   Click in: the **Category (x) axis** box and key in: **Team Members**.
    c   Click in: the **Value (y) axis** box and key in: **Contacts**.
    d   Click on: the **Legend** tab.
    e   Click in: the **Show legend** tick box to remove the tick.
    f   Click on: **Next**.

8 **Step 4 Chart Wizard** dialogue box appears: **Chart Location**.

    a   Click on: **As new sheet** option button and key in the name **Excluding Jack**.
    b   Click on: **Finish**.

The completed line graph is displayed as shown in Figure 7.20.

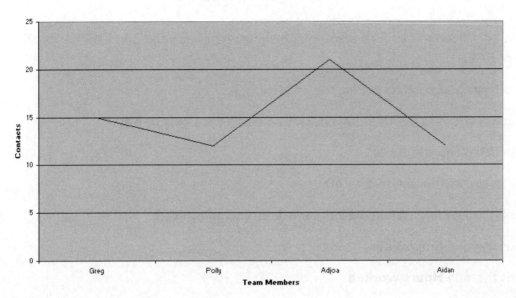

Figure 7.20 Completed line graph

4.2 Setting upper and lower limits for axes

Exercise 2

Set the y axis to display the range 5 to 30.

Method

Follow the instructions in Section 3.2.

4.3 Saving graph

Save the graph within the datafile with the original filename **Customers**, as in Section 2.3.

4.4 Print the graph as in Section 2.4

4.5 Close the datafile as in Section 2.5

Graphs and charts practice 3

Practice 5

The Team Leader has asked you to produce a line graph showing hours worked in WEEK1 for all the employees except KARL.

1   Load the datafile **Kym hours** saved in Practice 3, Section 3.

2   Produce a line graph showing the data for **WEEK1** all employees *except* **Karl**.

    a Display the names along the x axis.

    b Set the y axis to display the range **5** to **40**.

    c Give the graph the heading: **Week 1 Hours worked excluding Karl**.

    d Give the x axis the title **Employees**.

    e Give the y axis the title **Hours worked**.

3   Save the file using the name **Employees**.

4   Print one copy of the line graph.

5   Close the datafile.

Practice 6

The Store Manager has asked you to produce a line graph showing all book types sales on Monday.

1   Load the datafile **classics** saved in Practice 4, Section 3.

2   Produce a line graph showing the data for **MON** for all book types.

    a Display the book types along the x axis.

    b Set the y axis to display the range **40** to **220**.

    c Give the graph the heading: **Monday Sales**.

    d Give the x axis the title **Book Types**.

    e Give the y axis the title **Number of Sales**.

3   Save the file using the name **Monday sales**.

4   Print one copy of the bar chart.

5   Close the datafile.

5 Creating comparative graphs

In this section you will practise and learn how to create comparative graphs and charts.

5.1 Creating a comparative bar chart

Exercise 1

Using the datafile **Customers**, produce a comparative bar chart comparing the data for **Greg** and **Polly** from **Mon** to **Sat**.

1   Display the days along the x axis.

2   Set the y axis to display the range **5** to **30**.

3   Give the chart the heading: **Greg and Polly Customer Contacts**.

4   Give the x axis the title **Day**.

5   Give the y axis the title **Contacts**.

6   Use a legend to identify the bars. Make sure that the bars are distinctive and can be identified when printed.

Method

1   Load the datafile **Customers**.

2   Display the spreadsheet data.

3   Select the relevant data to chart, ie A1 to G3.

    Note: In this case we need to include the data range in row 1 in the selection so that the x axis labels (days) are automatically displayed on the chart.

4   Click on: the **Chart Wizard** button.

5   **Step 1 Chart Wizard**

    a   With the **Standard Types** tab selected, click on: **Column**.
    b   In the **Chart sub-type** box, click on: the first chart at the top left.
    c   Click on: **Next**.

6   **Step 2 Chart Wizard**. Click on: **Next**.

7   **Step 3 Chart Wizard**

    a   Select the **Titles** tab, click in: the **Chart title** box and key in: **Greg and Polly Customer Contacts**.
    b   Click in: the **Category (x) axis** box and key in: **Day**.
    c   Click in the **Value (y) axis** box and key in: **Contacts**.
    d   Click on: **Next**.

8   **Step 4 Chart Wizard**

    a   Click on: the **As new sheet** option button and key in **Greg and Polly Comparison**.
    b   Click on: **Finish**.

9   Set the y axis display as requested.

The completed comparative chart is displayed as shown in Figure 7.21.

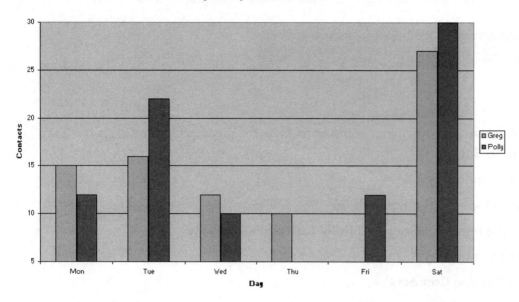

In this example, we need to show a legend to indicate which colour bars represent Greg and Polly. If you are printing in black and white, check that the bars and legend are displaying so that they are distinguishable. When necessary, use the **File** menu, **Page Setup** to select black and white printout.

5.2 Save the chart within the datafile as in Section 2.3

5.3 Print the chart as in Section 2.4

5.4 Creating a comparative line graph

Exercise 2

Produce a line graph comparing the data for Greg and Polly from Mon to Sat (as in Exercise 1).

1   Display the days along the x axis.

2   Set the y axis to display the range **0** to **30**.

3   Give the chart the heading: **Greg and Polly Customer Contacts**.

4   Give the x axis the title **Day**.

5   Give the y axis the title **Contacts**.

6   Use a legend to identify each line. Make sure that the lines and/or data points are distinctive and can be identified when printed.

Use the method as for Exercise 1, except at step 5 select: **Line**. In the **Chart sub-type** box select: the chart on the left of the second row, ie **Line with markers displayed at each data value**.

If you are printing a comparative line graph to a black and white printer, be careful to choose a chart type that displays different shapes on the lines to distinguish them. The type chosen above is suitable.

The chart will look like Figure 7.22.

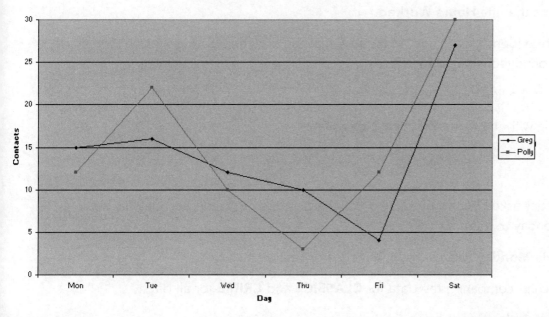

Greg and Polly Customer Contacts

Figure 7.22 Comparative line graph

5.5 Save the chart within the datafile as in Section 2.3

5.6 Print the chart as in Section 2.4

5.7 Close the datafile and exit Excel

Graphs and charts practice 4

Practice 7

The Team Leader has asked you to produce a line graph comparing Danny's hours with Kym's.

1 Load the datafile **Employees** saved in Practice 5, Section 4.

2 Produce a line graph comparing the data for **KYM** and **DANNY** for all weeks.

    a Display the weeks along the *x* axis.

    b Set the *y* axis to display the range **5** to **50**.

    c Give the graph the heading: **Comparison of Hours for Kym and Danny**.

    d Give the *x* axis the title **Week**.

    e Give the *y* axis the title **Hours Worked**.

    f Use a legend to identify each line. Make sure that the lines and/data points are distinctive and can be identified when printed.

3 Print one copy of the line graph.

4 Save the datafile with the name **Practice 7 compline**.

Practice 8

The Store Manager has asked you to produce a bar chart comparing crime and classics book types sales from Monday to Saturday.

1 Load the datafile **Monday sales** saved in Practice 6, Section 4.

2 Produce a bar chart comparing the data for **CLASSICS** and **CRIME** for all days.

    a Display the days along the *x* axis.

    b Set the *y* axis to display the range **0** to **300**.

    c Give the graph the heading: **Classics and Crime Genres**.

    d Give the *x* axis the title **Day**.

    e Give the *y* axis the title **Number of Sales**.

    f Use a legend to identify each bar. Make sure that the bars are distinctive and can be identified when printed.

3 Print one copy of the bar chart.

4 Save the datafile with the name **Practice 8 compbar**.

Graphs and charts quick reference for New CLAIT (Excel)

Action	Keyboard	Mouse	Right-mouse menu	Menu
Create a chart	Select the data to chart			
		Click: the ▥ **Chart Wizard** button		**I**nsert, **C**hart
	STEP 1	Select: the chart type Click: **Next**		
	STEP 2	Check that the source data is correct, if not change it Click: **Next**		
	STEP 3	Select: the **Titles** tab Key in the **Chart** title, the **Category (x) axis** title and the **Category (y) axis** title Select: the **Legend** tab Click: in the **Show legend** box to add/remove tick as appropriate (*For pie charts only*) Select: the **Data Labels** tab Click: **Show label** if appropriate Click: **Next**		
	STEP 4	Click: **As new s̲heet** or **As o̲bject in** Key in: the chart name Click: **F̲inish**		
Edit a chart	Select the chart by clicking on it			
			Right-click on the chart. Select from options	
Print a chart	With the chart displayed on screen			
	Ctrl + P Ensure **Active sheet** is selected Click: **OK**	Click: the 🖨 **Print** button (this will automatically print the sheet)		**F̲ile, P̲rint** Ensure **Acti̲ve sheet** is selected Click: **OK**
Save a chart	**Ctrl + S**	Click: the 💾 **Save** button		**F̲ile, S̲ave**
Set upper and lower limits on the y axis	*To set upper and lower limits for y (vertical) axis:* With the graph on screen Double-click: the **Value Axis** In the **Format Axis** dialogue box: Click: the **Scale** tab Key in: the new values in the **Maximum** and **Minimum** boxes Click: **OK**			

Hints and tips

- Reloading a saved chart – reload the spreadsheet from which the chart was produced. Click on: the **chartname** tab at the bottom of the sheet.
- When you change data in the spreadsheet, the data on the corresponding chart will change automatically to incorporate the amended data.
- Ensure that you create the type of chart requested.
- Have you labelled the charts as requested?

- Do you have the correct number of printouts?
- Ensure that you do not have any unwanted labels.
- Ensure that you do not have blank slices on the pie chart that do not relate to any data.
- Ensure that the printouts have easily distinguishable components where appropriate (eg on pie charts and comparative data charts and graphs) so that the chart is meaningful.

Graphs and charts: sample full practice assignment

Note: For this assignment you will need the datafile **Deliveries** on the CD-ROM.

Scenario

You are working as an Administrative Assistant for a company that makes musical instruments. Your job is to produce various reports on deliveries made to different towns in the West of England region.

Your Manager has asked you to produce a set of reports in graph format showing deliveries made over the past six months.

1   Open the datafile **Deliveries** that contains data on the number of deliveries to West of England towns from July to December.

    The first report will compare the number of deliveries to each town in July, using a pie chart.

2   Create a pie chart to display the **JUL** data for all towns.

    a   Give the chart the heading: **July Deliveries**.
    b   Ensure that each sector is shaded in such a way that the data can be clearly identified when printed.
    c   Each sector of the chart must be clearly labelled with the name of the town and the **number** or **percentage** of deliveries.

3   Save the file using the name **towns**.

4   Print one copy of the pie chart.

    Your manager would like to check the deliveries to Bristol until the end of October.

5   Produce a bar chart showing the data for **BRISTOL** from **JUL** to **OCT**.

    a   Display the months along the *x* axis.
    b   Set the *y* axis to display the range **5** to **55**.
    c   Give the bar chart the heading: **Deliveries to Bristol**.
    d   Give the *x* axis the title **Month**.
    e   Give the *y* axis the title **No of Deliveries**.

6   Save the file keeping the name **towns**.

7   Print one copy of the bar chart.

    Your manager would like to compare the deliveries to Bristol with those to Yeovil.

8   Produce a line graph comparing the data for **BRISTOL** and **YEOVIL** from **JUL** to **DEC**.

    a   Display the months along the *x* axis.
    b   Set the *y* axis to display the range **5** to **65**.
    c   Give the graph the heading: **Comparison Bristol and Yeovil**.
    d   Give the *x* axis the title **Month**.
    e   Give the *y* axis the title **No of Deliveries**.
    f   Use a legend to identify each line. Make sure that the lines and/or data points are distinctive, and can be identified when printed.

9   Save the file keeping the name **towns**.

10 Print one copy of the line graph.

11 Close the document and exit the software securely.

Web pages using FrontPage (Unit 9)

Getting started

In this section you will learn how to:

- appreciate the methods used to create and view web pages
- understand FrontPage basics
- insert a text file
- align page items
- set background colour
- view the page in Internet Explorer
- print the HTML source code

- load FrontPage
- create a new web page
- insert an image
- use three different font sizes
- save the page
- print the web page
- close and exit FrontPage

Note: For the exercises in this section you will need the files **celebrate.txt** and **balloon.gif**. These files should be stored in and accessed from the same folder.

1.1 Methods used to create web pages

There is a standard code that all web pages on the World Wide Web need to be written in. It is called *HTML (Hypertext Mark-up Language)* code. Web browser software (such as Internet Explorer) is able to convert this code into colourful and attractive *web pages* for everyone to view. HTML code is commonly created in text editors, such as Notepad. It is not difficult to learn but it can be extremely boring and time-consuming, especially now that we are used to having applications do all the repetitive work for us. However, it is worth looking at HTML code to see its characteristics. For CLAIT assignments you need to make printouts of the HTML code for the pages created and amended. Fortunately, there are many HTML editing applications available that are WYSIWYG (what you see is what you get, ie items are placed on the page exactly as they will appear in the browser), so you do not need to know HTML code.

Microsoft's FrontPage is one of these and we will be using it to create web pages in this chapter. DTP and word processing applications, such as Word, can be used to create documents that can then be converted into HTML automatically. However, capabilities are restricted and pages that you create will not necessarily look exactly as you have designed them (eg formatting may be lost) and the end result does not usually look very interesting or professional.

1.2 HTML code

HTML code (known as the web page's source code) consists mainly of text with HTML instructions, known as tags. Tags tell the browser how to display the text, eg centre, italicise, paragraph spacing, line breaks and so on. Tags usually come in pairs (known as containers), one at the start of the text and another at the end, and they use angle brackets. Here are some examples:

<B>Hello</B>   emboldens, producing **Hello.**
<I>Hello</I>   italicises, producing *Hello.*
<U>Hello</U>   underlines, producing <u>Hello.</u>

Most web pages are structured in a similar way with two main sections, the HEAD and the BODY. The HEAD contains the <TITLE>. The <TITLE> text will appear on the **Title** bar of the browser. The HEAD can also contain other invisible information, such as which application was used to create it. The <BODY> contains the main part of the web page and includes coding for text, images and anything else that is to appear on the page. An example of a simple web page's HTML code created in Notepad is shown in Figure 8.1. A table of common codes is given in the quick reference at the end of this chapter.

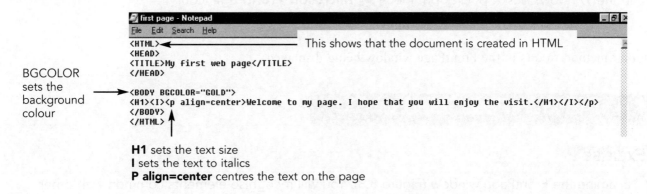

Figure 8.1   A simple web page's HTML code

Images can be added to pages but these remain as separate files and require coding to locate them. In order to move between pages, coding for hyperlinks (text or images that you click on to jump to another location on the web) needs to be added. You will see examples of this later in this chapter.

1.3 Loading FrontPage

Exercise 1

Load FrontPage.

Method 1

1   In the Windows 98 desktop, click on: the **Start** button.
2   Select: **Programs**, then click on: **Microsoft FrontPage** (Figure 8.2).

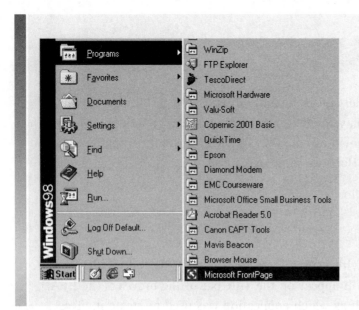

Figure 8.2 Loading FrontPage

Method 2

(Use if you have a shortcut icon to FrontPage on your desktop.)

In the Windows desktop, click on: the **Microsoft FrontPage** icon.

Either method results in the FrontPage window being displayed.

1.4 The FrontPage window

Exercise 2

Examine the FrontPage window (Figure 8.3). You will recognise elements common with other Microsoft applications.

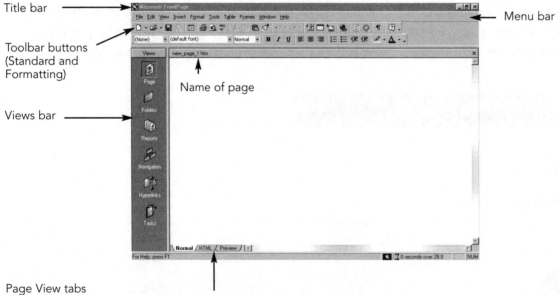

Page View tabs
Normal allows for editing in WYSIWYG (what you see is what you get)
mode, ie as content should display on a web page
HTML displays the HTML code for the page
Preview displays how the page will look as a web page in a browser

Figure 8.3 The FrontPage window

If the **Standard** and **Formatting** toolbars are sharing one row, you can display them on separate rows as follows:

1 From the **View** menu, select: **Toolbars**, then: **Customize**.

2 In the **Customize** dialogue box, select the **Options** tab.

3 Click in the: **Standard and Formatting toolbars share one row** box to remove the tick.

4 Click on: **Close**.

1.5 Inserting a text file

Exercise 3

Insert the file **celebrate.txt**.

Although you can key text directly onto the page, in the workplace it is common to receive files that have been created by other people that need to be inserted.

Method

1 In this instance a new page is already displayed. When it is not, you will need to click on: the 🗋 **New Page** button.

2 From the **Insert** menu, select: **File** (Figure 8.4).

Figure 8.4 Inserting a file

3 The **Select File** dialogue box is displayed (Figure 8.5).

4 In the **Look in** box, use the down arrow to select the location of the file to insert.

5 Double-click on: the folder that contains the file.

6 In the **Files of type** box, click on: the down arrow and select: **Text Files (*.txt)**.

7 Click on: the file and then on: **Open**.

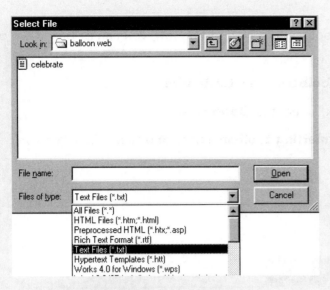

Figure 8.5 Selecting the file and file type to insert

8 The **Convert Text** box is displayed (Figure 8.6).

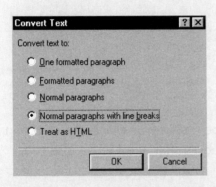

Figure 8.6 Convert Text box

9 Click in: the **Normal paragraphs with line breaks** option button. This option ensures that there is a line space between paragraphs.

10 Click on: **OK**.

11 The file is inserted on the page (Figure 8.7).
At this stage you can:
Click on: the **HTML** tab to view the HTML code (Figure 8.8).
Click on: the **Preview** tab to see what it looks like as a web page.
Click on: the **Normal** tab to switch back so that you can edit the page.

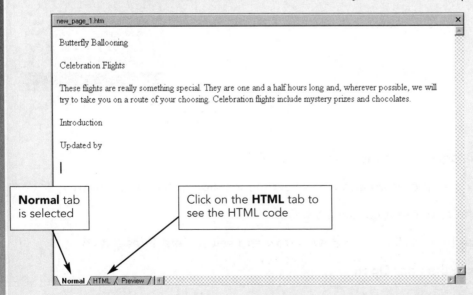

Figure 8.7 Web page in Normal View

```
new_page_1.htm                                                          ×
<html>

<head>
<meta http-equiv="Content-Type" content="text/html; charset=windows-1252">
<meta name="GENERATOR" content="Microsoft FrontPage 4.0">
<meta name="ProgId" content="FrontPage.Editor.Document">
<title>New Page 1</title>
</head>

<body>

<p>Butterfly Ballooning</p>
<p>Celebration Flights</p>
<p>These flights are really something special. They are one and a half hours
long and, wherever possible, we will try to take you on a route of your
choosing. Celebration flights include mystery prizes and chocolates.</p>
<p>Introduction</p>
<p>Updated by</p>

</body>

</html>

 \ Normal \ HTML / Preview / | ◄ |                                     ► | ◄ |
```

Figure 8.8 Web page HTML source code

1.6 Entering text directly on the page

Exercise 4

Enter your name after the text: **Updated by**.

Method

With the page in **Normal** View, click the cursor after the **Updated by** text, press the space bar to leave a space between **by** and **your name** and key in your name.

1.7 Aligning text on the page

Exercise 5

Format all the text so that it is centred on the page.

Method

1   Select all the text so that it is highlighted (**Ctrl + A**), drag the mouse over the text, or
    use another method that you prefer).

2 Click on: the ≣ **Center** button.

3 Click on: the page to remove highlighting.

Note: Use the ≣ **Align Left** and ≣ **Align Right** buttons when appropriate.

1.8 Emphasising text

Exercise 6

Embolden the text **Celebration flights**.

Method

1 Select the text to embolden.
To do this:

    a Position the cursor at the beginning of the text to select – in this case the **C** of **Celebration**.

    b Hold down the left mouse button and drag the I-beam pointer across the heading so that it is highlighted.

    c Release the mouse button.

2 Click on: the **B** **Bold** button.

 There are many ways to select text. These are given in the quick reference at the end of this chapter. There is no right or wrong way. Experiment to find your own preferred method.

Exercise 7

Italicise the text **mystery prizes and chocolates**.

Method

1 Select the text to italicise.

2 Click on: the *I* **Italic** button.

1.9 Setting font size

Exercise 8

Format the text as follows:

- **Butterfly Ballooning** as a Heading (large font size).
- **Celebration Flights** as a Subheading (medium font size).
- All other text as Body Text (small font size).

When sizing fonts for CLAIT assignments, use the following as a guide. *Note:* FrontPage has a different sizing format from other Office programs but it displays point sizes too:

Headings	Large font size	Size 7 (36 pt)
Subheadings	Medium font size	Size 5 (18 pt)
Body Text	Small font size	Size 3 (12 pt)

Method

1   Select the first text to resize.

2   Click on: the down arrow of the **Font Size** box (Figure 8.9) and click on: the required size.

3   Repeat for the other text.

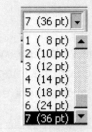

Figure 8.9   Setting font size

1.10 Separating paragraphs with a clear line space

Due to the option chosen in Section 1.5, the paragraphs are separated by a clear line space. If this were not the case, you would need to insert line spaces manually by positioning the cursor at the end of a paragraph and pressing: **Enter**.

You will be penalised in CLAIT assignments if there are extra line spaces or paragraph breaks.

1.11 Inserting an image file

Exercise 9

Insert the image file **balloon.gif** and position it below the text **...mystery prizes and chocolates** and above **Introduction**. Centre the image on the page.

1 Position the cursor at the end of the line ending in **chocolates** and press: **Enter**.

2 From the **Insert** menu, select: **Picture**, **From File** (Figure 8.10).

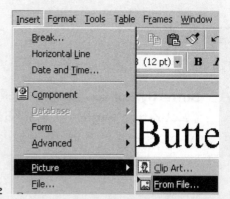

Figure 8.10 Inserting an image

3 The **Select File** box dialogue box is displayed (Figure 8.11).

4 In the **Look in** box, select: the location of the file.

5 Double-click on: the folder that contains the file.

6 Click on: the file.

7 Click on: **OK**.

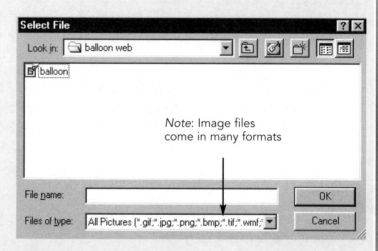

Note: Image files come in many formats

Figure 8.11 Selecting a file for insertion

The web page will now look something like Figure 8.12. *Note:* If the image is not centred, click on the image to select it, then click on the **Center** button. Use other alignment buttons to align when requested.

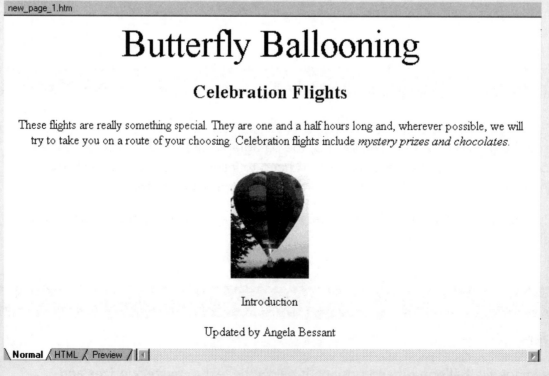

Figure 8.12 Image inserted

Exercise 10

Change the background colour to light blue.

Method

1   From the **Format** menu, select: **Background** (Figure 8.13).

2   The **Page Properties** dialogue box is displayed (Figure 8.14).

3   Ensure the **Background** tab is selected, in the **Colors** section, click on the down arrow of the **Background** box and click on a colour.

4   *Note:* If you do not see a colour you like, click on: **More Colors**. Click on: a colour in the colour palette, then on: **OK** and on **OK** again.

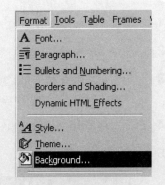

Figure 8.13 Changing the background colour

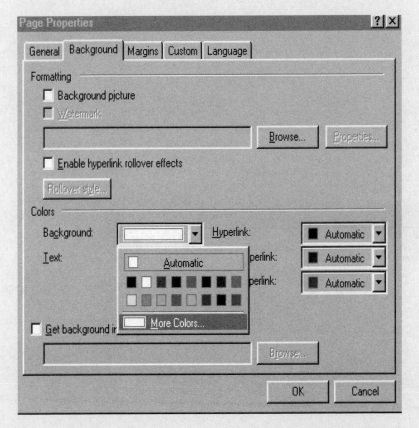

Figure 8.14 Page Properties dialogue box

Exercise 11

Save the web page with the name **ballooning**.

Method

1   From the **File** menu, select: **Save As**.

2   The **Save As** dialogue box is displayed (Figure 8.15).

3   In the **Save in** box, select the location to store the web page. *Note:* Store all the web components together for easy location of images.

4   In the **File name** box, key in the filename.

5   Click on: **Save**.

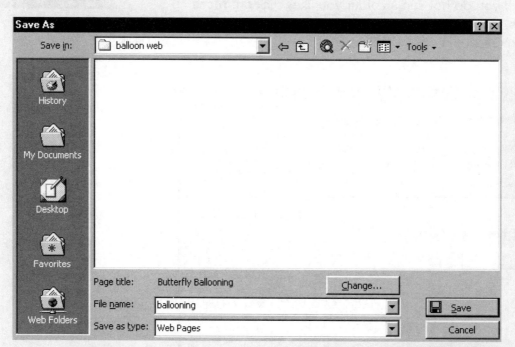

Figure 8.15 Saving the web page

   Web page files have the extension .htm

Exercise 12

Open the page you have just created in Internet Explorer.

Click on: the 🔍 **Preview in Browser** button.

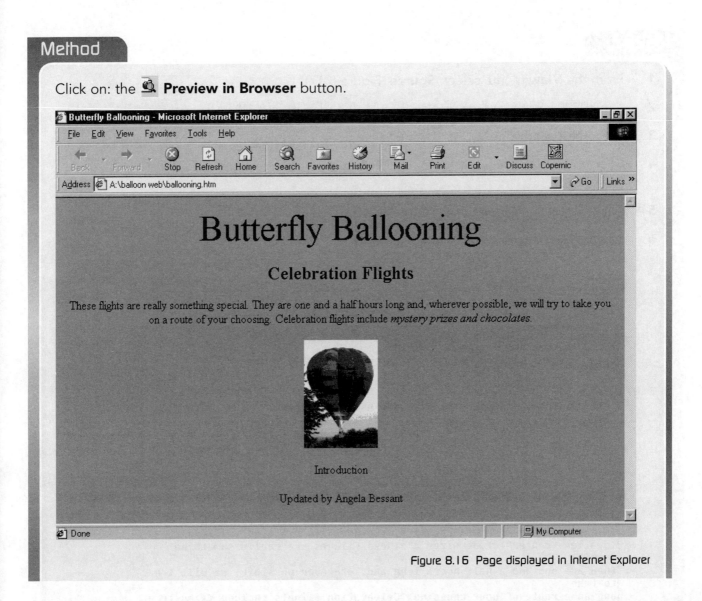

Figure 8.16 Page displayed in Internet Explorer

1.15 Printing the web page

Exercise 13

Print the web page from Internet Explorer.

Method

Click on: the 🖨 **Print** button.

Exercise 14

Print a copy of the HTML code for the web page.

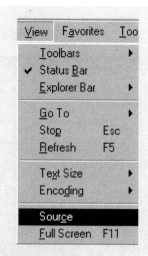

1   From the **View** menu, select: **Source** (Figure 8.17).

2   The HTML source code is displayed in Notepad (Figure 8.18).

3   In the **Notepad** window, from the **File** menu, select: **Print**.

4   Click on: the ⊠ **Close** button of the **Notepad** window to close Notepad.

5   Click on: the ⊠ **Close** button of Internet Explorer to close it.

6   You are returned to the FrontPage window.

Figure 8.17 Viewing the HTML code

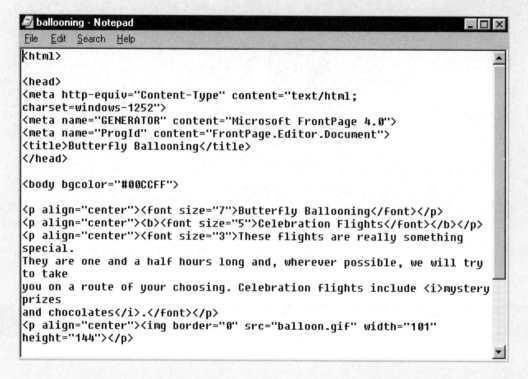

Figure 8.18 The HTML code for the web page

Note: You can now have a look at the printout to discover more about coding in HTML.

1.16 Closing the FrontPage file

Exercise 15

Close the file you have just created in FrontPage.

Method

From the **File** menu, select: **Close**.

1.17 Exiting FrontPage

Exercise 16

Exit FrontPage.

Method

From the **File** menu, select **Exit**.

Web pages practice 1

Note: For these exercises you will need access to the CD-ROM files **flats.txt** and **apartment.jpg** for Practice 1 and **nasturtiums.txt** and **orange.jpg** for Practice 2. The files relating to each web practice should be stored in and accessed from the same folder.

Practice 1

Make a new web page, to form part of a letting agency website as follows:

1   Create a new document and insert the file **flats.txt**.

2   Enter your name and centre number after the text **Updated by**.
Format the pages according to the company's web design policy as shown in the Figure 8.19 below.

3   Format the text **On the Move** as a Heading (large font size).
Format the text **Flats to Let** as a Subheading (medium font size).
Format all other text as Body Text (small font size and not bold).
Ensure that each of the five paragraphs is separated by a clear line space.

4   Format the text **Flats to Let** so that it is centred on the page. Ensure all other text is left aligned.
Embolden the text **Redland**.
Italicise the text **new**.

5   Import the graphic **apartment.jpg** and position it below the text **On the Move** and above the text **Flats to Let**.
Centre-align the graphic.

6   Change the background colour so that it is different from the text colour.

7   Save the new page.

8   Print the new page from Internet Explorer.

9   Print the HTML source code.

10 Close all files.

11 Exit FrontPage.

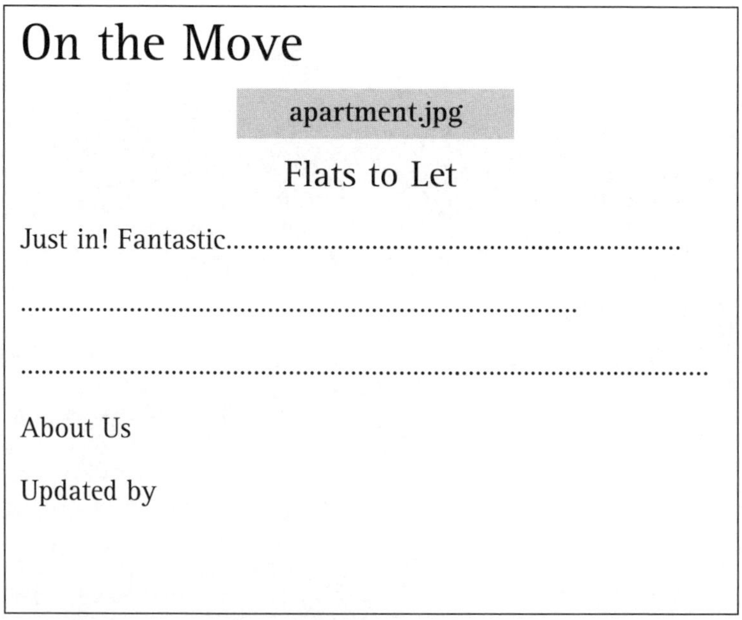

On the Move

apartment.jpg

Flats to Let

Just in! Fantastic...

....

....

About Us

Updated by

Figure 8.19 Diagram showing web design policy

Practice 2

Make a new web page that will form part of a Flower Facts website as follows:

1 Create a new document and insert the file **nasturtiums.txt**.

2 Enter your name and centre number after the text **Updated by:**
Format the pages according to the company's web design policy as shown in the Figure 8.20 below.

3 Format the text **Flower Facts** as a Heading (large font size).
Format the text **Nasturtiums** as a Subheading (medium font size).
Format all other text as Body Text (small font size and not bold).
Ensure that each of the five paragraphs is separated by a clear line space.

4 Format all the text so that it is centred on the page except the paragraph beginning **There are many...** which should be left-aligned.
Embolden the words **dwarf** and **climbing**.
Italicise the text **orange**.

5 Import the graphic **orange.jpg** and position it below the text ending **...roundish leaves** and above the text beginning **Click on the...** Centre-align the graphic.

6 Change the background colour so that it is different from the text colour.

7 Save the new page.

8 Print the new page from Internet Explorer.

9 Print the HTML source code.

10 Close all files.

11 Exit FrontPage.

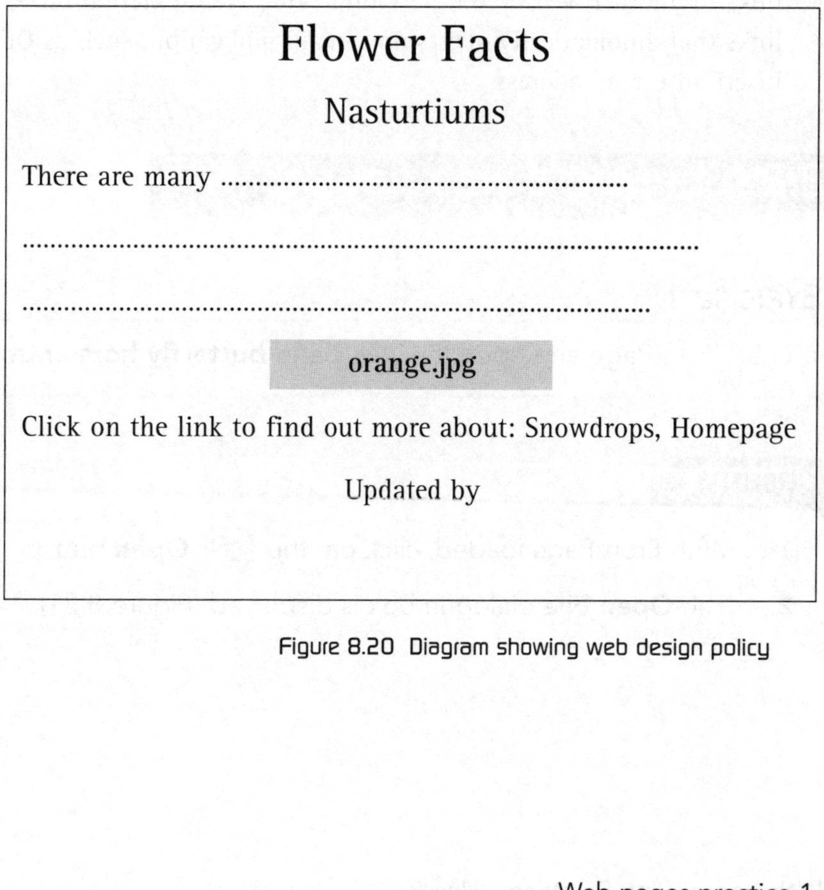

Flower Facts

Nasturtiums

There are many ....

....

....

orange.jpg

Click on the link to find out more about: Snowdrops, Homepage

Updated by

Figure 8.20 Diagram showing web design policy

2 Creating links

In this section you will learn how to:

- open prepared web pages
- insert an external link
- test links
- link pages
- insert an e-mail link
- insert link text

Note: For the exercises in this section you will need the files **butterfly home.htm** and **regular.htm**. These files should be stored and accessed in the same folder as the file ballooning.htm created in Section 1.

 OCR provide a web address and dummy e-mail address for the external links required in this unit.

2.1 Linking

One of the main ways of moving between web pages and websites (collections of related web pages) is using hyperlinks (links). When you click on a hyperlink you jump to a new location, ie the destination that has been set for the link. Hyperlinks can be text (usually underlined) or images. When you hover over a hyperlink, the pointer will (usually) turn into a hand symbol.

The links that you need to know how to create for CLAIT assignments are:

- links between web pages
- links to another website on the World Wide Web (external links)
- links that automatically access an e-mail application, such as Outlook Express, and automatically insert an e-mail address.

2.2 Opening a web page

Exercise 1

Load FrontPage and open the web page **butterfly home.htm**.

Method

1   With FrontPage loaded, click on: the 🖿 **Open** button.
2   The **Open File** dialogue box is displayed (Figure 8.21).

Figure 8.21 Opening an existing file

3 In the **Look in** box, select the location of the file.

4 Click on: the file and then on: **Open**.

 Whilst carrying out these exercises you may find it useful to know that you can load recently accessed files from the **File** menu, and selecting: **Recent Files**.

2.3 Creating links between prepared web pages

 It is important that you have a clear picture of what you are linking to what. Draw diagrams if necessary to assist you.

Exercise 2

Create a link in the **butterfly home.htm** web page as follows:

Text to be linked: **Regular Flights**
Link to: **regular.htm**

1 Ensure the **butterfly home.htm** page is displayed in **Normal** view (Figure 8.22).

Introduction

Butterfly Ballooning is part of the Bravado Ballooning Group. Let us take you on the flight of your dreams.
You can choose an early morning flight when the countryside is just waking or an evening flight when you can
have a breathtaking sunset backdrop. Book now for that special occasion.

Bravado Ballooning Group Home Page

Regular Flights

Updated by

Normal / HTML / Preview /

Figure 8.22 butterfly home.htm displayed in Normal view

2 Select the text to be linked, ie **Regular Flights**.

3 Click on: the 🖼 **Hyperlink** button.

4 The **Create Hyperlink** dialogue box is displayed (Figure 8.23).

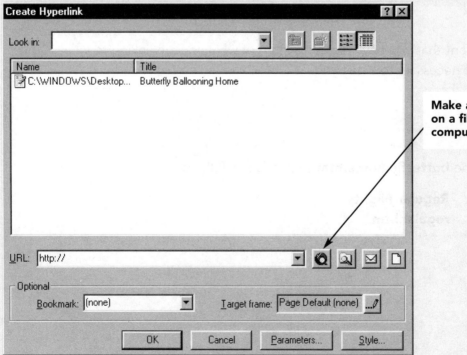

Make a hyperlink on a file on your computer button

Figure 8.23 Create Hyperlink dialogue box

5 Click on: the 🔍 **Make a hyperlink to a file on your computer** button.

6 The **Select File** dialogue box is displayed (Figure 8.24).

7 In the **Look in** box, select the location of the file **regular.htm**.

8 Click on: the file and then on: **OK**.

9 You are returned to the original web page. Notice that the link is now underlined and has changed colour.

10 Enter your name and centre number after the text **Updated by**.

11 Save the file by clicking on: the 💾 **Save** button.

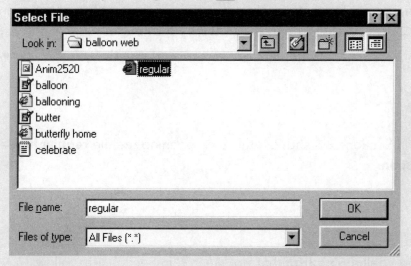

Figure 8.24 Selecting the 'Link to' file

2.4 Testing the link

Exercise 3

View the page in Internet Explorer and test the link.

Method

1 Click on: the 🔍 **Preview in Browser** button.

2 Click on: the link. The **regular.htm** web page is displayed and its name and location are displayed in the Internet Explorer's **Address bar**.

3 Close Internet Explorer by clicking on: the ⊠ **Close** button.

4 Close the page using the **Close** option on the **File** menu.

Exercise 4

Create a link in the **regular.htm** page as follows:

Text to be linked: **Introduction**
Link to: **butterfly home.htm**

Enter your name and centre number after the text **Updated by**.
Save the amended page with its original filename.
Check that the link works in Internet Explorer, ie when you click on the text **Introduction** in the **regular.htm** page, you automatically jump to the **butterfly home.htm** page.

Method

Follow the methods given in Sections 2.3 and 2.4, this time opening the file **regular.htm** and selecting the text **Introduction**.

Exercise 5

Create a link in the new page **ballooning.htm** that you created in Section 1 as follows:

Text to be linked: **Introduction**
Link to: **butterfly home.htm**

Save the amended page with the same filename **ballooning.htm** by clicking on: the **Save** button.

Check that the link works in Internet Explorer.

Method

Follow the methods given in Sections 2.3 and 2.4, this time opening the file **ballooning.htm** and selecting the text **Introduction**.

Exercise 6

The **butterfly home.htm** page should have a link to the new page that you created in Section 1, ie **ballooning.htm**.

In the **butterfly home.htm** page, on a separate line below the text **Bravado Ballooning Group Home Page** and above the text **Regular Flights**, add the text **Celebration Flights**. Format this text to be centre-aligned.

Link this text to the **ballooning.htm** page.

Save the amended page with the original filename **butterfly home.htm**.

Method

1 Open the page **butterfly home.htm** in **Normal** view.

2 Position the cursor after the **e** of **Page**.

3 Press: **Enter**.

4 Key in the new text: **Celebration Flights**.

5 Centre-align the text if necessary by using the **Center** button.

6 Create the link from this new text to the **ballooning.htm** page, as shown in the exercises above.

7 Resave the file.

8 Test the link.

You now have links to and from all three pages in place. Try them out in Internet Explorer to ensure that they are all working correctly.

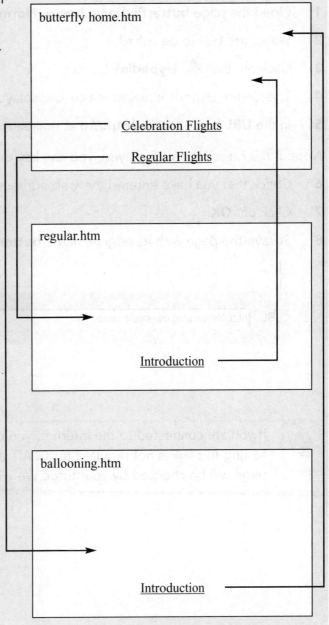

Figure 8.25 Links

Exercise 7

Create an external link in the **butterfly home.htm** page as follows:

Text to be linked: **Bravado Ballooning Group Home Page**
External link to: **www.progress-media.co.uk**

Method

 So far you have created only local links, ie links to pages that exist on your computer. This link will have a destination on the World Wide Web.

1   Open the page **butterfly home.htm** in **Normal** view.

2   Select the text to be linked.

3   Click on: the 🕷 **Hyperlink** button.

4   The Create Hyperlink dialogue box is displayed.

5   In the **URL** box, after the **http://** that is already there, key in the www address (Figure 8.26).

Note: If the http:// is not displayed, you can key that in too.

6   Check that you have entered the web address correctly.

7   Click on: **OK**.

8   Resave the page with its original name **butterfly home.htm**.

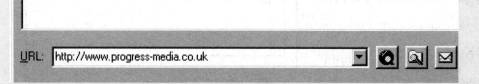

Figure 8.26 Create Hyperlink dialogue box

 If you are connected to the Internet, you can test this external link. However, testing this link is not required for CLAIT assignments. The HTML code for the page will be checked by your tutor. We will examine this later.

Exercise 8

Create an e-mail link in the **butterfly home.htm** page as follows:

Text to be linked: **your name and centre number**
External link to: **enquiries@progress-media.co.uk**

Save the amended file using the same filename **butterfly home.htm**.

Method

1   Ensure the **butterfly home.htm** page is displayed in **Normal** view.

2   Select the text to be linked, ie **your name and centre number**.

3   Click on: the 🌐 **Hyperlink** button.

4   The **Create Hyperlink** dialogue box is displayed.

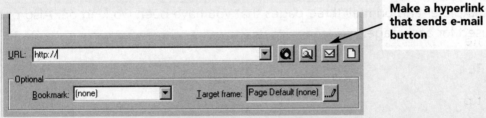

> Make a hyperlink that sends e-mail button

Figure 8.27 E-mail hyperlinking

5   Click on: the ✉ **Make a hyperlink that sends E-mail** button (Figure 8.27).

6   The **Create E-mail Hyperlink** box is displayed (Figure 8.28).

7   In the **Type an E-mail address** box, key in the appropriate address.

8   Check that you have entered it correctly.

9   Click on: **OK** and then on: **OK** again.

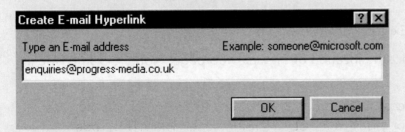

Figure 8.28 Entering the e-mail link

10   Save the web page file by clicking on: the **Save** button.

> You can check that this link works by clicking on: the 🔍 **Preview in Browser** button and then scrolling down (if necessary) and clicking on the link. It should take you to the Outlook Express window with the e-mail address already keyed in the **To:** box.

2.9 Close the open page on FrontPage and exit FrontPage

2.10 Print from Internet Explorer

Exercise 9

Load Internet Explorer and print all three pages that you have been working on. Also print the HTML code used for each page.

Method

1   Load Internet Explorer (**Start**, **Programs**, **Internet Explorer**).

Note: If the Dial-up Connection box is displayed, click on: the **Work Offline** button, unless you want to check the external link.

2   From the **File** menu, select: **Open**.

3   The Open box is displayed.

4   Click on: **Browse**.

5   The Microsoft Internet Explorer box is displayed.

6   In the **Look in** box, select the location of the first web page. *Note:* It is an HTML file type.

7   Click on: the file and then on: **OK**.

8   The Open box is displayed again, now displaying the location of the file.

9   Click on: **OK**.

10   The page is displayed in the browser.

11   Print as in Section 1.

12   Close the file.

Repeat for the other pages.

When carrying out assignments, your tutor will look for evidence that you have completed the linking correctly by examining the HTML code. Have a look at the code now to see if you can recognise the links. The code **<a href** indicates a hyperlink. Check through to find the links you have inserted.

If you need to update or amend anything in the HTML code in the browser, you will need to click on: the **Refresh** button to display the latest changes and don't forget to save them.

2.11 Close Internet Explorer

Web pages practice 2

Note: For these exercises you will need access to the CD-ROM files **moving.htm** and **houses.htm**, for Practice 3, and **flower facts.htm** and **snowdrops.htm**, for Practice 4. The files relating to each web practice should be stored in and accessed from the same folder and from the same folder as the pages produced in the Section 1 practice.

Practice 3

Two unlinked pages have been prepared. They are:

moving.htm, the 'On the Move' home page
houses.htm, a page about houses to let

1   Create a link in the **moving.htm** page as follows:

Text to be linked: **Houses**
Link to: **houses.htm**

Enter your name and centre number after the text: **Updated by**.
Save the amended **moving.htm** page.

2   Create a link in the **houses.htm** page as follows:

Text to be linked: **About Us**
Link to: **moving.htm**

Enter your name and centre number after the text: **Updated by**.
Save the amended **houses.htm** page.

3   Check the links function correctly by viewing them in the browser.

4   Open the new page that you created in Section 1, Practice 1 (about flats).

Create a link in the new page that you created as follows:

Text to be linked: **About Us**
Link to: **moving.htm**

Save the page.

5   On the **moving.htm** page, on a separate line below the text **Houses** and above the text **Head Office**, add the text:

Flats
Ensure that this is left-aligned on the page.
Ensure that there is consistent spacing between the paragraphs.
Link this text to the page that you created about flats.
Save the amended page.

6   Load all three pages into the browser and test the new links.

7 Create an external link in the **moving.htm** page as follows:

Text to be linked: **Head Office**
External link to: **www.progress-media.co.uk**

Save the amended **moving.htm** page.

8 Create an e-mail link in the **moving.htm** page as follows:

Text to be linked: **Your name and centre number**
E-mail link to: **enquiries@progress-media.co.uk**

Save the amended **moving.htm** page.

9 Load the **moving.htm** page into your browser and print a copy.
Load the **houses.htm** page into your browser and print a copy.
Load your new page about flats into your browser and print a copy.
Print a copy of the HTML code used for each of the three pages.

10 Close each document and exit from the application(s) following the correct procedures.

Practice 4

Two unlinked pages have been prepared. They are:

flower facts.htm, the 'Flower Facts' home page
snowdrops.htm, a page about snowdrops

1 Create a link in the **flower facts.htm** page as follows:

Text to be linked: **Snowdrops**
Link to: **snowdrops.htm**

On a new line at the bottom of the page after the line ending **...the webmaster**, enter the text: **Updated by [your name]**

Save the amended **flower facts.htm** page.

2 Create a link in the **snowdrops.htm** page as follows:

Text to be linked: **Homepage**
Link to: **flower facts.htm**

Enter your name and centre number after the text: **Updated by**.
Save the amended **snowdrops.htm** page.

3 Check the links function correctly by viewing them in the browser.

4 Open the new page that you created in Section 1, Practice 2 (about nasturtiums).
Create a link in the new page that you created as follows:

Text to be linked: **Homepage**
Link to: **flower facts.htm**

Save the page.

5 On the **flower facts.htm** page, after the text **Click on the links for: Snowdrops**, add the text:

Nasturtiums

Link this text to the page that you created.
Save the amended page.

6 Load all three pages into the browser and test the new links.

7 Create an external link in the **flower facts.htm** page as follows:

Text to be linked: **Click here for more Flower Facts**
External link to: **www.progress-media.co.uk**

Save the amended **flower facts.htm** page.

8 Create an e-mail link in the **flower facts.htm** page as follows:

Text to be linked: **webmaster**
E-mail link to: **enquiries@progress-media.co.uk**

Save the amended **flower facts.htm** page.

9 Load the **flower facts.htm** page into your browser and print a copy.
Load the **snowdrops.htm** page into your browser and print a copy.
Load your new page into your browser and print a copy.
Print a copy of the HTML code used for each of the three pages.

10 Close each document and exit from the application(s) following the correct procedures.

Web pages quick reference for New CLAIT (FrontPage)

Action	Keyboard	Mouse	Right-mouse menu	Menu
Align text	Select the text to be aligned			
		Click: the relevant alignment ▦ ▦ ▦ button		
Background, colour			**Page Properties**, **Background**	**Format**, **Background**
Bold text	**Ctrl + B**	Click: the **B** **Bold** button	**Font**	**Format**, **Font**
			Select: **Bold** from the **Font style:** menu	
Capitals (blocked), when keying in	**Caps Lock** Key in the text **Caps Lock** again to remove			
Centre text	Select the text			
	Ctrl + E	Click: the ▤ **Center** button		
Close a file		Click: the ⊠ **Close** button		**File**, **Close**
Cut text	Select the text to be cut			
	Ctrl + X	Click: the ✂ **Cut** button	**Cut**	**Edit**, **Cut**
Delete a character	Press: **Delete** to delete the character to the right of the cursor Press: ← (Backspace) to delete the character to the left of the cursor			
Delete a word	Double-click: the word to select it. Press: **Delete**			
Delete/cut a block of text	Select the text you want to delete			
	Delete or **Ctrl + X**	Click: the ✂ **Cut** button	**Cut**	**Edit**, **Cut**
Exit FrontPage	**Alt + F4**	Click: the ⊠ **Close** button		**File**, **Exit**
Font	Select the text you want to change			
		Click: the ▾ down arrow next to the **Font** box Select: the font you require	**Font**	**Format**, **Font**
			Select: the required font from the **Font** menu	
Font size	Select the text you want to change			
		Click: the ▾ down arrow next to the **Font Size** box Select: the font size you require	**Font**	**Format**, **Font**
			Select: the required size from the **Size** menu	
Help	**F1**			**Help** **Microsoft FrontPage Help**
	Shift + F1			**What's This?**
Hyperlink, add	Select text or object to link			
	Ctrl + K	Click: the 🔗 **Hyperlink** button	**Hyperlink**	**Insert**, **Hyperlink**

Action	Keyboard	Mouse	Right-mouse menu	Menu
Insert graphic		Click: the 🖼 **Insert Picture From File** button		**Insert**, **Picture**, **From file**
Insert text	Position the cursor where you want the text to appear Key in the text			
Insert text file				**Insert**, **File**
Italicise text	Select the text to italicise			
	Ctrl + I	Click: the *I* **Italic** button		
Load FrontPage	In the Windows 98 desktop			
		Double-click: the **FrontPage** shortcut icon		**Start**, **Programs**, **Microsoft FrontPage**
Open an existing file	**Ctrl + O**	Click: the 📂 **Open** button		**File**, **Open**
	Select the appropriate folder and filename Click: **Open**			
Print from browser, as web page	**Ctrl + P**	Click: the 🔍 **Preview in Browser** button		**File**, **Print**
as HTML code				**View**, **Source** and print from **Notepad**
Redo	**Ctrl + Y**	Click: the ⤳ **Redo** button		**Edit**, make selection
Remove/add text emphasis	Select text to be changed			
	Ctrl + B (bold) **Ctrl + I** (italics) **Ctrl + U** (underline)	Click: the appropriate button **B** *I* **U**	**Font** Select from the **Font Style** menu	**Format**, **Font**
Resize objects	Select the object. Resize using the handles. To preserve aspect ratio (proportions), resize from a corner			
Save	**Ctrl + S**	Click: the 💾 **Save** button		**File**, **Save**
	If you have not already saved the file you will be prompted to specify the directory and to name the file			
Save using a different name or to a different folder or drive				**File**, **Save As**
	Select the appropriate drive and folder, change the filename if relevant. Click: **Save**			
Select All	**Ctrl + A**			**Edit**, **Select All**
Spell check	**F7**	Click: the ✓ **Spelling** button		**Tools**, **Spelling**
Underline text	Select text to underline			
	Ctrl + U	Click: the **U** **Underline** button		
Undo	**Ctrl + Z**	Click: the ↰ **Undo** button		**Edit**, make selection
View	Click on: **Normal**, **HTML** or **Preview** tab			
Zoom		Click: the 100% ▾ **Zoom** button		**View**, **Zoom**

Selecting text

Selecting what	Action
Whole document	**Ctrl + A**
One word	Double-click on word
Any block of text	Click cursor at start of text, hold down: **Shift**. Click cursor at end of text and click
Deselect text	Click in any white space

Some common HTML codes

Code	Meaning
HEAD	Contains head information
TITLE	Sets HTML page title
BODY	Defines the body area
P	Paragraph
A	Hyperlink
IMG	Image
HR	Horizontal line
BR	Line break
FONT	Font size, colour and so on

Hints and tips

- Always check that all links are correct.
- Remember to insert an image when requested and position it correctly.
- Check thoroughly for errors in keying in text.
- Check that you have aligned page items as specified.
- Check that you have changed background colour when requested.
- Check for correct line spacing and text flow. There should not be breaks within paragraphs.
- Have you formatted text as specified?
- Web pages must be printed from the browser and not from FrontPage's Preview. Check that you have all the printouts requested.

Web pages: sample full practice assignment

For this assignment you will need the files **animals.htm** and **tall.htm**. The animals.htm page requires the graphic **drawing.gif**. The tall.htm page requires the graphic **giraffe.jpg**. You will also need the file **bird.txt** and **penguin.jpg**. All these files are on the CD-ROM and when working on this assignment must be located in the same folder.

Scenario

You work as an administrative assistant for a university research department. You have been asked to help develop some web pages for a forthcoming open day for schools.

Your supervisor has two unlinked pages already prepared that need to be linked. These are:

- **animals.htm**, the 'Animals and Birds' home page
- **tall.htm**, a page about giraffes

1   Create a link in the **animals.htm** page as follows:

Text to be linked: **Giraffes**
Link to: **tall.htm**

Enter your name and centre number after the text: **Last updated by**.
Save the amended **animals.htm** page.

2   Create a link in the **tall.htm** page as follows:

Text to be linked: **Homepage**
Link to: **animals.htm**

Enter your name and centre number after the text: **Last updated by**.
Save the amended **tall.htm** page.

3   Check the links function correctly by viewing them in the browser.

You have been asked to make a new page about penguins.

4   Create a new document and insert the text file **bird**.

5   Enter your name and centre number after the text: **Last updated by**.

The new page must be formatted according to the university's web design policy as shown in Figure 8.29.

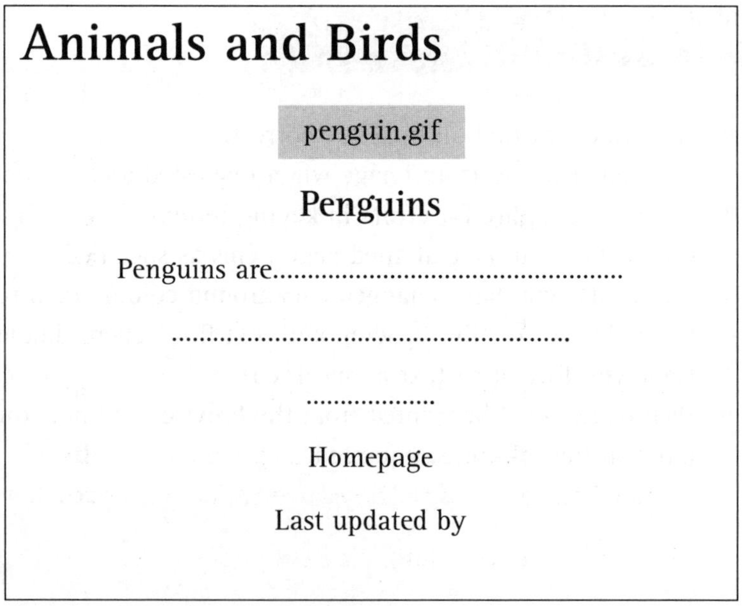

Figure 8.29 The university's web design policy

Animals and Birds

penguin.gif

Penguins

Penguins are...

....

....

Homepage

Last updated by

6. Format the text **Animals and Birds** as a Heading (large font size).
   Format the text **Penguins** as a Subheading (medium font size).
   Format all other text as Body Text (small font size and not bold).
   Ensure that each of the five paragraphs is separated by a clear line space.

7. Format all the text except the heading **Animals and Birds** to be centred on the page.
   Embolden the text **flightless**.
   Italicise the text **flexible elbow joint**.

   The page must include an image of a penguin.

8. Import the graphic **penguin.jpg** and position it below the text **Animals and Birds** and above the text **Penguins**. Centre-align the graphic on the page.

   The new page should link back to the **animals** home page.

9. Create a link in the new page as follows:

   Text to be linked: **Homepage**
   Link to: **animals.htm**

   Save the new page.

   The home page should have a link to the new page.

10. In the **animals.htm** page, on a separate line below the text **Giraffes** and above the text **Click here to visit the Fish site**, add the text:

    Penguins

    Format this to be centred on the page.
    Link this text to your newly created page.
    Save the amended **animals.htm**.

11. Load all the pages into the browser and test the new links.

12. Change the background colour of the **animals.htm** page ensuring that it is a different colour from the text colour.

    Save the amended **animals.htm** page.

13. Some of the links on the home page have not been completed.

    Create an external link in the **animals.htm** page as follows:

    Text to be linked: **Click here to visit the Fish site**
    External link to: **www.progress-media.co.uk**

    Save the amended **animals.htm** page.

14. Create an e-mail link in the **animals.htm** page as follows:

    Text to be linked: **Your name and centre number**
    E-mail link to: **openday@progress-media.co.uk**

    Save the amended **animals.htm** page.

    You have been asked to provide printouts showing the amendments you have made.

15 Load the **animals.htm** page into your browser and print a copy.

Load the **tall.htm** page into your browser and print a copy.

Load the new page that you created into your browser and print a copy.

Print a copy of the HTML code used for each of the three pages.

16 Close each document and exit from the application(s) following the correct procedures.

Presentation graphics using PowerPoint (Unit 10)

 Getting started

In this section you will learn how to:

- understand PowerPoint basics
- create a new presentation
- create text areas
- insert a graphic
- close the file

- load PowerPoint
- set up a master slide
- apply background
- save the presentation
- exit PowerPoint

1.1 What is PowerPoint?

PowerPoint is an application that enables the creation of professional-looking and interesting presentations. A PowerPoint presentation consists of a number of slides (pages) that you design and create and then display as a slide show, either on a computer or via a computer attached to a projection system. Whilst creating the slides you can also create presenter notes, handouts and an outline of the presentation. All these are saved together in the same PowerPoint presentation file.

The slides can be given a common look with the aid of master slides. This would be appropriate when needing to adhere to a house style (a particular style that is always used by an organisation when creating documents). Master slides enable you to set out the design you want (eg background colour, size and emphasis of text) and then automatically apply it to all the slides in the presentation. This gives the presentation a more co-ordinated look and makes for easier reading. For CLAIT assessments it is essential that you create a master slide for your presentation. This section shows you how to do this.

You are not able to key text directly onto a slide, as you would on a page in Word for example. All content must be inserted into frames, known in PowerPoint as placeholders. You can either create these frames yourself, or PowerPoint can present various AutoLayouts for you to choose from as a basis for each slide. All these (except Blank AutoLayout) contain frames in which to insert the content. The AutoLayout you choose will be determined by what elements you want to appear on the slide. The elements on PowerPoint slides are called objects. These can include text, Clip Art, graphics or charts. Most AutoLayouts have placeholders for title text (the main heading) and body text (the main detail). The body text is in the form of a bulleted list of points. Bulleted lists are often used on slides to help structure the presentation.

1.2 Loading PowerPoint

Exercise 1

Load PowerPoint.

1 In the Windows desktop, click on: the **Start** button.

2 Select: **Programs** (by moving the mouse over it), then **Microsoft PowerPoint** (Figure 9.1).

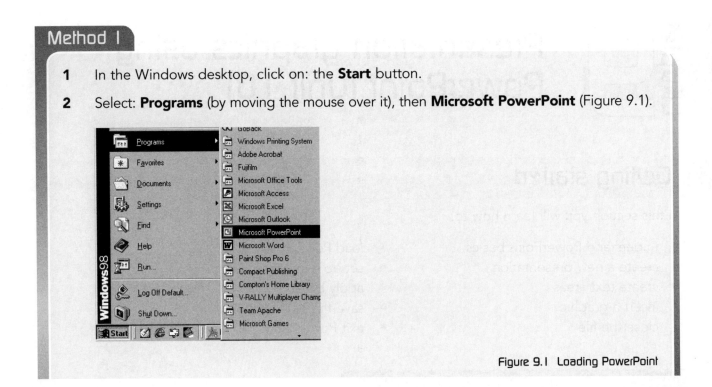

Figure 9.1 Loading PowerPoint

Method 2

(Use if you have a shortcut icon to PowerPoint on your desktop.)

In the Windows desktop, click on: the **Microsoft PowerPoint** shortcut icon.

Either method results in the PowerPoint window being displayed (Figure 9.2).

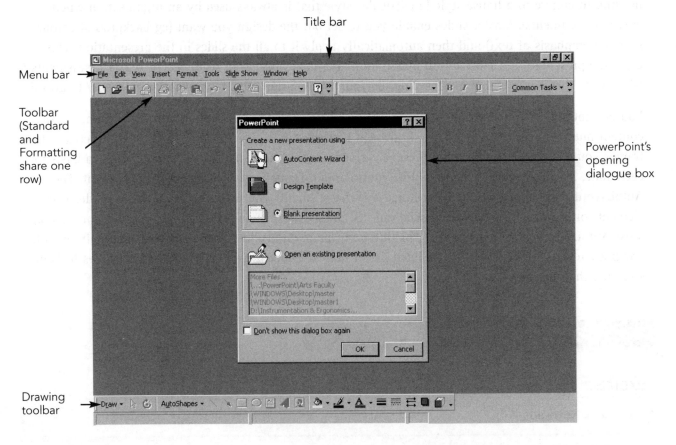

Figure 9.2 PowerPoint's opening window

Exercise 2

Set up a master slide for the presentation.

Method

1 Click in: the **Blank presentation** option button, then on: **OK**.

2 The **New Slide** dialogue box is displayed (Figure 9.3).

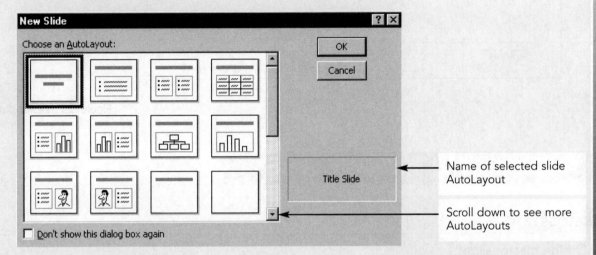

Figure 9.3 New Slide dialogue box

 Many different **AutoLayouts** are displayed for you to choose from. To give an idea of the sort of slides you can create, have a look at these by clicking once on each. Notice that the AutoLayout name changes accordingly. Use the scroll bar to access other AutoLayouts.

3 Select: **Blank** slide and click on: **OK**.

4 From the **View** menu, select: **Master**, **Slide Master** (Figure 9.4).

Figure 9.4 Accessing the slide master

5 The master slide is displayed (Figure 9.5).

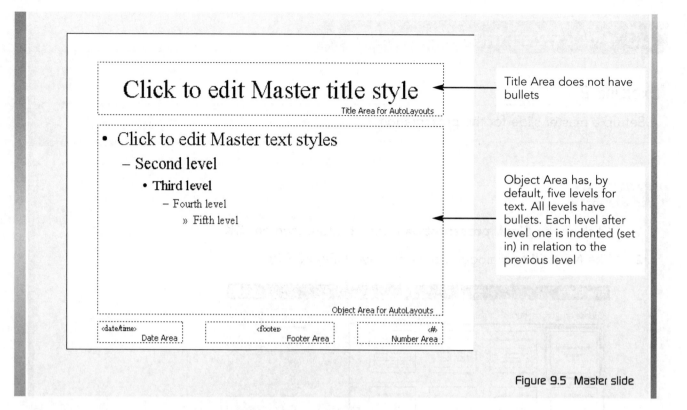

Figure 9.5 Master slide

1.4 Customising the master slide

On the master slide:

* Create a page-wide title frame (placeholder) at the top of the page.
* Create a page-wide main frame (placeholder) below the title frame.
* Set up the following text styles within these frames as follows:

Frame	Style	Emphasis	Size	Bullets	Alignment
title	title	bold	48	no	centre
main	1st level	italic	28	yes	left
main	2nd level	none	24	yes	left and indented

The master slide already contains page-wide title and main frames so we only need to set the styles for these areas. When necessary alter the size of a frame as follows:

a Select the frame (placeholder).
b Resize it by dragging the handles.

Move the frames by holding down the left mouse in the frame border; the cursor turns into a four-headed arrow. Drag the frame to the required position.

Using Undo and Redo

As with most Office applications, the **Undo** and **Redo** buttons can be used to undo or redo actions.

Method

1   Click in: the **Title** area frame.

2   Using the Formatting toolbar buttons, refer to the table above and select:

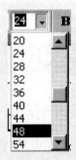

- Font size: click on: the down arrow of the **Font Size** box, click on: **48** (Figure 9.6).

Figure 9.6 Selecting font size

Note: If the font size is not listed, click in: the **Font Size** box and key in the required size.

- Enhancement: click on: the relevant enhancement button (Figure 9.7), in this case the **Bold** button.

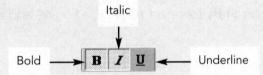

Figure 9.7 Enhancing text

- Alignment: click on the relevant alignment button (Figure 9.8), in this case the **Center** button.

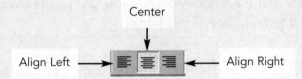

Figure 9.8 Setting alignment

Method

The main (Object) area frame contains five text levels as shown in Figure 9.5.

1   Delete levels 3, 4 and 5 by selecting them and pressing: **Delete**.

2   Set the text styles for level 1 and 2 as above. *Note:* Both levels already have bullets and level 2 is already indented.

When you need to remove/add a bullet, position the cursor in the line containing/not containing the bullet and click on: the ⬛ **Bullets** button.

1.7 Deleting frames

Exercise 4

Delete the frames **Date Area**, **Footer Area** and **Number Area**.

Method

Select the frames (hold down **Shift** to select them all at once) and press: **Delete**.

1.8 Inserting a frame

Exercise 5

Create a frame (placeholder) at the bottom of the slide, below the main frame. Enter your name, centre number and today's date in this frame.

Method

1 On the **Drawing** toolbar (at the bottom of the window), click on: the ▣ **Text Box** button. (*Note:* If the **Drawing** toolbar is not displayed, from the **View** menu, select: **Toolbars**, then **Drawing**.)

2 Using the mouse, position the cross hair where you want the top of the text box to be. Hold down the left mouse button and drag out a text box. Release the mouse button.

3 Set the text to a smallish size, eg 14 pt.

4 Key in your name, centre number and today's date.

1.9 Applying a background colour

Exercise 6

Set the background to be white.

Method

1 From the **Format** menu, select: **Background**.

2 The **Background** dialogue box is displayed (Figure 9.9).

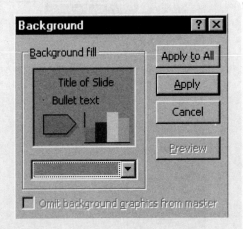

Figure 9.9 Changing the background colour

3 In the **Background Fill** section, click on: the down arrow of the colour box and click on: a colour.

4 Click on: **Apply**.

 The default is white. If you do not see the required colour, at step 3, select: **More Colors** and click on a colour on the colour palette. Click on: **OK** and then on: **Apply**.

1.10 Inserting a graphic

Note: For this exercise you will need to access the file **exhibition** from the CD-ROM.

Exercise 7

Place the graphic **exhibition** at the bottom right corner of the slide. Ensure that the logo does not overlap the frames.

Method

1 From the **Insert** menu, select: **Picture**, **From File** (Figure 9.10).

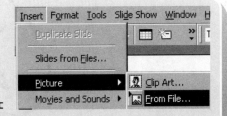

Figure 9.10 Inserting a graphic

2 The **Insert Picture** dialogue box is displayed (Figure 9.11).

3 In the **Look in** box, click on: the down arrow and select the location of the graphic file.

4 Click once on the filename to see a preview.

5 Click on: **Insert**.

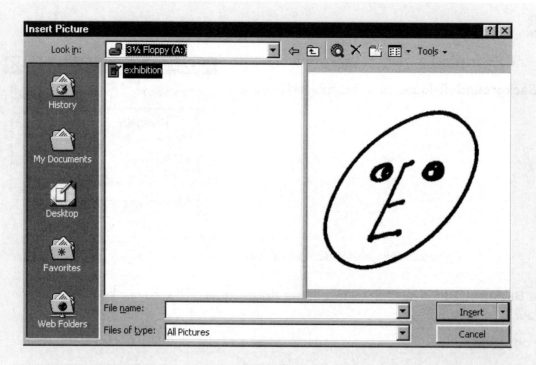

Figure 9.11 Insert Picture dialogue box

6   The graphic is inserted as in Figure 9.12. It is too big!

7   Resize the graphic by dragging the handles inwards. *Note:* Drag from the corners to keep the graphic's aspect ratio, ie not make it too narrow, short, tall or wide.

8   Reposition the graphic to the required location by holding the left mouse over it (the mouse pointer turns into a four-headed arrow) and dragging. Release the mouse. *Note:* Do not overlap any of the frames.

Figure 9.12 Graphic inserted

9   The master slide now looks like Figure 9.13.

Figure 9.13 Master slide created

1.11 Saving the presentation

Exercise 8

Save the master slide with the filename **paintings**.

Method

1 From the **File** menu,
   select: **Save As**.

2 The **Save As** dialogue
   box is displayed (Figure
   9.14).

3 In the **Save in** box, click
   on: the down arrow and
   select the location where
   you want to save.

4 In the **File name** box,
   key in the filename
   paintings.

5 Click on: **Save**.

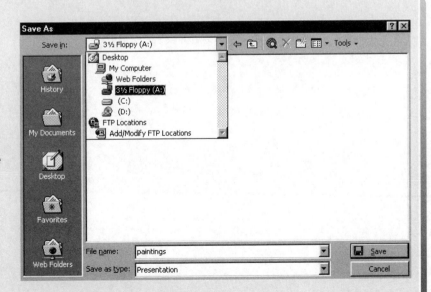

Figure 9.14 Saving a file

1.12 Closing the file

Exercise 9

Close the file.

Method

From the **File** menu, select: **Close**.

1.13 Exiting PowerPoint

Exercise 10

Exit PowerPoint.

Method

From the **File** menu, select: **Exit**.

Note: When you have closed a PowerPoint presentation but have not exited PowerPoint, you can start a new presentation by clicking on the ☐ **New** button. You can open an existing presentation by clicking on the ☞ **Open** button. (If your toolbars share one row, you may need to click on the ❯❯ **More Buttons** button first.)

 Now that the master slide has been created, it can be used as the basis for the other slides in the presentation in Sections 2 and 3.

Presentation graphics practice 1

Note: For these exercises you will need access to the files **computer** and **build** on the accompanying CD-ROM.

Practice 1

1 Load PowerPoint and a new presentation.

2 Create or amend the master slide as follows:

    a Create a page-wide title frame at the top of the page.
    b Create a page-wide frame below the title frame.
    c Set up text styles in these frames as follows:

Frame	Style	Emphasis	Size	Bullets	Alignment
title	title	italic and bold	40	no	centre
main	1st level	bold	30	yes	left
main	2nd level	none	26	yes	left and indented

    d Insert the image **computer** at the bottom left corner of the slide. Ensure it does not overlap the text frames.
    e Create a frame at the bottom of the slide, below the main frame. Enter your name, centre number and today's date in this frame.
    f Format the background to be light blue.

3 Save the master slide using the filename **training**.

4 Close the file and exit PowerPoint.

Practice 2

1 Load PowerPoint and a new presentation.

2 Create or amend the master slide as follows:

    a Create a page-wide title frame at the top of the page.
    b Create a page-wide frame below the title frame.
    c Set up text styles in these frames as follows:

Frame	Style	Emphasis	Size	Bullets	Alignment
title	title	bold	54	no	centre
main	1st level	none	42	yes	left
main	2nd level	italic	28	yes	left and indented

    d Insert the image **build** at the bottom left corner of the slide. Ensure it does not overlap the text frames.
    e Create a frame at the top of the slide, above the title frame. Enter your name, centre number and today's date in this frame.
    f Format the background to be yellow.

3 Save the master slide using the filename **heritage**.

4 Close the file and exit PowerPoint.

In this section you will learn how to:

- create a new slide in an existing presentation
- insert text
- print slides and audience notes

2.1 Opening an existing presentation

Exercise 1

Load PowerPoint and open the presentation **paintings** saved at the end of Section 1.

Method

1 Load PowerPoint.

2 In the PowerPoint opening dialogue box (Figure 9.15), click in: the **Open an existing presentation** option button.

3 Click on: the filename.

4 Click on: **OK**.

Note: If the filename is not visible, to locate it double-click on: **More files**.

Click in: the option button

Click on: the filename

Click on: **OK**

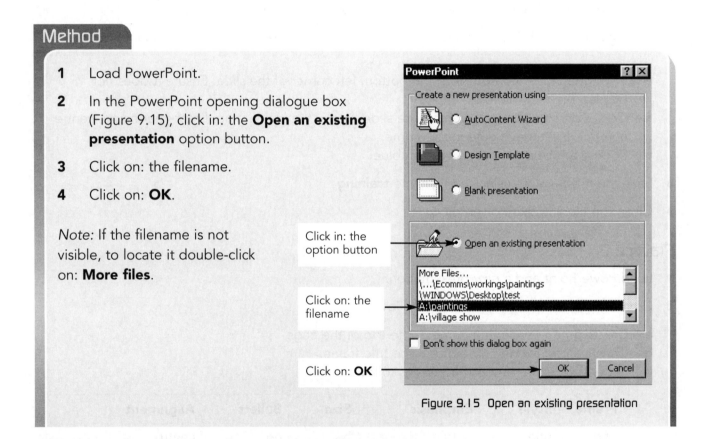

Figure 9.15 Open an existing presentation

2.2 Creating a new slide

Exercise 2

Create the first slide in the presentation with the following content:

Enter the title:
ILLEY COMMUNITY COLLEGE

Leave the main frame blank for this slide.

1 With the master slide displayed, change to **Normal View** by clicking on: the **Normal View** button (Figure 9.16) at the bottom left of the window.

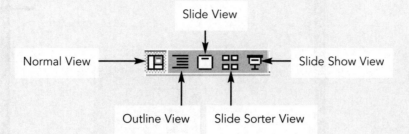

Figure 9.16 Types of View

Slide Views

Normal View	Use this view or **Slide View** to create/edit slides. It contains three panes: Outline, Slide and Notes. The pane sizes can be adjusted by dragging the pane borders. **Normal View** displays slides individually and can be used to work on/view all parts of your presentation. The Outline pane gives an overview of your presentation (currently there is only one slide). The Notes pane allows you to input any notes that you want to make about the slide. This is helpful when delivering a presentation.
Outline View	Displays an outline of your presentation. You can enter/review the text in your presentation in this view.
Slide View	Displays one slide at a time. Use this view or **Normal View** to create/edit slides.
Slide Sorter View	• You can view all your slides in this view as miniatures (small versions or thumbnails). • Zoom in and out for more/less detail using **Zoom** Control. • Sort slides into a different presentation order, by clicking on the slide you want to move and dragging it to a new location. • Add a new slide by placing the pointer between the slides where you want the new slide to appear and clicking on the **New Slide** toolbar button. • Delete a slide, by selecting it and pressing the **Delete** key (use the **Undo** toolbar button to reinstate the deleted slide).
Slide Show View	Shows your slides on a full screen, as they will appear when you set a slide show in motion. Select the first slide. Click the **Slide Show** button. To view the next slide, press: **Page Down**. When all the slides have been viewed you will be returned to the previous view.

2 Right-click in the **Slide** pane (Figure 9.17).

3 From the pop-up menu, select: **Slide Layout**.

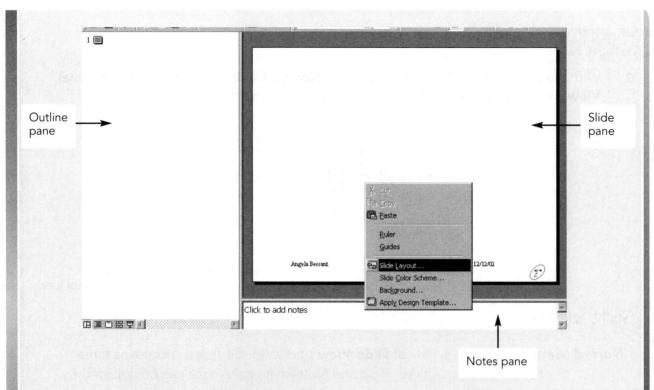

Outline pane

Slide pane

Notes pane

Figure 9.17 Slide in Normal View

4 The **Slide Layout** box is displayed (Figure 9.18).

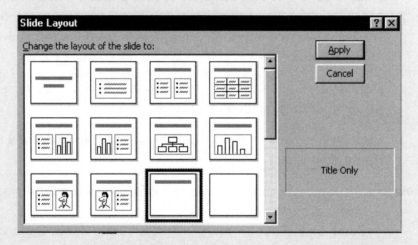

Figure 9.18 Slide Layout box

5 Select a slide that will best fit your content. In this case select: **Title Only**.

Note: Do not select **Title Slide** since this will not automatically take the master slide styles and layout.

6 Click on: **Apply**.

7 The slide is displayed.

8 Key in the text in the title frame.

9 The slide will now look like Figure 9.19.

Notice that the text is also displayed in the **Outline** pane. As an alternative, it can be keyed directly into this pane if preferred.

For CLAIT assignments you must ensure that the slides are created in the correct order. If you find that you have failed to do this, you can move the slides as follows:

1   Click on: the **Slide Sorter View** button.
2   Hold down the left mouse button on the slide to move and drag to the required position.
3   Release the mouse button.

To delete a slide:

1   Click on: the **Slide Sorter View** button.
2   Click on: the slide to delete.
3   Press: **Delete**.

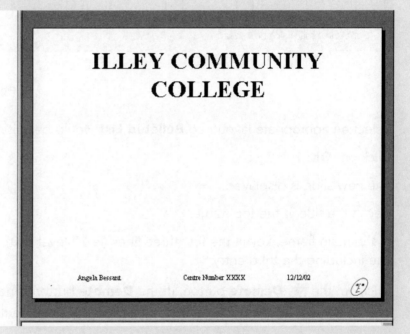

Figure 9.19 Slide 1

2.3 Creating a slide with levels

Exercise 3

Create slide 2 with the title **EXHIBITORS**.

Enter the following text in the main frame with the levels shown:

Art and Design Ltd	1st level
Graphics to Go	1st level
Picture and IT	1st level
Landscape Views	2nd level
Impressionist Echoes	1st level
Mulberry Interiors	2nd level

1   Click on: the 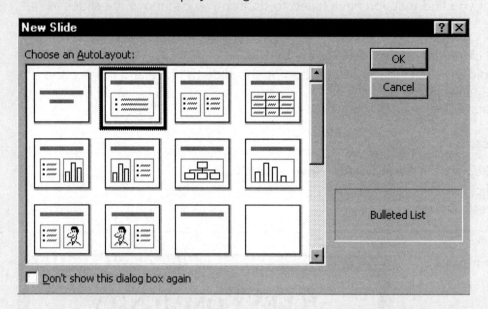 **New Slide** button.

2   The **New Slide** box is displayed (Figure 9.20).

Figure 9.20 New Slide dialogue box

3   Select an appropriate layout, eg **Bulleted List** would be suitable for this slide's content.

4   Click on: **OK**.

5   The new slide is displayed.

6   Key in the title in the top frame.

7   In the main frame, key in the first three lines (ie 1st level text), pressing: **Enter** after each line including the third entry.

8   Click on: the **Demote** button. (If the **Demote** button is not displayed on the toolbar, click on: the **More Buttons** button first.) The line is indented to the 2nd level.

9   Key in the text for this line and press: **Enter**.

10 The next line is at 1st level again. Click on: the **Promote** button.

11 Key in the text for this line and press: **Enter**.

12 The next line is at 2nd level again, so click on: the **Demote** button.

13 Key in the text.

14 The slide now looks like Figure 9.21.

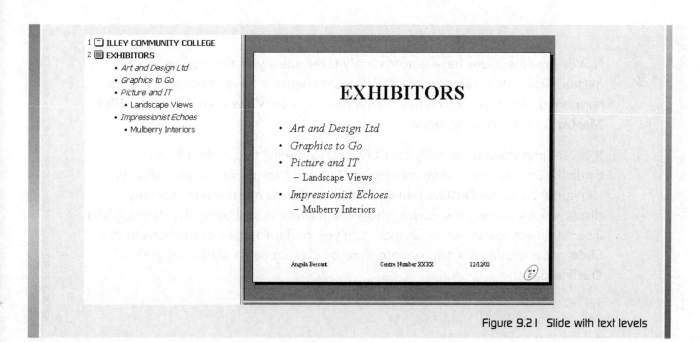

Figure 9.21 Slide with text levels

Exercise 4

Create slide 3 with the following content:

Enter the title: **EXHIBITIONS**

Interior Project	1st level
Carpets	2nd level
Curtaining	2nd level
Wall Project	2nd level
Garden Project	1st level
Plants and Pots	2nd level

Method

Use the same method as in Exercise 3. The slide will look like Figure 9.22.

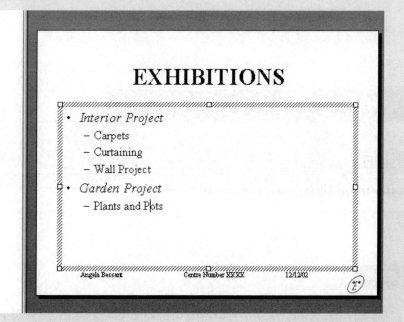

Figure 9.22 Slide 3

Notice how the slides have automatically taken the styles that you set on the master slide. When carrying out CLAIT assessments, always check that this has happened. If not, you can return to the master slide (**View** menu, **Master**, **Slide Master**) to amend as necessary.

It is very important (especially for CLAIT assessments) to proofread very carefully. Do this now before moving on. If you do spot an error on a slide you can correct it in the **Outline** pane, even if the slide is not the one currently displayed, by clicking the cursor where the mistake is and using the deleting and inserting methods shown in Chapter 1. If you prefer to make corrections in the **Slide** pane, display the appropriate slide by clicking on its slide icon in the **Outline** pane.

2.4 Saving with existing filename

Exercise 5

Save the presentation keeping the same filename **paintings**.

Method

Click on: the 🖫 **Save** button.

 Saving by this method overwrites the original file, ie you will not be able to access the original. When you want to keep the original, select: **Save As** from the **File** menu and give the file a different name.

2.5 Printing the presentation

Exercise 6

Print the three slides, one per page.

Method

1   From the **File** menu, select: **Print**. The **Print** dialogue box appears (Figure 9.23).
2   With the **Slides** option selected in the **Print what** section, click on: **OK**.

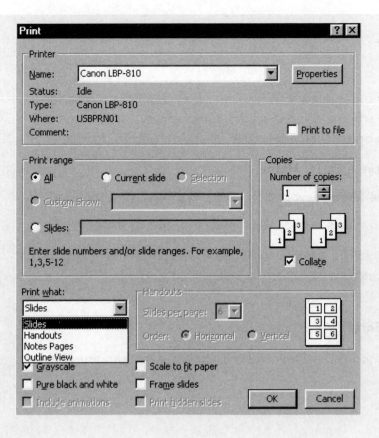

Figure 9.23 Print dialogue box

Exercise 7

Print a set of audience notes with three thumbnail slides on one page.

Method

1 From the **File** menu, select: **Print**. The **Print** dialogue box appears (Figure 9.23).

2 In the **Print what** section, click on: the down arrow and select: **Handouts**.

3 In the **Handouts** section, click on: the down arrow of the **Slides per page** box and select (in this case): 3 (Figure 9.24).

4 Click on: **OK**.

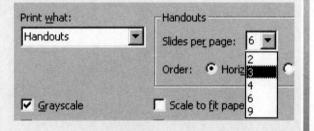

Figure 9.24 Selecting number of slides per page

5 The printout will have three slides on the left side of the page and spaces for notes on the right.

Examining different views

Side Show View

At this stage, although not required for CLAIT, you may be interested to see what the slides look like when displayed on the computer as a slide show (without the distractions of the toolbars, scrollbars and so on). To do this:

1 Go to the first slide (press **Ctrl** + **Home**).

2 Click on: the 🖵 **Slide Show** view button (at the bottom left of the window).

3 Use the keyboard arrow keys or click the mouse to move to the next slide.

The slides can be set up to run automatically and even special effects can be added, such as sounds and display effects (scrolling in, flying in).

Slide Sorter View
Click on: the ⊞ **Slide Sorter View** button.

All slides are displayed. You can reorder slides in this view by dragging them to the required location.

2.6 Close the file and exit PowerPoint

Presentation graphics practice 2

Practice 3

1 Load PowerPoint and the file **training** saved in Section 1, practice 1.

2 Create slide 1 and enter the title **RACEAHEAD TRAINING**.
Leave the main frame blank for this slide.

3 Create slide 2 and enter the title **REGIONAL OFFICES**.
Enter the following text in the main textframe, with the styles shown:

Bristol Centre	1st level
Bath Crescent	1st level
Oxford Circus	1st level
Exeter Buildings	1st level
Cambridge Cam	1st level
Swindon Hitech	1st level

4 Create slide 3 and enter the title **COURSES**.

Enter the following text in the main text frame, with the styles shown:

Spreadsheets	1st level
Beginners	2nd level
Advanced	2nd level
Desktop Publishing	2nd level
Beginners	2nd level
Beginners Web Pages	1st level

5 Save the slide show, keeping the name **training**.

6 Print out each of the slides, one per page.

7 Print out a set of audience notes with three thumbnail slides on one page.

8 Close the file and exit PowerPoint.

Practice 4

1 Load PowerPoint and the file **heritage** saved in Section 1, Practice 2.

2 Create slide 1 and enter the title **WORLD HERITAGE PLACES**.
Leave the main frame blank for this slide.

3 Create slide 2 and enter the title **FRANCE**.

Enter the following text in the main textframe, with the styles shown:

ORANGE	1st level
ROMAN THEATRE	2nd level
TRIUMPHAL ARCH	2nd level
REIMS	1st level
CATHEDRAL NOTRE-DAME	2nd level
ST REMY ABBEY	2nd level

4 Create slide 3 and enter the title **TIMES OF EXCURSIONS**.

Enter the following text in the main text frame, with the styles shown:

ROMAN PLACES	1st level
MONDAYS	2nd level
THURSDAYS	2nd level
FRIDAYS	2nd level
OTHER PLACES	1st level
WEEKENDS	2nd level

5 Save the slide show, keeping the name **heritage**.

6 Print out each of the slides, one per page.

7 Print out a set of audience notes with three thumbnail slides on one page.

8 Close the file and exit PowerPoint.

3 Editing and amending slides

In this section you will learn how to:

- delete text
- replace specified text
- promote/demote text

3.1 Deleting a line of text

Exercise 1

Open the file **paintings** saved in Section 2. On slide 2, delete the line **Graphics to Go**.

Method

1   Load PowerPoint and open the file **paintings**.

2   Ensure that you are in **Normal View**. If not click on: the ▣ **Normal View** button (bottom left of the window).

3   In the **Outline** pane, position the cursor after the **o** in **Go** on slide 2.

4   Press: the ← **Del** (Backspace) key until all the text in this line and the line space are deleted.

 There are many ways of selecting text. These are given in the quick reference at the end of this chapter. Once selected you can delete/copy/cut and paste it using the toolbar buttons or keyboard shortcuts. This makes for greater efficiency since it saves duplication of effort but needs to be carried out carefully to prevent text being duplicated or deleted accidentally.

3.2 Inserting a line of text

Exercise 2

Add the following line to slide 3, after **Garden Project** and before **Plants and Pots**:

Hanging Baskets   2nd level

Method

1   In the **Outline** pane, position the cursor after the top of **Garden Project** on slide 3.

2   Press: **Enter**.

3 To demote the text on this line, click on: the ➡ **Demote** button.

4 Key in the new text.

3.3 Demoting existing lines of text

Exercise 3

On slide 2, demote the line **Picture and IT** to become 2nd level text.

Method

1 In the **Outline** pane, position the cursor on the line to demote.

2 Click on: the ➡ **Demote** button.

3.4 Promoting a line of text

Exercise 4

On slide 3, promote the line **Curtaining** to become 1st level text.

Method

1 In the **Outline** pane, position the cursor on the line to promote.

2 Click on: the ⬅ **Promote** button.

3.5 Searching and replacing

Exercise 5

Replace the word **Project** with **Design** wherever it appears in the presentation (three times in all).

With a short presentation like this one, it would be easy to search and replace manually. However when working with longer presentations, it is more efficient to use PowerPoint's search and replace facility. This should be used in CLAIT assessments.

Figure 9.25 Replacing text

1 Move the cursor to the start of the presentation by pressing: **Ctrl + Home** or click the cursor at the start.

2 From the **Edit** menu, select: **Replace** (Figure 9.25).

3 The **Replace** dialogue box is displayed (Figure 9.26).

4 In the **Find what** box, key in the word you want to replace, ie *Project*.

5 In the **Replace with** box, key in the replacement word, ie *Design*.

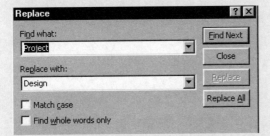

Figure 9.26 Replace box

6 You now have a choice. You can click on: **Replace All**. You will be advised how many replacements have been made as in Figure 9.27. Alternatively, you can click on: **Find Next**. The searched word is highlighted. You can then click on: **Replace**. This can be repeated until all words are found and replaced. You will need to keep a tally of them since you will not be advised how many replacements have been made.

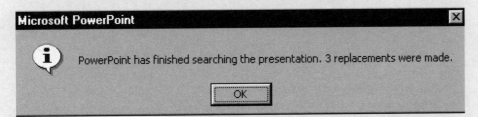

Figure 9.27 Number of replacements made

 In Figure 9.26, the **Replace** box, notice the check boxes for **Match case** and **Find whole words only**. **Match case** will only find words that have the same upper and lower case pattern as the one in the **Find what** box. For example, in Figure 9.26 if **Match case** were selected, it would only find *Project* with a capital P and not *project* with a lower case p. The **Find whole words only** option will do just that. For instance, if you are looking for the word **all** and you have not ticked to find whole words only, the search could find b**all**, b**all**oon, **all**igator.

In CLAIT assessments you need not be too concerned about setting these options. Since the presentations are very short, it is unlikely that you would encounter problems.

3.6 Save the file with the filename paintings2

3.7 Print a set of audience notes with three thumbnails per page

3.8 Close the file and exit PowerPoint

Presentation graphics practice 3

Practice 5

1 Load PowerPoint and open the presentation **training** saved in Section 2, Practice 3.

2 On slide 2, delete the line **Cambridge Cam**.

3 Add the following line to slide 3, after **Spreadsheets** and before **Beginners**:

Introductory   2nd level

4 On slide 3, promote the line **Desktop Publishing** to become 1st level text.

5 Replace the word **Beginners** with the word **Basic** wherever it appears (three times in all).

6 Save the amended slide show as **training2**.

7 Print a set of audience notes with three thumbnail slides on one page.

8 Close the presentation and exit the software securely.

Practice 6

1 Load PowerPoint and open the presentation **heritage** saved in Section 2, Practice 4.

2 On slide 2, delete the line **ROMAN THEATRE**.

3 Add the following line to slide 3, after **OTHER PLACES** and before **WEEKENDS**:

TUESDAYS   2nd level

4 On slide 3, promote the line **WEEKENDS** to become 1st level text.

5 Replace the word **PLACES** with **SITES** wherever it appears (three times in all).

6 Save the amended slide show as **heritage2**.

7 Print a set of audience notes with three thumbnail slides on one page.

8 Close the presentation and exit the software securely.

Presentation graphics quick reference for New CLAIT (PowerPoint)

Action	Keyboard	Mouse	Right-mouse menu	Menu
Align text	Select the text to be aligned			
		Click: the relevant alignment ⬛⬛⬛ button		
Background, colour			**Background**	**F**ormat, **B**ackground
Bold text	**Ctrl + B**	Click: the **B** **Bold** button	**F**ont	**F**ormat, **F**ont
			Select: **Bold** from the **F**ont style: menu	
Bullets	Position the cursor on the line to insert/remove bullet			
		Click: the ⬛ **Bullets** button		
Capitals (blocked), when keying in	**Caps Lock** Key in the text **Caps Lock** again to remove			
keyed in text	Select text to be changed			
				Format, Change Cas**e**, **UPPERCASE**
Centre text	Select the text			
	Ctrl + E	Click: the ≡ **Center** button		**F**ormat, **A**lignment, **C**enter
Change case	Select the text to be changed From the **Format** menu, select: **Change Cas**e Select the appropriate case			
Close a file	**Ctrl + W**	Click: the ⊠ **Close** button		**F**ile, **C**lose
Cut text	Select the text to be cut			
	Ctrl + X	Click: the ✂ **Cut** button	**Cut**	**E**dit, **C**ut
Delete a character	Press: **Delete** to delete the character to the right of the cursor Press: ← (Backspace) to delete the character to the left of the cursor			
Delete a word	Double-click: the word to select it. Press: **Delete**			
Delete/cut a block of text	Select the text you want to delete			
	Delete or **Ctrl + X**	Click: the ✂ **Cut** button	**Cut**	**E**dit, **C**ut
Demote text	In **Outline** View			
	Tab	Click: the ➡ **Demote** button		
Exit PowerPoint	**Alt + F4**	Click: the ⊠ **Close** button		**F**ile, **E**xit
Font	Select the text you want to change			
		Click: the ▾ down arrow next to the **Font** box Select: the font you require	**F**ont	**F**ormat, **F**ont
			Select: the required font from the **Font** menu	

Action	Keyboard	Mouse	Right-mouse menu	Menu
Font size	Select the text you want to change			
		Click: the ▾ down arrow next to the **Font Size** box	**Font**	**F**ormat, **F**ont
		Select: the font size you require	Select: the required size from the **Size** menu	
Frame, insert delete, resize	On the **Drawing** toolbar, click: the 📄 **Text Box** button, drag out a text box in the required position			
	Click on the frame, press: **Delete**			
	Select the frame, resize using the handles			
Help	**F1**			**Help** **Microsoft PowerPoint Help**
	Shift + F1			**What's This?**
Insert graphic				**Insert**, **Picture**, **From File**
Insert text	Position the cursor where you want the text to appear Key in the text			
Italicise text	Select the text to italicise			
		Click: the *I* **Italic** button		
Load PowerPoint	In the Windows 98 desktop			
		Double-click: the **PowerPoint** shortcut icon		**Start**, **Programs**, **Microsoft PowerPoint**
Master slide Slide master				**View**, **Master**, **Slide Master**
Move frames, containing text or graphic	Select the frame			
		Position the mouse in the frame (placeholder), hold down the left mouse and drag to the required position		
New presentation, create	**Ctrl + N**	Click: the 📄 **New** button		**File**, **New**
New slide	**Ctrl + M**	Click: the 🗔 **New Slide** button		**Insert**, **New Slide**
Open an existing file	**Ctrl + O**	Click: the 📂 **Open** button		**File**, **Open**
	Select the appropriate folder and filename Click: **Open**			
Page setup				**File**, **Page Setup**
Placeholder, delete				**Edit**, **Cut**
Print – slides, handouts	**Ctrl + P**			**File**, **Print**
	Select from the **Print what:** drop-down menu			
Promote text	In **Outline** View			
	Shift + Tab	Click: the ← **Promote** button		
Redo		Click: the ⤳ **Redo** button		**Edit**, make selection

Action	Keyboard	Mouse	Right-mouse menu	Menu
Remove/add text emphasis	Select text to be changed			
	Ctrl + B (bold) **Ctrl + I** (italics) **Ctrl + U** (underline)	Click: the appropriate button: B I U	**F**ont	**F**ormat, **F**ont
			Select from the **Font Style** menu	
Resize objects	Select the object. Resize using the handles. To preserve aspect ratio (proportions), resize from a corner			
Save	**Ctrl + S**	Click: the 💾 **Save** button		**F**ile, **S**ave
	If you have not already saved the file you will be prompted to specify the directory and to name the file			
Save using a different name or to a different folder or drive				**F**ile, Save **A**s
	Select the appropriate drive and folder, change the filename if relevant Click: **Save**			
Select all	**Ctrl + A**			**E**dit, Select A**l**l
Slide master				**V**iew, **M**aster, **S**lide Master
Spell check	**F7**	Click: the 📝 **Spelling** button		**T**ools, **S**pelling
Underline text	Select text to underline			
	Ctrl + U	Click: the U **Underline** button		
Undo	**Ctrl + Z**	Click: the ↶ **Undo** button		**E**dit, make selection
View		Click: a **View** button		**V**iew, make selection
Zoom		Click: the 100% ▾ **Zoom** button		**V**iew, **Z**oom

Selecting text

Selecting what	Action
All text in selected frame	**Ctrl + A**
One word	Double-click on word
Any block of text	Click cursor at start of text, hold down: **Shift**. Click cursor at end of text and click
Deselect text	Click in any white space

Hints and tips

- Are the slides in the order specified? Ensure that you create and print them in the correct order.
- Have you inserted the image as requested?
- Have you missed out words or lines of text? Always proofread carefully.
- Alignment of text and graphic not as specified.

- Have you set up the master slide correctly? Is the layout of slides consistent? Do not use PowerPoint's Title slide AutoLayout since this does not take on the layout of the master slide.
- Check for consistency of font size, correct font emphasis and alignment.
- Check for incorrect use of bullets.
- Have you deleted/inserted/replaced text as specified?
- Have you promoted/demoted text as specified?

Check your work thoroughly. Have you done everything asked?

Presentation graphics: sample full practice assignment

For this assignment you will need the image file **world** from the CD-ROM.

Scenario

You work as an administrative assistant for a university research department. You have been asked to produce a slide show presentation for a forthcoming event.

Your line manager has asked you to produce a short presentation of three slides.

1   Create or amend the master slide as follows:

   a   Create a page-wide title frame at the top of the page.
   b   Create a page-wide main frame below the title frame.
   c   Set up the text styles in these frames as follows:

Frame	Style	Emphasis	Size	Bullets	Alignment
title	title	bold and italic	48	no	centre
main	1st level	none	30	yes	left
main	2nd level	italic	26	yes	left and indented

   d   Place the image **world** at the bottom right corner of the slide, below the main frame. Ensure that the image does not overlap the text frames.
   e   Create a frame at the bottom of the slide, below the main frame. Enter your name, centre number and today's date in this frame.
   f   Format the background to be white.

2   Save the master slide using the filename **climate**. This master slide is to be used for all three slides.

3   Create slide 1 and enter the title **WORLD GEOGRAPHY**.

   Leave the main frame blank for this slide.

4   Create slide 2 and enter the title **WORLD VEGETATION**.

   Enter the following text in the main frame, with the styles shown:

Ice and Snow	1st level
Mosses and Lichens	1st level
Tundra	1st level
Coniferous Forest	1st level
Deciduous Forest	1st level
Tropical Forest	1st level

5 Create slide 3 and enter the title **WORLD CLIMATES**.

Enter the following text in the main frame, with the styles shown:

Subtropical	1st level
Semi-arid	2nd level
Arid	2nd level
Polar Caps	1st level
Tropical	2nd level
Mediterranean	1st level

6 Save the slide show keeping the name **climate**.

7 Print out each of the three slides, one per page.

Some changes need to be made to the presentation.

8 On slide 2, delete the line **Coniferous Forest**.

9 Add the following line to slide 3, after **Tropical** and before **Mediterranean**:

Boreal   1st level

10 On slide 3, promote the line **Tropical** to become 1st level text.

11 Replace the word **WORLD** with the word **EARTH** wherever it appears (three times in all).

12 Save the amended slide show as **climate2**.

13 Print a set of audience notes with three thumbnail slides on one page.

14 Close the presentation and exit the software securely.